Hans Peter Hahn, Kristin Kastner (eds.)
Urban Life-Worlds in Motion

Hans Peter Hahn, Kristin Kastner (eds.)
Urban Life-Worlds in Motion
African Perspectives

[transcript]

Gedruckt mit Unterstützung des Zentrums für Interdisziplinäre Afrika-Forschung (ZIAF) der Goethe-Universität Frankfurt a.M.

Bibliographic information published by the Deutsche Nationalbibliothek
The Deutsche Nationalbibliothek lists this publication in the Deutsche Nationalbibliografie; detailed bibliographic data are available in the Internet at http://dnb.d-nb.de

© 2012 transcript Verlag, Bielefeld

All rights reserved. No part of this book may be reprinted or reproduced or utilized in any form or by any electronic, mechanical, or other means, now known or hereafter invented, including photocopying and recording, or in any information storage or retrieval system, without permission in writing from the publisher.

Cover concept: Kordula Röckenhaus, Bielefeld
Cover illustration: Photo taken by Hans Peter Hahn in September 2005, showing New Tafo Motor Park, Okomfo Anokye Road, Kumasi, Ghana
Proofread by Hans Peter Hahn, Kristin Kastner
Printed by Majuskel Medienproduktion GmbH, Wetzlar
ISBN 978-3-8376-2022-1

Global distribution outside Germany, Austria and Switzerland:

Transaction Publishers
New Brunswick (U.S.A.) and London (U.K.)

Transaction Publishers	Tel.: (732) 445-2280
Rutgers University	Fax: (732) 445-3138
35 Berrue Circle	for orders (U.S. only):
Piscataway, NJ 08854	toll free 888-999-6778

Content

Preface | 7
Hans Peter Hahn, Kristin Kastner

Introduction
Urban Life-Worlds in Motion
Hans Peter Hahn | 9

**The Urban Poor, the Informal Sector
and Environmental Health Policy in Nigeria**
Geoffrey I. Nwaka | 29

'I go chop your Dollar'
Scamming Practices and Notions of Moralities among Youth
in Bamenda, Cameroon
Bettina Frei | 41

Women and Magic in Dakar
Rural Immigrants Coping with Urban Uncertainties
Amber Gemmeke | 73

'They behave as though they want to bring heaven down'
Some Narratives on the Visibility of Cameroonian Migrant Youths in
Cameroon Urban Space
Primus M. Tazanu | 101

Movements into Emotions
Kinetic Tactics, Commotion and Conviviality among Traffic Vendors
in Accra
Gabriel Klaeger | 131

The Transnational Choice
Young Tuareg Traders between Niger and Nigeria
Tilman Musch | 157

The Issue of the Diaspo in Ouagadougou
Ludovic Kibora | 173

Haalpulaar Migrants' Home Connections
Travel and Communication Circuits
Abdoulaye Kane | 187

Epilogue
Images and Spaces
Kristin Kastner | 207

Abstracts and Information on Authors | 217

Preface

HANS PETER HAHN, KRISTIN KASTNER

Urban agglomerations in Africa are among the most astonishing places in the world. Characterized by outstanding growth rates, these places are also known for being chaotic, dangerous, or at least a challenge for everyday life. Whereas many urban settlements in Africa are classified as slums by UN-Habitat, cities in Africa are fertile places for arts and among the best connected ones in matters of communication, circulation of goods and migration.

This book aims to tackle these contradictions not by looking at cities as static and coherent structures, but through the perspectives of the people living in them. It focusses on the life-worlds of the city dwellers whose experiences and expectations are very often linked to movements and mobility. By adopting a comprehensive understanding of urban life in Africa, the book endeavours to gain a new and broader understanding of how these places are locally constituted and – simultaneously – connected to other places. Throughout all contributions, the dynamics of urban life-worlds and their role in embedding the experiences of the city dwellers into local realities are evident. We do not claim to present a solution as to how the conundrum of contradicting notions might be put together to form a coherent image of cities in Africa. By adopting the perspective of those concerned, we rather aim at showing how life-worlds are experienced and how the urbanites' different perspectives constitute the puzzle of cities in Africa.

An edited volume is a project that needs many hands to come into being. We therefore want to thank all those who contributed in various ways to the preparation of the present book. First of all, we appreciate the decision of the contributors to publish in this volume. Many thanks also go to the organizers of the German African Studies Association (VAD) conference in Mainz in 2010 who made the meeting of the authors possible. We also would like to thank the German Research Foundation (DFG) that covered the travel expenses for our guests from Africa. All but one contribution (Kane) were initially presented at this event. Furthermore, we want to thank the Centre for Interdisciplinary African Studies of the Goethe-University (ZIAF, Goethe-Universität, Frankfurt) for sponsoring this book. Finally, we would like to express our gratitude to Geraldine Schmitz for editing and formatting and to Robert Parking for proofreading.

Introduction

Urban Life-Worlds in Motion

HANS PETER HAHN

DYNAMICS OF THE URBAN IN AFRICA

Cities in Africa are experiencing highly dynamic growth and they are attracting people to an outstanding degree. If it is true that the future and past of any society are closely related to each other, then it is even more important to consider urban life as a particular and complex setting of cultural and economic phenomena. Cities played a salient role in the history of many countries in Africa in pre-colonial times and throughout the period of colonialism (Genova 2005), particularly during the years of the independence movements (Coquery-Vidrovitsch 1991). Obviously, they have also played a significant role since independence. Urban cultures will also be highly relevant for the future due to their creativity and innovative character. This also applies to the perception of societies in Africa beyond the spatial limits of the continent and to their contribution to the so-called global community.

Most of the contributions in this book originate from a panel of the same title at the VAD (Vereinigung der Afrikanisten in Deutschland, Association of Africanists in Germany) conference, 'Continuities and Dislocations: Fifty Years of African Independence', held in Mainz in April 2010 and jointly organized by the author and Kristin Kastner. Among the reasons why the perspective on urban life-worlds is combined here with motion, movement and mobility is that these count among the most important features of the recent history of cities in Africa. On a global scale, cities in Africa are the fastest growing urban centres worldwide (Swiaczny 2005). In contrast to South Asian cities, which likewise have similar growth rates, the dynamic in Africa is not the result of a direct governmental impact, centralised planning or an official policy, but rather the consequence of spontaneous and very often unplanned population movements. The growth of cities in Africa is much higher than the demographic increase of these countries in general, which indicates that it must be based on migration from the villages to the cities, and not just on the increase of urban populations through reproduction.

The focus of this book is on mobile urban life-worlds and the wide range of different movements which are constitutive of the shape of cities. The book deals with movement within the inner city as well as from rural areas to the cities. Furthermore, there is considerable mobility between cities. Individuals who take part in inter-urban mobility often have a high professional profile and are seeking new fields of activities in other cities. Movement is also relevant for those people who live in a city in Africa but expect to be leaving the continent and emigrating to Europe or the USA. Although for such people the city is just an intermediate place on their itinerary, they provide an important contribution to the mobile character of urban life-worlds. As the contributions to this volume illustrate, the different forms of mobility and movement are helping shape the image of cities in Africa (Beauchemin and Bocquier 2004).

From a cultural anthropological perspective, the issues of urban societies and their ethnography have been a somewhat neglected topic (Horn 1989; Wildner 1995). This becomes clear when one examines the issues of the journal *Urban Anthropology*, which was established in 1972 but faded approximately ten years later (Al-Zubaidi 1998). However, cities in Africa represent an exception to the problematic disengagement of anthropology from the field of urban studies. As early as the 1950s, the towns of the so-called *copper belt* in southern Africa (Zambia, Zimbabwe and other nations), but also some cities in West Africa like Lagos and Freetown, were important fields of ethnographic research. Back then, anthropologists were mainly interested in the migration of men and women from rural areas to the cities. It is not unreasonable to argue that anthropologists actually accompanied their subjects of study on their way from the villages along the new roads into the cities, where many new job opportunities had been created and new life-styles waited to be discovered by the former villagers (Ferguson 1992; Moore 1994: 67-73).

The simultaneous character of inherited social institutions (often labelled 'traditional'), in particular those that regulate kinship networks and the so-called 'modern' practices which seemed to dominate social life in the cities, led to a critique of some widespread contemporaneous assumptions concerning cultural change. Empirical findings revealed that the rural-urban migrants were able to tie together both life-worlds: that of the village and that of the towns. They did so at the individual level of their biographies, that is, by movement, in particular by travelling back and forth between their villages of origin and the city (Gutkind 1965; Gugler 1971). The presupposition repeatedly articulated by the colonial administration – and sometimes even by anthropologists (Skinner 1974) – that it would be necessary for migrants to abandon their traditions in order to come to terms with the standards of urban life proved to be wrong. In fact, several studies of the new urbanites' social life did show how the mobile members of urban societies had been able to create new practices and new social institutions. Through these new practices, traditions and urban structures were integrated in a creative manner (Cohen 1969; Epstein 1961; Mitchell 1956; Mitchell and Epstein 1959).

During the 1960s, this debate had a considerable impact on the sociology of the city on a more general level. The main aspect, namely why these ethnographic studies were able to pave the way for an improved theoretical framework, was related to the acknowledgement of cultural diversity within the towns. As was evident in studies of cities like Lusaka or Lagos, men and women were living simultaneously in several social and culturally divergent networks, one related to their traditions, the culture of origin and the place of birth, others to their neighbourhoods and to the contexts of their professional lives. The mere theoretical aspect of this debate affects the question of whether this link between the different worlds was permanent in character, or whether the intermingling was due to migrants' specific situations and therefore merely of an ephemeral and non-permanent character. One of the noteworthy outcomes of this debate was the recognition of similarities between US-American cities and those in Africa, particularly with regard to their rapid growth and their capacity to host a wide range of different cultures (Otiso and Owusu 2008).

NEW APPROACHES TO THE STUDY OF URBAN LIFE-WORLDS IN AFRICA

In the following, it is not intended to reanimate these old debates. Although the intellectual objective of the contributions to this book is related to the aforementioned findings of earlier ethnographic approaches to the city in Africa, it is suggested that there are at least two new and complementary aspects that constitute innovative approaches to a better understanding of urban life-worlds and that allow the phenomena related to mobility and movement in the urban context to be grasped in a more differentiated way.

One of these approaches is the concept of transnationalism, which has increasingly been acknowledged during the last fifteen years. Based on studies of men and women of Caribbean origin who currently live in New York, Nina Glick Schiller (1992) and others (Wimmer and Glick Schiller 2003; Vertovec 2009) have shown that these migrants maintain transnational networks characterized by the engagement of particular people at the place of origin and specific 'fields of social action' at both places, that of origin and that of the migrants' destination. An important example of these 'fields of social action' is the organization of funerals (Mazzucato and Kabki 2006). Also the professional fields of action that provide the basis for economic survival at both places receive greater awareness in recent studies. This can be illustrated by the activities of transnational individuals related to mobile telephony and communication centres (Hackenbroich and Vöckler 2007; Paragas 2005). On a more general level, transnational networks do have a direct impact on urban life-worlds in so far as mobile people find places and niches in cities like New York, London and Paris. They do not limit their activities to economic survival but also articulate their esteem for their cultures and societies of origin. Furthermore, it is obvious that these networks are based on kinship. Remittances made by individuals from the place of destination to their parents or children they have left behind constitute one of the crucial aspects of these networks (Nieswand 2009).

The concept of transnationalism is not only important for the understanding of social networks of migrants and their economic activities; it is also relevant for an appropriate description of urban life-worlds. Mobile individuals in a city who maintain permanent ties to places elsewhere provide a particular contribution to the city's image or, more precisely, to its specificity. The impact of these individuals and groups consists of cultural, social and economic practices which refer to the remote place. At the very same time, these aspects become part of the city's image. Investigations of the transnational relations of urbanites should start with actors like mobile individuals and groups that have a particular influence on urban life-worlds (Smith 2005). On the methodological level this requires a broadened perspective, which must not be restricted to the logic of a single nation or city. The call for a spatial extension of the field of study might be the most important contribution of the concept of transnationalism to the study of urban life-worlds. It would be misleading to confine a city to a spatially delimited object dominated by only one culture and one nation. Instead, cities are always composed of a wide range of identities and belongings (Smith 2001; Glick Schiller and Çağlar 2009). Thus, a more careful examination of the biographies of the mobile lives is required. This will also bring these people into the focus of analysis. Their meaningful ties stretching beyond the spatial context of their current life-worlds and its time frame need to be integrated into urban studies.

A second approach that is closely related to this conceptual framework also transgresses the limited perspective in older debates on the ethnography of particular spatially confined urban societies. It deals with images of the city that are important for the self-understandings of people living in urban contexts. Generally speaking, the images of cities in Africa that circulate in the media reflect a highly ambivalent evaluation of these places. On the one hand, they are associated with the fastest growing societies worldwide and are considered to be hotbeds of creativity (UN-Habitat 2003). There are no other places worldwide that are exposed to such explicit expectations of innovation with regard to political and social developments (Koolhaas and van der Haak 2005). Cities in Africa are perceived to be of increasing relevance as centres of modern art and exhibitions. In some cases, like Dakar (Dak'art), Ouagadougou (FESPACO) and Johannesburg (Biennale), they are already playing an important role in the global discourse on new forms of art (Vincent 2005).

On the other hand, cities in Africa are represented in the global media as hotspots of violence and misery. This refers in particular to sites of civil war (Mogadiscio, N'Djamena, Abidjan, Freetown and others). Cities in Africa are also burdened with their unbearable mismanagement with regard to infrastructure, for example, the decay of the congested roads, the deficient water supply or the malfunctioning of waste disposal. This deplorable state of affairs has led some authors to the general assumption that all cities in Africa are merely slums and that any further growth will lead to a worsening of their living conditions (Davis 2006; Pieterse 2008).

The contradiction between cities' quite high esteem – as creative places – and the repeated reference to their existential deficits should be read as an indicator of an inadequate and fragmented understanding of urban life-worlds in Africa as such. Against the background of these contradictions, the current challenge for a more appropriate description is to provide a more consistent basis for an understanding of urban places and societies. This basis requires linking expectations and disappointments, experiences of creativity and experiences of despair (Murray and Myers 2007).

To manage this challenge, the focus on mobility and movement appears to be particularly helpful, because it refers to the experiences and expectations of many urban dwellers. Thus, cities are intermediate places that represent a transitory stage for many of its inhabitants. These people's biographies refer to the rural contexts or other cities from which they came. At the very same time, cities are places where people stay in order to prepare for the next step in a journey which might lead to another city on the continent, or to a place beyond the African continent. Future places, destinations of intended journeys, are also important for many people in cities. In sum, urban life-worlds are not spatially or culturally confined places, but rather segments in broader networks that link them to other cities, countries, cultures and societies. In the framework of this expanded understanding, the city might therefore be approached as an 'invisible city' since many links exist beyond the immediate horizon of perception (De Boeck and Plissart 2004).

This kind of contextualization, which does not prioritize any direct link to a single place or image, has quite concrete consequences for the understanding of urban life-worlds. Cities in Africa are full of references to forms of urbanity and life-styles, which can be associated with European, US or Asian cities (Malaquais 2004; Weiss 2002, 2009). Mobility, in this context, does not just address the question of factual access to other cities, places and urban cultures. Mobility, in this extended definition, is a technique to make particular use of names, practices and images associated with these towns on other continents and to create associations and ties (Salazar 2010; Syed 2007). This notion of mobility has an outstanding relevance, reaching far beyond the urban life-worlds in Africa, and it explains the 'African' character of some *quartiers* in Paris and New York (Copeland-Carson 2004; MacGaffey and Bazenguissa-Ganga 2000; Stoller 2002).

Obviously it is not unproblematic to associate globally circulating images with a life-world which can still be located in Africa (Garcia Canclini 1995; Nutall 2004). Any exclusive or privileged link to an 'African character' (whatever that might mean) of the life-worlds described here should be denied. The very idea of 'not having a purely African character' may contribute to the perception of these urban life-worlds as highly dynamic and vital. Furthermore, it is precisely the affirmative attitude regarding this hybrid character and the often enthusiastic appreciation of cultural phenomena from all parts of the world that generate the power for cities' momentum of expansion. It is justified to call this a 'hybrid character' because the combination of different sources is explicitly confirmed and regarded as an appealing feature of these images. Against the background of this hybrid character, cities in Africa should not be understood as devices of (cultural) integration, but merely as heterogeneous, expanding and sometimes aggressive entities (Behrens 2007).

Recently there has been a more theoretically inspired debate over whether transnational communities can be associated with a concept of 'locality' at all. Some authors argue that, in spite of their transnational character, there is a struggle over power that defines the superior relevance of locality (Lentz 2000; Smith 2005). Others define the 'transnational community' in a more complex way and insist on the intermingling of interests and power between different levels. Locality could then only be identified through a process of 'scaling', where the local is the bottom end of the scalar effect, which includes translocal and transnational phenomena (Levitt 1999; Glick Schiller 2005). Although the contributions to this book do not claim to provide the final argument in this debate, the notion of the life-world focuses on perceptions and avoids unnecessary spatial definitions.

One consequence of the focus on transgressing boundaries and self-consciously adopting new cultural elements from different parts of the world is the difficulty in delimiting cities in Africa spatially. Cities in Africa grow at such a speed that it is often unclear whether a particular settlement is part of the city or not. Thus, the study of the peri-urban has become a field in its own right, investigating the question of specific contributions by these 'in-between' areas of urban life (Drechsel, Graefe and Fink 2007).

The territoriality of cities in Africa has not only become questionable due to their rapid growth: the difficulty of delimiting a city is also linked to the problem of identifying a 'centre'. Very often, a given city has several centres, depending on whether economic activities, cultural life or traffic are considered the dominant criteria. But, even if such a scale is defined, peripheral places have sometimes very quickly turned into central locations, while old city centres may lose their relevance (Heeg 2008). Therefore, these different dynamics allow one to refer to the deterritorialization of cities, as it becomes impossible to delimit the space and structure of the urban in Africa (Guèye and Fall 2005; Boesen and Marfaing 2007).

FURTHER METHODOLOGICAL REMARKS

In order to provide an adequate framework that includes the two complementary approaches mentioned above, a specific methodology is needed. Methods developed in transnational studies (network analysis and biographical enquiries) should be combined with appropriate ways of documenting and analysing imaginations and images of the city.

These two aspects can only be related to each other through in-depth studies on a micro-scale. The aim should be to highlight the entanglement of people and places without neglecting the meaningful aspects linking these people to other places. The most promising approach here is phenomenology, which makes it possible to link the immediate character of a situated perception with the chronologically deeper horizons of past experiences (Waldenfels 1997). Compared to other approaches, the phenomenological perspective also manages to grasp the current and intended mobility in urban life-worlds in concrete contexts (Pelican and Tatah 2009). An example of this is the detailed documentation of the moments of the departure and arrival of migrants (Klute and Hahn 2007). In these moments the hidden dimensions of mobility become clear. This refers not only to the persons who actually migrate, but also to the families and others present at the moment of bidding goodbye or welcome.

Moreover, a phenomenological approach has the advantage of detaching the experience of movement from the present and linking it to experiences connected with movements in someone's life history. Being mobile, having the experience of moving from one place to another, is part of the biographies of many urbanites. A phenomenological perspective may also include a detailed description of moving along a street. Sounds, lights and impressions of other mobile people in the street result in a specific perception of what the character of a street is (Kusenbach 2003). Phenomenology more generally suggests that motion is the combined outcome of the bodily experience of 'being on the move' and the biographical dimension, i.e. embodying the experience of past migrations (Kastner 2010). Both of them refer to the level of the individual as well as to the expectations of the social environment, as has been stressed by the notion of the 'migratory project' (Boyer 2005).

Within this framework, it is important to consider the wide range of different rhythms of movement. In the case of urban dwellers, movement can be observed on their daily trip from a place outside town or from a peripheral sector to the city's centre, a path that is travelled in both directions on the same day. Movement can also consist of periods of stasis when someone is preparing for the moment when he will have the means and contacts required to engage in labour migration. Other movements are exemplified in Geoffrey I. Nwaka's contribution on the forced resettlement of slum-dwellers from a city's centre to its periphery. This practice currently creates new social tensions in many cities in Africa. Another example of a particular urban rhythm of movement, focused on by Gabriel Klaeger, is the incessant search of mobile traders for more promising locations, for markets that might reveal a higher turnover and more profit.

An appropriate description of urban life-worlds in motion will not only address the multitude of movements at different speeds and in different directions, it will also consider their intermingling: none of them exists without interference from the other. Each one is – although to different degrees – a precondition for or an obstacle to the others. It is only the sum of all these movements that draws an adequate picture of the everyday life-worlds of African cities.

In his work *Rhythmanalysis*, Henry Lefebvre (2004) proposed a methodological paradigm to address the connections between the different levels of mobility. He develops his suggestions precisely in the context of urban life-worlds. He also underlines the importance not only of the actual migrations, but also of the expectations and experiences of movement and, in particular, the possibility to change one's own life through specific movements. All these aspects are relevant for the constitution of transnational communities within cities.

The context of an individual's evaluation of himself depends on whether, at a given moment, his 'migration project' to the intended destination will be possible or not (Carling 2002). Vice versa, the self-conscious statement of someone that has the means and knowledge to move to any place he likes can be decisive for his identity. Thus, the image of a city is marked by the perspectives of the people who live there, but who are also gazing upon other horizons that extend beyond the city. For them, the city is a 'stepping stone' on their journey to somewhere else (Sinatti 2008). This might appear to be an abstract statement, but it has been made evident by Idrissou Mora-Kpai's film about the northern Nigerien town of Arlit (Mora-Kpai 2005: *Arlit, deuxième Paris*). Mora Kpai forcefully shows that all those portrayed in the film have a migratory biography; each of them understands his role in Arlit by referring to his own story. Every man, every woman, every family has the experience of past movement. Some found a profitable business in Arlit, and many of them expect to move on one day, heading towards Europe. Some of the expectations become reality, most of them fail, but this is not very important for one's perception of one's lifeworld. The key to the subjective perceptions of these people's self-evaluations is the idea of other places (back to the village of origin, forward to Europe) to which the future might bring them. In this perspective, the whole city becomes a crossroads of migratory projects following different rhythms.

Henry Lefebvre (2004: 5ff.) called his approach a 'critique of the thing', because he wanted to distinguish his method from approaches that treat the city as a kind of material, spatially bounded object, or as a collection of objects, like buildings, roads and places. This is a valuable clarification on the methodological level and supports the argument mentioned above about the deterritorialization of urban life-worlds. However, there is a particular 'materiality' to most movements. This perspective on material items contributes to a better understanding of urban life-worlds. The materiality of movements can be a matter of fact on a macroeconomic scale, as is the case for the slum and the seemingly unacceptable dwellings of its inhabitants. Poverty is a material fact, and many administrative decision-makers are convinced that 'getting rid' of the slums' materiality is only possible through forced resettlement from the centre to peripheral sectors (Marris 1961; Pellow 1991, 2002).

The materiality of mobile moments in urban life-worlds can also be found in other places that serve the movements of urbanites, such as bus stations, taxi stands, hotels and market places. These places have been categorized by James Clifford (1988: 237) as 'chronotopes', a reference to their temporal character, which may be considered indicators of the temporality and 'rhythmization' of urban life-worlds. The list of the objects of regular movements in specific life-worlds can be extended to encompass luggage, electronic devices usually associated with travellers, mobile people and, last but not least, clothing. A closer look at the various kinds of objects indicating movements provides even more evidence of the materiality of migration (Basu and Coleman 2008).

CONTRIBUTIONS

The theoretical considerations and methodological issues discussed so far constitute the framework for the contributions summarized in the following. Although these contributions presented at the VAD conference mentioned above seem to address quite distinct topics, they all focus on urban life-worlds and diverse movements on a micro-scale. At the same time, all of them deal with negotiations about the perceptions and valuations of movement in urban societies. Most probably, it is not by chance that almost all contributions also talk about conflicts when focusing on specific groups and the particular modes of mobility and specific life-styles that distinguish them from other people's movements.

One of the most concrete ways to describe movement is by referring to mobile street-vendors in Accra, the main topic of Gabriel Klaeger's contribution. Here, the speed of the vehicles and the speed of the hawkers decide the success of the petty traders' business. Speed is also an issue in the context of the forced resettlement of slum-dwellers in Nigeria. Geoffrey I. Nwaka stresses that there is no evidence for the contribution of resettlement schemes to the development of a city; instead, forced resettlement leads to a deterioration of the former slum-dwellers' lives. The range between the speedy micro-movements of street-vendors and the slow movements of people who are subjected to resettlement shows the spectrum in the use of the notion of mobility when describing the complexity of urban life-worlds.

Another motive for movement may be the chance to adopt a certain lifestyle. The way moving people are in conflict or at least unsatisfied with particular lifestyles is the main theme of Primus Tazanu's contribution on young returnees in Cameroon. Those who suffered abroad in order to find a way to survive or to support their families in Cameroon are subjected to mockery at the place of origin, as they do not correspond to the expectations of those who did not travel. Life-style – of which Tazanu's contribution is a good example – is based on the logic of coherence and separation. It is due to those who do not take part in migration and who critically dissociate themselves from the migrants that migrants are forced to articulate a particular stylization.

Another example of conflicts over life-styles is the contribution of Bettina Frei, which deals with the controversial practice of 'scamming', or various fraudulent internet business practices. These create a direct link to their European and US-American victims by underlining the smartness of the young Cameroonians who succeed in convincing their communication partners of their invented business stories.

Life-styles are unavoidably part of any form of mobility. However, they are also connected to the materiality of movement. As already mentioned, the acquisition of material objects can be a driving force for movement. This becomes evident in the contribution of Tilman Musch, who deals with young Tuareg men and women who travel between Niger and Nigeria in order to purchase goods in the latter. Apart from the economic incentive, it is the search for adventure and the image of Nigeria as an example of prosperity and a modern life-style that make these young people move.

Frequent journeys are also undertaken by Haalpulaar people between their home villages in the Senegal river valleys and the capital of Dakar, which is the location of Abdoulaye Kane's case study. Thanks to new communication technologies these Haalpulaars also maintain strong relations to their diasporas in other African, European and North American cities. Thus, this case study provides further evidence of how spatial boundaries between village, town and the 'global world' are blurred.

Obviously, concepts like motion, mobility and movement cannot be measured in terms of statistics or quantitative criteria. Neither distance nor rhythms of movement are predictable and, very often, migration projects never become a reality. Furthermore, it is evident that quantitative criteria have little meaning in explaining why motion has such high esteem for a self-conscious perspective on one's own society. A good example of the contradictions between actual immobility and a clear reference to (non-) existent migration is the contribution by Ludovic Kibora, who deals with a diaspora group in Ouagadougou. The setting is the place of origin of its members; thus, mobility in this case is purely a topic, a debate not related to concrete actions.

The redefinition of the prestige concerning the place of origin may be a typical strategy of diasporic groups and is examined in the contribution by Amber Gemmeke, who shows that the high esteem that certain marabouts enjoy within their translocal community in Dakar is linked to their strategy of conspicuously demonstrating a rural habitus. With their habitus referring to a remote place, these marabouts contribute to the establishment of a shared set of norms and values among their clients.

CONCLUSION

The questionable character of any definition of motion, mobility and movement may be regarded as an underlying hypothesis of all these contributions. They all deal with mobility and movement, not exclusively in the concrete sense of 'moving from one place to the other' (Casey 1996), but rather in a more complex way through the idea of the deterritorialization of life-worlds. In this way, the questioning of the concept of a spatially bounded locality is one of the coherent messages in this book. The protagonists who are in focus here, namely people on the move, understand their actions in contexts which draw their relevance from origins or destinations far beyond the place of the actual event.

This has some important methodological consequences. It is no longer possible to consider only the place of origin or the destination of migration. This means more particularly that any urban life-world cannot be limited to just one city. The ethnography of these places requires more complex strategies, which must also take into account inspirations, experiences and interfaces with other places. Deterritorialization may be an important clue to a better understanding without abandoning the concept of locality. The diversity of links to other places and the range of different movements do not mean that the concrete life-world has lost its emplaced and local character.

Transnationalism and the globally circulating images of urbanity constitute a substantial development in the study of cities in Africa. The current reframing of urban studies is of equal relevance to the methodological milestones of the situated emergence of urban networks and the creation of new social forms of everyday life and rituals of the 1960s. At that time, authors like Mitchell, Epstein and Cohen provided methods for studying culture beyond the culturally bounded spaces of villages and 'ethnic territories'. Currently, authors like Glick Schiller, de Boeck, Malaquais, Nutall and Weiss are providing a framework for dealing with locality in a new way. Their inspiring studies of cities in Africa not only acknowledge the role of urban cultures in the context of understanding societies in Africa, they also expand the methodology of ethnographic studies in general. They urge Africanist scholars to reconsider the interconnectedness between different – and sometimes distant – places on the globe, without neglecting the notion of locality.

All the contributions in this volume stress the ideas of the transgression of the local and of deterritorialization concerning the notion of cities in Africa. However, none of the texts makes an assumption about 'what African cities are'. In contrast, it is more appropriate to refer to the dynamics of the expansion of urban life-worlds as a characteristic, which does not imply any specific notion about the actors' 'Africanness' and their networks. This is actually one of the reasons why it is possible for urbanites in and from Africa to become cosmopolitans and – in the following – to redefine 'Africa' as a topic, as a set of practices that are also lived and dealt with in Europe. Questions about African cultures are no longer answered in Africa alone but must also be linked to Dubai, Paris or New York, among other places. This new dynamic takes urban life-worlds as a starting point and will probably play a decisive role in the future of African societies.

REFERENCES

Al-Zubaidi, Layla. 1998. *Urban Anthropology*. Bloomington: Indiana University. http://www.indiana.edu/~wanthro/URBAN.htm (accessed 05 October 2010).

Basu, Paul and Simon Coleman. 2008. 'Introduction: Migrant Worlds, Material Cultures', *Mobilities*, 3(3): 313-330.

Beauchemin, Cris and Philippe Bocquier. 2004. 'Migration and Urbanisation in Francophone West Africa: An Overview of the Recent Empirical Evidence', *Urban Studies*, 4(11): 2245-2272.

Behrens, Roger. 2007. 'Kritische Theorie der Stadt', *Widerspruch. Münchner Zeitschrift für Philosophie,* 46: 13-38.

Boesen, Elisabeth and Laurence Marfaing (eds.). 2007. *Les nouveaux urbains dans l'espace Sahara-Sahel: Un cosmopolitisme par le bas*. Paris: Karthala.

Boyer, Florence. 2005. 'Le projet migratoire des migrants touaregs de la zone de Bankilaré: la pauvreté désavouée'. In: Veronika Bilger and Albert Kraler (eds.). *African Migrations: Historical Perspectives and Contemporary Dynamics*. Wien: Arbeitsgemeinschaft Angewandte Afrikanistik: 47-67.

Carling, Jørgen. 2002. 'Migration in the Age of Involuntary Immobility: Theoretical Reflections and Cape Verdean Experiences', *Journal of Ethnic and Migration Studies*, 28(1): 5-42.

Casey, Edward S. 1996. 'How to Get from Space to Place in a Fairly Short Stretch of Time? Phenomenological Prolegomena'. In: Steven Feld and Keith H. Basso (eds.). *Senses of Place*. Santa Fe: School of American Research: 13-52.

Clifford, James. 1988. *The Predicament of Culture: Twentieth-Century Ethnography*. Cambridge: Harvard University.

Cohen, Abner. 1969. *Custom and Politics in Urban Africa: A Study of Hausa Migrants in Yoruba Towns*. Berkeley: University of California.

Copeland-Carson, Jacqueline. 2004. *Creating Africa in America: Translocal Identity in an Emerging World City*. Philadelphia: University of Pennsylvania.

Coquery-Vidrovitch, Catherine. 1991. 'The Process of Urbanization in Africa (From the Origins to the Beginning of Independence)', *African Studies Review*, 34(1): 1-98.

Davis, Mike. 2006. *Planet of Slums*, London: Verso.
De Boeck, Filip and Marie-Françoise Plissart. 2004. *Kinshasa: Tales of the Invisible City*. Tervuren: Luidon.
Drechsel, Pay, Sophie Graefe and Michael Fink. 2007. *Rural-urban Food, Nutrient and Virtual Water Flows in Selected West African Cities*. Colombo: IWMI.
Epstein, Arnold L. 1961. 'The Network and Urban Social Organization', *Rhodes-Livingstone Journal*, 29: 29-62.
Ferguson, James. 1992. 'The Cultural Topography of Wealth: Commodity Paths and the Structure of Property in Rural Lesotho', *American Anthropologist*, 94: 55-73.
Garcia Canclini, Néstor. 1995. 'Cultural Globalization in a Disintegrating City', *American Ethnologist*, 22: 743-755.
Genova, James E. 2005. 'Africanité and Urbanité: The Place of the Urban in Imaginings of African Identity during the Late Colonial Period in French West Africa'. In: Steven J. Slam and Toyin Falola (eds.). *African Urban Spaces in Historical Perspective*. Rochester: University of Rochester: 266-286.
Glick-Schiller, Nina. 1992. 'Towards a Definition of Transnationalism'. In: Nina Glick-Schiller (ed.). *Towards a Transnational Perspective on Migration: Race, Class, Ethnicity, and Nationalism Reconsidered*. New York: New York Academy of Sciences: IX-XIV.
---. 2005. 'Transnational Social Fields and Imperialism: Bringing a Theory of Power to Transnational Studies', *Anthropological Theory*, 5(4): 439-461.
Glick Schiller, Nina and Ayse Çağlar. 2009. 'Towards a Comparative Theory of Locality in Migration Studies: Migrant Incorporation and City Scale', *Journal of Ethnic and Migration Studies*, 35(2): 77-202.
Guèye, Cheikh and Abdou Fall. 2005. *Urbain-rural: L'hybridisation en marche*. Dakar: ENDA.
Gugler, Josef. 1971. 'Life in a Dual System: Eastern Nigerians in Town, 1961', *Cahiers d'Etudes Africaines*, 11(3): 400-421.
Gutkind, Peter C. W. 1965. 'African Urbanism, Mobility and the Social Network', *International Journal of Comparative Sociology*, 6: 48-60.
Hackenbroich, Wilfried and Kai Vöckler. 2007. 'Call Center in Kolkata. Aufgespaltene Räume, aufgespaltene Identitäten'. In: Regina Bittner,

Wilfried Hackenbroich and Kai Vöckler (eds.). *Transnationale Räume - Transnational Spaces*. Berlin: Jovis: 112-120.

Heeg, Susanne. 2008. 'Megacities am Rande des Kollaps? Von Slums and „Gated Communities": Wie der städtische Raum zerfällt', *Forschung Frankfurt* 3: 34-40.

Horn, David G. 1989. 'Culture and Power in Urban Anthropology', *Dialectical Anthropology*, 13(2): 189-198.

Kastner, Kristin. 2010. 'Moving Relationships: Family Ties of Nigerian Migrants on their Way to Europe', *African and Black Diaspora*, 3(1): 17-34.

Klute, Georg and Hans Peter Hahn. 2007. 'Cultures of Migration: Introduction'. In: Hans Peter Hahn and Georg Klute (eds.). *Cultures of Migration. African Perspectives*. Berlin: Lit: 9-27.

Koolhaas, Rem and Bregtje van der Haak. 2005. *Lagos, Wide and Close: An Interactive Journey into an Exploding City*. Amsterdam: Submarine.

Kusenbach, Margarete. 2003. 'Street Phenomenology: The Go-Along as Ethnographic Research Tool', *Ethnography*, 4(3): 355-385.

Lefebvre, Henri. 2004. *Rhythmanalysis. Space, Time, and Everyday Life*. London: Continuum.

Lentz, Carola. 2000. '"This is Ghanaian Territory!" Land Conflicts in Transnational Localities on the Burkina Faso-Ghana Border', *Berichte des Sonderforschungsbereichs 268*, 14: 477-495.

Levitt, Peggy. 1999. 'Social Remittances: A Local-Level, Migration-Driven Form of Cultural Diffusion', *International Migration Review*, 32(124): 926-949.

MacGaffey, Janet and Rémy Bazenguissa-Ganga. 2000. *Congo-Paris: Transnational Traders on the Margins of Law*. London: James Currey.

Malaquais, Dominique. 2004. *Douala / Johannesburg / New York: Cityscapes Imagined*. Cape Town: Isandla Institute.

Marris, Peter. 1961. *Family and Social Change in an African City: A Study of Rehousing in Lagos*. London: Routledge.

Mazzucato, Valentina, Mirjam Kabki and Lothar Smith. 2006. 'Transnational Migration and the Economy of Funerals: Changing Practices in Ghana', *Development and Change*, 37(5): 1047-1072.

Mitchell, Clyde J. 1956. *The Kalela Dance: Aspects of Social Relationships among Urban Africans in Northern Rhodesia*. Manchester: Manchester University.

Mitchell, Clyde J. and Arnold L. Epstein. 1959. 'Occupational Prestige and Social Status among Urban Africans in Northern Rhodesia', *Africa*, 29: 22-40.

Moore, Sally F. 1994. *Anthropology and Africa: Changing Perspectives on a Changing Scene*. Charlottesville: University of Virginia.

Mora-Kpai, Idrissou. 2005. *Arlit, deuxième Paris* (DVD). Stuttgart: EZEF.

Murray, Martin J. and Garth Andrew Myers. 2007. 'Introduction: Situating Cities in Contemporary Africa'. In: Martin J. Murray and Garth A. Myers (eds.). *Cities in Contemporary Africa*. New York: Palgrave: 1-25.

Nieswand, Boris. 2009. 'Development and Diaspora: Ghana and its Migrants', *Sociologus*, 59(1): 17-31.

Nutall, Sarah. 2004. 'City Forms and Writing the "Now" in South Africa', *Journal of Southern African Studies*, 30(4): 731-749.

Otiso, Kefa M. and George Owusu. 2008. 'Comparative Urbanization in Ghana and Kenya in Time and Space', *GeoJournal*, 71: 143-157.

Paragas, Fernando. 2005. 'Migrant Mobiles: Cellular Telephony, Transnational Spaces, and the Filipino Diaspora'. In: Kristof Nyíri (ed.). *A Sense of Place: The Global and the Local in Mobile Communication*. Wien: Passagen: 241-249.

Pelican, Michaela and Peter Tatah. 2009. 'Migration to the Gulf States and China: Local Perspectives from Cameroon', *African Diaspora*, 2(2): 229-244.

Pellow, Deborah. 1991. 'The Power of Space in the Evolution of an Accra Zongo', *Ethnohistory*, 38(4): 414-450.

---. 2002. *Landlords and Lodgers: Socio-Spatial Organization in an Accra Community*. Westport: Praeger.

Pieterse, Edgar. 2008. *City Futures: Confronting the Crisis of Urban Development*. London: Zed.

Salazar, Noel B. 2010. 'Towards an Anthropology of Cultural Mobilities', *Journal of Migration and Culture*, 1(1): 53-68.

Sinatti, Giulia. 2008. 'The Making of Urban Translocalities: Senegalese Migrants in Dakar and Zingonia'. In: Michael P. Smith and John Eade (eds.). *Transnational Ties: Cities, Migrations and Identities*. New Brunswick: Transaction: 61-76.

Skinner, Elliott P. 1974. *African Urban Life: The Transformation of Ouagadougou*. Princeton: Princeton University.

Smith, Michael P. 2001. *Transnational Urbanism: Locating Globalization.* Oxford: Blackwell.

---. 2005. 'Power in Place/Places of Power: Contextualizing Transnational Research', *City & Society*, 17(1): 5-34.

Stoller, Paul. 2002. *Money has no Smell: The Africanization of New York City.* Chicago: University of Chicago.

Swiaczny, Frank. 2005. 'Regionalisierte Ergebnisse der World Population Prospects 2002. Teil 7: Verstädterung', *BiB-Mitteilungen*, 3: 24-30.

Syed, Ali. 2007. '"Go West Young Man": The Culture of Migration among Muslims in Hyderabat, India', *Journal of Ethnic and Migration Studies*, 33(1): 37-58.

UN-Habitat. 2003. *The Challenge of Slums: Global Report on Human Settlements.* London: Earthscan.

Vertovec, Steven. 2009. *Transnationalism.* London: Routledge.

Vincent, Cédric. 2005. 'De Sim City au Musée: Mégalomanie urbaine dans la globalisation de l'espace artistique', *Mouvements*, 39/40: 83-95.

Waldenfels, Bernhard. 1997. *Topographie des Fremden: Studien zur Phänomenologie.* Frankfurt a.M.: Suhrkamp.

Weiss, Brad. 2002. 'Thug Realism: Inhabiting Fantasy in Urban Tanzania', *Cultural Anthropology*, 17: 93-124.

---. 2009. *Street Dreams and Hip Hop Barbershops: Global Fantasy in Urban Tanzania.* Bloomington: Indiana University.

Wildner, Kathrin. 1995. 'Picturing the City: Themen und Methoden der Stadtethnologie', *Kea. Zeitschrift für Kulturwissenschaften*, 8: 1-22.

Wimmer, Andreas and Nina Glick-Schiller. 2003. 'Methodological Nationalism, the Social Sciences and the Study of Migration: An Essay in Historical Epistemology', *International Migration Review*, 37(3): 576-610.

The Urban Poor, the Informal Sector and Environmental Health Policy in Nigeria

GEOFFREY I. NWAKA

INTRODUCTION

Ideally, well-managed cities should promote both development and environmental health, but most African cities face severe health challenges arising mainly from widespread poverty, which constitutes 'the largest roadblock to good health' (Global Forum for Health Research 2004: 15). More than midway to the 2015 delivery date for attaining the Millennium Development Goals, it looks very unlikely that the development targets in health, education, environmental sustainability and poverty reduction will be met in Africa, despite noticeable improvements in some areas. Poverty, slum conditions and infectious diseases remain pervasive and persistent. The level of preventable child and maternal deaths is still high, and Africa contributes least to but suffers most from the worsening consequences of climate change. The current global economic recession and poor coordination among donor agencies have undermined the impact of international development assistance.

Up to the 1980s, poverty was largely associated with rural areas in developing countries, but the situation has changed, with the dramatic increase in the numbers and proportion of the population living in urban areas and the corresponding increase in the level of urban poverty (Carr 2004). Many now argue that it is best to target poverty where it is growing fastest – in the cities. The assumption that city-dwellers are better off than their rural counterparts often obscures the wide and growing gap in health status and amenity levels between the wealthy few and the urban poor majority who are presumed to be illegal squatters in the city and are therefore excluded from due recognition and access to health, education and other services. Although some of the elite neighbourhoods in African cities enjoy relatively high-quality housing and residential environment, the bulk of the urban poor live in squalid and health-threatening conditions. The supply of water for personal and domestic hygiene is grossly inadequate, as is the coverage of sanitation facilities. The state of waste management and drainage is rudimentary, nutritional standards are low and food contamination occurs frequently, especially in the extensive street food industry. Rapid urbanization also increases the demand for energy for industrial uses, transport and the domestic consumption of households. Electricity supply is usually unreliable, and petroleum products (especially kerosene) and gas are often unavailable or unaffordable. The vast majority of townspeople, especially those who live in small and medium urban centres, rely almost entirely on traditional fuels (firewood and charcoal), which not only deplete rural forests, but have the adverse health effect of air pollution. Indoor pollution from open fires and stoves in poorly ventilated homes is known to be responsible for a wide variety of respiratory ailments among women and children, who are exposed constantly to toxic fumes in cooking areas (Hosier 1992).

Environmental and health problems overlap. As poverty increases the risk of ill health, the urban poor suffer disproportionately from the effects of environmental problems in the cities. The appalling state of affairs described above has serious adverse implications for public health, as seen in the high incidence of water-borne and filth-related diseases (Hardoy and Satterthwaite 1990). Unfortunately, the current pattern of government spending on the health sector is clearly inequitable as it tends to benefit the better off, the principal users of health services, who can in fact afford to pay for these services, which are provided and subsidized by government.

The main policy challenge is how best to reach the poor and decrease the inequalities in access to health services; how to support and regulate the urban informal sector and irregular settlements in a way that promotes shelter and livelihood for the poor while at the same time ensuring a safe, healthy and socially acceptable environment; and how to ensure that the struggle against urban poverty and slum dwelling does not result in a campaign against the urban poor and slum-dwellers themselves. What are the essential elements of a strategy to improve the informal sector and the conditions of the poor?

POLICY DILEMMA

Opinions differ widely on what the appropriate attitude and policies towards the informal sector and the urban poor should be. Some of the more optimistic advocates of the informal sector see it as a vital source of employment and income for the poor, the seedbed of local entrepreneurship, and a potent instrument in the campaign to combat poverty and social exclusion. They condemn the large number of regulations and bureaucratic procedures that tend to stifle entrepreneurship and inhibit the realization of the full potential of the informal sector in socio-economic development and poverty reduction (Danida 1997; De Soto 1989). Others, however, dismiss the sector as an anomaly, a source of disorder and an obstacle to the development of a modern city and a modern economy. They condemn the slums, health risks, insecurity and exploitation associated with the sector, and hope that, like other transitory phases in the course of development, the sector will wither away quickly with time and economic progress. They accordingly argue that public policy should actively seek to speed up the process of its eradication (Abumere 1998; Maegher and Yanusi 1996). Even those who tend to idealize the informal sector acknowledge that it is at best a mixed blessing. In so far as informal sector activities do not respect legal, health and quality standards, and furthermore do not pay taxes, they violate the rules of fair competition. They maintain that the informal sector has now run its course, is now saturated, and may just be replicating the problems of rural areas in urban contexts.

These conflicting positions pose a difficult dilemma for planners and policy-makers and tend to reinforce the ambivalence and hostility of African governments towards the sector. For many African governments and planners, the main policy dilemma is how best to uphold the rule of law and contain the adverse health and environmental effects of slums and irregular settlements without disrupting the livelihoods of the poor, as well as how to protect the vulnerable groups that work in the informal sector, especially women, children and apprentices, from harm and exploitation. In most slums and informal settlements there is no officially registered owner to whom government officials can offer services, and officials consider it ill-advised to extend services like water and electricity to 'illegal settlements' that may soon be pulled down by government. Insecure housing and tenure also discourage the poor from investing as much as they might to improve their homes and environment (Satterthwaite and McGranahan 2007). This explains why some African governments have sometimes adopted a misguided policy of blaming the victims, trying in vain to outlaw and repress the informal sector, as well as forcibly evict hundreds of thousands of so-called squatters from urban slums. This was the case in the so-called 'War Against Environmental Indiscipline' and 'Operation Clean and Green' in Nigeria, which, like the recent 'Operation Restore Order' in Zimbabwe, destroyed the homes and businesses of millions of poor townspeople, thus worsening the problems of poverty and social exclusion. This chapter argues that human beings ought to be at the centre of the concern for urban sustainability in Africa. While acknowledging the importance of the 'green agenda' for protecting natural resources and ecosystems in order to secure long-term global sustainability and make cities healthy and beautiful, the chapter maintains that the proper starting point in the quest for urban sustainability in Africa is the 'brown agenda' that prioritizes improving people's living and working environments of the urban poor. The latter face a more immediate environmental threat to their health and well-being. UN-Habitat has rightly observed that, 'in pursuit of protecting the environment, we must first protect the people', as it is absolutely essential 'to ensure that all people have a sufficient stake in the present to motivate them to take part in the struggle to secure the future for humanity' (Habitat Day Speech of the Executive Secretary of UN-Habitat, cf. Ramachandran 1990). Current research suggests that the path to urban sustainability in Africa lies in trying to build and manage more inclusive and socially equitable cities where everybody, regardless of economic means, gender, age, ethnic origin or religion, is enabled and empowered to participate productively in the social, economic and political opportunities that cities offer. This human-centred approach to development calls for rethinking the traditional engineering solutions and broadening the narrow technical focus of conventional town-planning and urban management. It would also involve revising the large number of regulations and bureaucratic procedures from different levels of government that tend to stifle individual initiative, as well as inhibit the realization of the full potential of the informal sector and the poor in the development of the cities.

THE URBAN CHALLENGE IN NIGERIA AND AFRICA

Africa is the world's least urbanized but most rapidly urbanizing continent, although the rate of urban growth may be slowing down in some areas (Potts 2009). Nonetheless the total urban population is expected to exceed 200 million in the next few years. Unlike the historical experience of Europe and North America, where the growth of cities and general population growth occurred slowly over centuries, allowing sufficient time for the institutions and structures of urban management to develop apace, the extremely rapid rate of urbanization in Africa is occurring in the context of widespread poverty, with little industrialization to provide jobs, and ahead of the development of the requisite institutions for managing and providing adequately for townspeople. Many analysts have observed in Africa a process of instant urbanization (Mabogunje 1992).

Almost everywhere in Africa, urban conditions have grown from bad to worse. Good quality housing is scare and very expensive, and critics have complained about the 'ruralization' of the African city – with the weakening of land and planning controls, close urban-rural ties, extensive urban agriculture, the deterioration of the physical environment and the almost mindless horizontal sprawl.

The urban situation in Nigeria is particularly disturbing. Successive administrations have at best been ambivalent in their attitude to the cities and the informal sector. Nigeria is one of the largest oil-producing countries in the world and potentially the richest country in Africa, but most of the country's 140 million people, especially those in the rapidly expanding urban informal sector and slums, are extremely poor by all accounts. The rate of urban population growth is about 5.8 per cent, and the country's urban population is expected to exceed 100 million by 2020. More than seven cities have populations that exceed one million, and over five thousand towns and cities have populations of between twenty and five hundred thousand. Lagos, the former national capital grew from 1.4 million in 1963 to 3.5 million in 1975; its current population is estimated to be six million, and it is projected to reach 24 million by 2020. Although most Nigerian towns owe their growth largely to activities generated by European presence in the colonial period, British officials neither anticipated nor approved of the growth of a large urban population and therefore tended to see cities as an unfortunate by-product of colonial activities which had to be firmly contained in order to avoid political subversion and social disorganization. The policies and institutions introduced for urban development were generally very restrictive, myopic and ineffective, especially in the critical areas of land-use control, town planning, urban administration and the provision of urban services. Housing and planning policies were used as instruments of segregation and social exclusion. Consequently, the rapid urban expansion which occurred in the post-independence period has quickly overtaken and overwhelmed the local capacity to cope with the crises of inadequate shelter and services, unemployment and the worsening deterioration of the urban environment (Nwaka 1996; UN-Habitat 2006).

Sadly, these colonial laws, codes, regulations and institutions (embodied in the colonial Town and Country Planning Ordinance of 1946), which were designed for the small populations envisaged in the cities of the colonial period, have been inherited with little rethinking by post-colonial administrations, even as the cities expand rapidly in response to many aspects of post-colonial transformation (Egunjobi 2000; Nwaka 1996). The concern about a presumed 'urban bias' has also led to the negative response of anti-urbanism and to urban neglect. Many still believe that the cities attract a disproportionate share of national development resources but contribute little to national development and welfare. Urban problems have therefore tended to be addressed indirectly through rural development programmes, migration control and other policies to contain or reverse the trend of urbanization. However, these have not only failed to stop the inevitable and irreversible process of urbanization, they have also created a policy vacuum, pushing cities to grow in a disorderly manner and allowing urban problems to accumulate. Most of the current legislation and by-laws for environmental health and sanitation appear to townspeople as reminders of colonial segregation and oppression and have therefore often been evaded or resisted. Some of the urban-related policies and reforms introduced in recent years, such as the Nigerian Land Use Decree and the Nigerian Urban and Regional Planning Law of 1992 (which forms the basis of the National Urban Development Policy of 1997), have proved hopelessly inadequate to deal with the accumulated problems of past neglect.

Land is central to the slum problem and urban informality in Nigeria. The Habitat Agenda (Habitat II; New Delhi Declaration 1996) has rightly emphasized that 'access to land and security of tenure are strategic prerequisites for the provision of adequate shelter for all [...] for the development of sustainable settlements, and a way of breaking the vicious circle of poverty' (The Government of India et al.: 1996). The Nigerian Land Use Decree/Act was introduced in 1978 ostensibly to streamline the wide variety of pre-existing land practices in the country, to curb land speculation and to facilitate equitable access to land for bona fide public and private users. But the law has been marred in its application by official arbitrariness, corruption, bureaucratic delays and other forms of abuse, which have turned it into a major blockage on land supply to all except the very rich and well-connected individuals. There is an urgent need to find a more appropriate, more efficient and transparent system of land control and allocation that moves from the present centralized state monopoly of land control towards a more decentralized land delivery system that serves local needs and protects the rights and development concerns of the poor.

With the failure of planning and land-use control, the informal urban sector expanded rapidly in the 1980s and 1990s as a result of the austerity measures introduced as part of the Structural Adjustment Programmes. The reduction in public spending, especially for the social sector, the drop in real wages and public-sector retrenchment swelled the ranks of the informal sector and led to the greater informalization of many formal sector enterprises. Unfortunately, the government response to the social crisis and the 'safety nets' introduced in the 1990s have not affected the conditions of the poor in any significant way. Government officials have tended to blame the environmental problems of the cities on the lawlessness of the informal sector and have sought to deal with the challenges of informality through increased powers of control and regulation, by insisting on legal titles to land, public housing, mortgage finance and so on – conventional approaches that have usually by-passed the poor, still leaving the informal sector as the dominant provider of land and housing in large parts of urban and peri-urban areas.

A number of more promising policy initiatives have been introduced in recent years. These include the establishment of People's Banks and Community Banks (now Micro-Finance Banks), based on the Asian model, and meant to provide small credits and other forms of financial services to the urban poor. Also, the National Directorate for Employment and the National Open Apprenticeship Scheme were set up to promote self-employment by providing training and financial support for unemployed youth. However, a recent survey has shown that only about ten per cent of the informal sector workers interviewed were aware of how to take advantage of these opportunities (Dike 1997; Maeghar and Yanusi 1996). More recently the Nigerian government has introduced a number of Poverty Alleviation Programmes and adopted the National Economic Empowerment and Development Strategy (NEEDS) with its state counterparts (SEEDS) as a social charter and reform agenda meant to strengthen governance, transform values, combat corruption and alleviate poverty. But the impact of these progressive new initiatives on the urban poor remains to be seen.

THE WAY FORWARD

The way forward appears to lie in well-coordinated partnerships among the various stakeholders in the pursuit of urban sustainability. In this regard, useful insights could be drawn from a number of recent UN-sponsored conferences and global initiatives which provide guidance on practical approaches to dealing with urban poverty. Agenda 21 of the Rio Earth Summit sees the creation of sustainable human settlements as integral to the achievement of sustainable development, while the Habitat Agenda of the Istanbul City Summit outlines approaches to developing sustainable human settlements. In particular, WHO's Healthy Cities Programme seeks to promote coordination and collaboration among various government agencies and other stakeholders in support of health and the environment, as well as ensure equitable access to preventive and curative health services. Other such initiatives include ILO's Decent Work Agenda, the World Bank-sponsored Cities Alliance for Cities without Slums (cf. www.cities alliance.org), the NEPAD Cities Programme, and the UN Habitat's twin Campaigns for Good Urban Governance and Secure Tenure. There is a growing international consensus that the crisis of governance in developing countries is at the heart of the worsening urban crisis and that good governance is perhaps the single most important factor in eradicating poverty and promoting development.

There is an urgent need for improved governance structures that provide for greater social inclusion in setting priorities and providing services. State and local authorities need to promote a more decentralized, accountable and effective system of governance that would allow for the broad participation of all interest groups, including the private sector and civil society organizations. They should also evolve a general framework of laws and regulations for planning and development that are more realistic and compatible with local conditions. In particular, there is a need to change the way health care is organized and financed in order to remove or lower the financial barriers to the use of preventive and curative health services and to tackle the social and economic causes of health inequalities. It is essential not only to improve the various aspects of urban health infrastructure, but even more to introduce well-targeted programmes to address the lack of knowledge among the poor, cultural barriers to good health and programmes that ensure greater access to public health education and services for the poor.

Since resolving the urban crisis is central to Africa's economic and social progress, the international development community genuinely needs to address the global economic context of underdevelopment and the structural roots of urban poverty in Africa, especially in the critical areas of fair trade, debt relief and development assistance. Donor agencies and NGOs should provide more technological and financial assistance to help strengthen local public health capacity, as far as possible channelling their aid directly to organizations that work with and for the poor.

Finally, for their part the urban poor and informal sector enterprises should also try to organize and regulate themselves better in order to engage more constructively with government and other development partners. Collectively they must actively seek to curb some of the socially unacceptable aspects of their activities, such as the adulteration of goods and services, crime and other sharp practices, and confine themselves to genuine activities for livelihoods that may technically be 'illegal' in the sense of not conforming with bureaucratic norms and regulations, many of which are arbitrary and inequitable. After all:

"[…] a modern economy can be made up of sectors and activities with very different sizes, types of technology, styles of organization and degrees of integration into local, national and international markets […]. The fundamental raison d'être of any economic system is the well-being of the individuals, their families, and communities. Economic power, the growth of national income, the increase of profit, the enlargement of a firm are only instruments. Deified, they become obstacles to the welfare of the population. To modernize the economy is to use the best technologies available to allow the individual to work, to create, to earn an income, and to enforce the rights of employees and workers." (DANIDA 1998:18)

REFERENCES

Abumere, S. I. *et al.* 1998. *The Informal Sector in Nigeria's Development Process*. Ibadan: DPC.

Allen, Adriana *et al*. 2002. *Sustainable Urbanization: Bridging the Green and Brown Agendas*. London: DPU.

AMCHUD (African Ministerial Conference on Housing and Urban Development). 2006. *African Cities Driving the NEPAD Initiative: An introduction to the NEPAD Cities Programme*. Durban, South Africa. http://www.sarpn.org/documents/d0001681/index.php (accessed 10 January 2012).

Carr, Dara. 2004. 'Improving the Health of the World's Poorest People', *Health Bulletin of the Population Reference Bureau*, 1: 1-34.

DANIDA. 1998. *Conditions for Social Progress: Humane Markets for Humane Societies*. Report of the 1997 Copenhagen Seminar for Social Progress. Copenhagen: Ministry of Foreign Affairs.

De Soto, Harnando. 1989. *The Other Path – Invisible Revolution in the Third World*. London: Tauris.

Dike, Enwere. 1997. *Structural Adjustment and Small Scale Industrial Enterprises in South Eastern Nigeria*. Geneva: UNRISD.

Egunjobi, Layi. 2002. 'Planning the Nigerian Cities for Better Quality of Life'. In: O. O. Oyesiku and Samuel Onakomaiya (eds.). *Environment, Physical Planning and Development in Nigeria*. Ibadan: College: 89–107.

Fernandes, Edeso and Ann Varlery (eds.). 1998. *Illegal Cities: Law and Urban Change in Developing Countries*. London: Zed.

Hardoy, Jorge Enrique and David Satterthwaite. 1989. *Environmental Problems of Third World Cities: A Global Issue Ignored*. London: IIED.

Hosier, Richard H. 1992. 'Energy and Environmental Management in East African Cities', *Environment and Planning A*, 24: 1231-1254.

IIED/DANIDA. 2001. *Urban Environmental Improvement and Poverty Reduction*. London: Earthscan.

Mabogunje, Akin L. 1992. 'A New Paradigm for Urban Development'. In: The World Bank (ed.). *Proceedings of the World Bank Annual Conference on Developing Economies*. Washington DC: World Bank: 191-219.

McAuslan, Patrick. 1987. 'Legislation, Regulation and Shelter -Hindrance or Help to the Homeless', *Cities*, 2: 22–27.

McGranahan, Gordon *et al*. 1999. *Environmental Change and Human Health in Countries of Africa, the Caribbean and the Pacific*. Stockholm: Stockholm Environment Institute.

Meagher, Kate and Mohammed-Bello, Yunusa. 1996. *Passing the Buck: Structural Adjustment and the Nigerian Informal Sector*. Geneva: UNRISD.

Nwaka, Geoffrey I. 1996. 'Planning Sustainable Cities in Africa', *Canadian Journal of Urban Research*, 5(1): 119-136.

Potts, David. 2009. 'The Slowing of Sub-Saharan African Urbanization: Evidence and Implications for Urban Livelihoods', *Environment and Development*, 21(1): 253-259.

Ramachandran, Arcot. 1990. 'Urbanization in Global Perspective. Concluding Remarks', *Cities*, 7(1): 81-86.

Stock, Robert. 1988. 'Environmental Sanitation in Nigeria: Colonial and Contemporary', *Review of African Political Economy*, 42: 19–31.

The Government of India *et al*. 1996. *Habitat II: New Delhi Declaration. Global Platform on Access to Land and Security of Tenure as a Condition for Sustainable Shelter and Urban Development*. http://www.spatial.maine.edu/~onsrud/Courses/SIE526/New_Delhi_De claration.htm (accessed 08 February 2012).

UN-Habitat. 2003. *The Challenge of Slums: Global Report on Human Settlements*. London: Earthscan.

---. (ed.). 2006. 'Introduction.' In: *African Cities Driving the NEPAD Initiative*. Nairobi: UN-Habitat: 7-11.

Westendorff, David. 2004. *From Unsustainable to Inclusive Cities*. Geneva: UNRISD.

'I go chop your Dollar'

Scamming Practices and Notions of Morality among Youth in Bamenda, Cameroon

BETTINA FREI

> [...] I don scamming no be small, upon say I get sell
> Poverty no good at all, oh
> Na im make I join internet
> Overscamming no be thief, it is just a game, everybody dey play em
> If any white man fall mugu, I go internet, oh, I go scam em
> Chihuahua, parrots na mi get em
> Any good thing na mi sell em
> DJ Skipper na my sister brother
> You be the mugu, I be the master
> I go chop your Euro, I go take your money and disappear,
> 419 is just a game, you are the loser, I am the scammer [...][1]

'TO CHOP MONEY', OR NORMATIVE DIMENSIONS OF 'USING (OR MISUSING) MONEY'

In this chapter, the notion of 'eating', 'to chop' in Pidgin English, will serve as a background for reflections and for exploring the dimensions of peo-

---

1 Excerpt from DJ Skipper, Bamenda, a local production, selling the CD 'underhand' (I go chop your Euro). Song text covering Nkem Owoh (I go chop your Dollar, soundtrack Master I + II).

ple's normative notions about 'using (or misusing) money', related to fraudulent business practices of 'scamming' in Bamenda, Cameroon. 'Scammers',[2] as I will describe later in this paper, are seen as trespassing conventional societal hierarchies and norms by 'making fast money' and by acquiring it through illegal practices, which have become possible through the availability of new media of communication and information. This is an example of how some young people in this setting negotiate their lifeworld's conditions, in view of the relatively high level of dissatisfaction and economic insecurity, and apparently abundant opportunities elsewhere. In this context I would like to introduce the wider meaning of the notion of 'to chop (money)' in order to shed light on respective negotiations of moralities and social legitimacies related to notions of 'success', 'responsibility' and 'solidarity'. The 'scammer' and 'scamming practices' are thus seen as an epitome of opposition to moral values, reflected in diverse local narratives.

With reference to the title of this chapter, and the above quoted excerpt from a local popular song, as far as the colloquial expression 'to chop money' is concerned, it is often used in the setting of Anglophone Cameroon, but also beyond it, in various fields and situations. It refers to 'misusing the money'[3] and misusing power, in the sense of not using it in an acceptable and morally justifiable way. 'Eating', in general, is a term widely used in Africa to refer to the accumulation of wealth and power, implying a negative connotation, in particular related to the nepotism of the state apparatus and its representatives, as has been widely discussed by others (e.g. Bayart 1993; Mbembe 2001; Jua 2003; Argenti 2007; Geschiere 1997). This is, on the one hand, a perspective of the everyday experiences of people related to practices of corruption as acts of the display of power as performed by state representatives, officials, functionaries, the police and the military, who ar-

---

2   When talking about 'scammers', I denote the importance of these fraudulent – and doubtlessly criminal – activities for some young men in this setting as a source of livelihood. Their being involved in such activities is not a fixed but a transient state, forming a part of their identity performance in a certain setting and peer group. A scammer is not only a scammer – when I use the term, I emphasize that it is not meant in an exclusive or pejorative sense.

3   'Misusing money' corresponds to an expression often used by people in everyday discourses.

bitrarily collect money, for example, at checkpoints in the streets, in tax collections, in offices and in any other situation when people come in contact with them (cf. Bayart *et al*. 1999; Bayart 1993). Related to the situation in the North West Province, the notion also expresses a feeling of political and economic marginalization (cf. Jua and Konings 2004) in the country and of mistrust in relation to the state authorities.[4] In everyday popular narratives, 'to chop money' is often related to, on the other hand, the reality that people spend money quickly, instantly and continuously in order to provide and maintain their daily livelihoods, and at a low level of performance. It also points to the difficulties and living reality of most people in this setting, whose economic situations are determined by the insecurity and unreliability of resources, and to the consequently needed flexibility regarding sources of income and social networks. The fact that money is continuously 'chopped' for everyday survival is also linked to the difficulty of accumulating wealth that could be used in order to improve one's life situation, to 'break out' of the cycle of poverty, to save and invest money and 'turn things for the better'. This kind of 'immobility' or invariability of the situation and lack of a perspective of ever changing it is expressed by people in statements such as: 'things are not moving', 'we are managing', or, 'we are just there hustling'[5] and many other expressions relating to the 'futility of everyday life struggles'.

In this sense, the notion of 'to chop' can be seen as a normative expression related to practices of accumulation and redistribution, and thus also in the context of people's daily economic struggles. When economic resources are secured and shared with others, there is a success: 'success', or being 'successful' does have a moral dimension in this context. This moral di-

---

4　Similarly, when extending this situation of visible state power, the notion 'to chop money' is relating to the wide state apparatus and to a (not clearly defined) group of people who are somehow related to this privileged group and thereby profiting from them. Argenti (2007: 172, 173) points to an allusion to crime, and refers to the 'similar extractive practices' of the gendarmerie compared to bandits and thieves, due to difficulties in distinguishing the spheres of accumulation of criminals and state representatives respectively.

5　In this chapter, I am using quotes and statements of people, which are at least literally taken from interviews and informal conversations. All names are changed.

mension involves ideals regarding how money should be used, not used or accumulated. The expression 'to chop money' thus relates on the one hand to how money is spent and used under conditions of constraints regarding economic resources, conflicting with the ideal of accumulation. On the other hand, it points to unjust distribution, or to a power gradient regarding those who 'chop the money' or figuratively 'put on weight',[6] become a 'big man' (Jua 2003: 18) at the expense of others. The moral claim related to success, which is not fulfilled in the examples mentioned, is related to, first, solidarity: for whom is the money used, including meeting moral notions of redistribution, supporting and strengthening one's family or those towards whom one has certain moral duties (cf. Nyamnjoh 2005).

Secondly, it relates to how money is used in the sense of 'morally restricted accumulating', a lifestyle characterised by one's taking over of responsibility, and the wise and sustainable spending of money. Thirdly, it refers to the acquisition of wealth through honest and hard work. By meeting such preconditions, one can be seen as 'a responsible person'. Negotiations regarding success that does not integrate these normative realms could include discourses about, first, disregarding notions of solidarity, secondly, a careless handling of financial resources expressed in a neglectful and 'extravagant lifestyle', and thirdly, the acquisition of money through illegal practices, which altogether are the attributes of an 'irresponsible person'. The expression 'to chop money' is thus very much related to considerations of 'using money in an irresponsible way' (or misusing it), as well as to respective moral notions of responsibility, to which people often relate in everyday discourses. However, there seem to be various contradictions and tensions between the different ideals involved in being or becoming a 'responsible person': tensions arise between the ideal of solidarity and redistribution of wealth on the one hand, and the accumulation of wealth and displaying it in the sense of indicating one's potentiality to others on the other hand. A successful and capable person thus acts in responsible and supportive ways towards others, including in the sense that such a person uses money wisely and in 'sustainable' ways, thus contributing to the economic stability of one's family. Furthermore, displaying status and power is important to 'let others know' about one's position, including 'acts of gen-

---

6   The belly is the locus of power, and similarly, eating and the belly are related to misuse of power, too (Argenti 2007: 106,109-110).

erosity' and redistribution.[7] Status, which is devolved from observing certain moral conditions, is, as we have seen, very much dependent on moral legitimacy in a certain setting and with a certain group of people, and is thus an ambivalent, situational and transient issue, always negotiated between 'having' and 'giving', between 'being a big man', and 'being a responsible man' (cf. Nyamnjoh 2005; Argenti 2007; Goheen 1996; Warnier 1996; Bayart 1993).

BECOMING A RESPONSIBLE PERSON: YOUTH'S CONSTRAINTS AND OPPORTUNITIES

According to Jua (2003: 14), the problem of the social integration of young people into Cameroonian society started in the 1980s, when structural adjustment programmes were cutting back the state, causing a lack of job opportunities in an economy where the state was the main employer. Along with the general economic downturn in most African countries in the last two or three decades and failures of the Cameroonian government to stimulate the private business sector, this lack of perspectives has hit young people especially hard. The word 'cadets' (Bayart 1985) denotes young males who are regarded as classificatory children, regardless of their respective ages, as their status in society does not permit them to participate in social life as adults by starting their own families and taking over responsibility, which needs as a basis an economic foundation (cf. Argenti 2007; Warnier 1996). Having a responsible position in one's family and society is very much associated with power, and power in this society is most often attributed to certain groups, gender and age. 'Traditional' power usually be-

---

[7] These ambivalences, related to power and wealth, can be transferred to discourses about witchcraft and occult forces that are often seen to be involved with it. On the one hand, empowering occult forces provides (dangerous) powers with which one can become successful, which is, however, often realized at the expense of others (as kin). On the other hand, accusations of witchcraft can serve to claim redistributions of accumulated wealth and thus participation in another's success. Geschiere calls the former the accumulation, the latter the levelling side of witchcraft (Geschiere 1997: 3, 4, 10).

longs to male 'elders' in society, as is generally true of state power, the two realms being interrelated. Regarding positions of power, young people in general do not have much say, or can only go through influential elders to access connections and financial means (Argenti 2007: 7, 8). As today, according to Jua (2003: 17, 18), the willingness to work hard or acquire a good education as guarantees of a successful future alone are failing, and youths are forced to search for opportunities elsewhere. This is probably one of the main explanations for why some young people become involved in illegal businesses, such as scamming. Scamming practices, the central topic of this chapter, provide opportunities for young people to achieve success, despite their lack of connections and financial means, and despite their young age. Scammers can thus be seen as trespassing on the conventional social hierarchies and norms by bypassing such networks of power relations[8] that are linked to seniority and affiliation. However, scamming practices do not seem to offer any opportunities for social recognition, as does, for example, migration, which for most youths in this setting is seen as the ultimate goal.[9] Some (young, male) interviewees said that, as soon as they went abroad for their studies, they could finally start leading a 'responsible life' and 'become a man', in the sense that they could finally work (besides studying), earn some money, accumulate savings and contribute to the support of their families back home. Thus the search for opportunities, the hopes for a better future, are, in this setting, transferred to a more global level, where the chances of fulfilling them are considered better.

In this sense, the new media provide a means of challenging and deploying new spaces, of in this sense contesting the given norms and hierarchies of society (cf. Macamo and Neubert 2008; Burrell 2009). Media spaces can offer a distinct realm within youth's life-worlds where young people acquire new rights and have opportunities to 'make themselves heard'.

---

8 This was expressed as follows: 'They want to take a shortcut to success' (Cletus 26 September 2009).

9 Abroad is where hard work is still the way to become successful, maybe allowing one to accumulate wealth in order to become a 'successful person', and where education is considered favourable and prestigious, so much that it even helps in the Cameroonian setting.

Figure 1: Signboards of cyber cafés in the streets of Bamenda, Cameroon

Source: photo by the author

Above all it is a realm beyond the control of those who control spaces of power, wealth and expression in society. Young people have always deployed alternative new spaces, as Argenti puts it, related to the period of colonial rule and the beginning of independence, by migrating and seeking salaried employment 'from a third force that was independent of local authority, indeed superior to it' (Argenti 2007: 8). Related to the new media (spaces), we could say that seeking education, migrating, scamming or just emulating a 'global youth culture' are strategies young people employ in search of new perspectives. Information gathering and 'browsing' the internet, as well as media features such as chat-rooms and forums, blogs and dating sites, are perceived as offering opportunities for self-realization, pointing to images of success and providing a space and conditions in which to reach one's aims, as well as to create new identities that can sometimes even stretch out to 'invention' in the sense of fiction and the 'duping' of others, for example, in the field of scamming practices.[10]

Popular discourses run along threads of normative discussions related to the re-interpretation of notions of 'success' (cf. Nyamnjoh 2005; Ndjio 2008; Simone 2005; Diouf 2003; Bucholtz 2002) and to challenging the

---

10 Important in this illegal business is also the possibility of changing identity. For example, having several identities in the sense of possessing various identity cards is common in Cameroon (and not only related to illegal activities). Furthermore, in the scamming business, scammers play different roles by representing different contact persons vis-à-vis their scam victims, as I show later in this chapter.

ideals of reciprocity and solidarity, as well as what it means to be or to become a 'responsible person'. Furthermore, it relates to the behaviour and 'lifestyles' or practices of conspicuous consumption of (some) young people, and, regarding the scammers especially, the illegal nature of 'making money' and thus inverting power relations.

BEYOND MORAL LEGITIMACY: SCAMMING AS A BUSINESS PRACTICE

In Bamenda, youth's visibility and appearance in the public sphere greatly determine social perceptions of the scamming phenomena. The practices of scamming themselves, however, are less transparent, even though they are observable in public cyber cafés, performed more or less openly, but only comprehensible for internet users with a certain level of internet literacy and experience. Scamming can be related to a set of specific business practices, the notion being derived from 'scam' (fraud, cheat, deceit or swindle). General, more encompassing terms are 'feymania' (Ndjio 2006; Malaquias 2001) and '419', practices 'relating to the respective section of the Nigerian criminal code that deals with business malpractices at large and specifically fraud' (Ndjio 2008: 4). The 'classic' 419 frauds are 'counterfeiting' (which means selling or buying fake cheques) and advanced payment fraud, though 419 practices existed long before the advent of the internet in the area (cf. Smith 2007). From the popular discourses that I witnessed, the expression '419' was used as a general term for fraudulent business practices, whereas 'scamming' was used for internet-related practices, the term 'feymania' being less common. Ndjio (2008: 6) writes that the terms 'scamming' and '419':

"[...] have become an all-purpose concept for explaining illicit forms of wealth accumulation, unlawful economic activities, riches acquired by occult means, ill gotten fortunes, and above all fantastic forms of wealth creation, which are officially unsanctioned because they derive from business activities or economic practices which contravene conventional norms and moral values, and especially circumvent official economic regulatory channels."

In general the term 'scamming' was used synonymous of deceiving people, of duplicity, dishonesty and trickery, as well as of any behaviour that relies on illusion or manipulating the truth in order to facilitate a gain or advantage (Smith 2007; Ndjio 2008). A large percentage[11] of the young, mainly male internet users in the public cyber cafés in Bamenda seemed to be involved in scamming activities at different levels of intensity and 'professionalism'. In this chapter, I will specifically refer to the setting of Bamenda and the practices that are mainly observable in public cyber cafés there, which constitute rather 'small-scale' scamming' on a more informal level.

Regarding the internet-related fraud practices in this setting, most activities are related to the field of the so-called 'puppy-fraud', which includes advertising and attempting to sell non-existent puppies (and sometimes other animals or items) on ad sites, or, less commonly, on self-created homepages. Thus, the main working practices involve posting ads, which needs a certain know-how and experience, since almost all (free) ad sites are blocked for Cameroonian IP addresses. So part of the work involves searching for proxy lists where unprotected (transparent) IP addresses[12] can be found, in order to replace the existing IP address in the local computer's configurations. By doing this, it is possible to post an ad on an ad site by pretending to post it in another location, whereby scammers try to find a match with a certain geographical category in the respective ad site. By doing this, and depending on the site, scammers use translation machines in order to translate ad texts (or correspondence) into other languages (other

---

11 In some cyber cafés I estimated that about 70-80 per cent of internet users were involved in scamming practices.

12 In data transmission, computers communicate through an IP (Internet Protocol), which is based on a numerical code. This code, the IP address, provides geographical information (about the internet domain and network) through which a computer can be located and thus identified. Most often, IP addresses are protected in the sense that it is not possible to use them, but on various so-called proxy lists in the internet open or unprotected IP addresses can be found, which can be copied and used. If a scammer has a credit card at his disposal, such work is no longer necessary because ad sites that charge a fee are not blocked. Thus, some try to obtain access to credit-card numbers, which they might use a few times to pay to post ads before they get blocked by their holders.

than English). Once the ads have been posted, the main work consists in checking the various (and often changing) e-mail addresses which can be contacted by potential buyers. Responses can consist of standard messages that are inserted by copying and pasting, but often individual compositions are necessary, depending on how advanced the process is and 'how much they (the potential buyers) need to be convinced' (Augustus 15 July 2009). Regarding the 'puppy sale' scam, payments are asked at different stages in the process, from the selling price, via payments for shipping, transport, insurance, custom duties and quarantine, to various extra 'incidental' expenses along the way, depending on how long a buyer continues paying. In order to create credibility in the course of these procedures, the sites of shipping companies, airports and insurance companies are needed, and correspondence is held in various threads, dealt with by such institutions and by the pretending breeder or seller of the puppy, by e-mail, chat or mutual phone calls.

Figure 2: Examples of ads for puppies on pet ads sites: the pet scam in the field of advanced fee scam

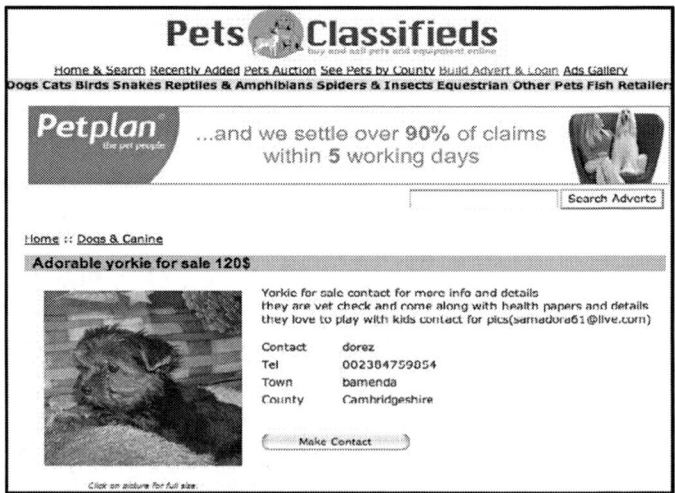

Source: Screenshot from http://www.pets-classifieds.co.uk/

As most of the scammers do not possess a bank account for international transactions, the payments are usually done more or less anonymously by money transfer companies as Western Union and Money Gram. Apart from the daily 'business procedures', many scammers, especially when they are well versed and experienced, are continuously engaged in searching for information or improving their sites to enhance their business practices, in the sense of 'trying to professionalize', or else they carry out 'research' in order to acquire 'new business ideas' related to internet fraud. Many scammers, also depending on their experience and level of prior computer education, are thus internet savvy at a high level, but some also work with a limited array of technological means and know-how. Usually, they are doing several things at the same time, have several windows open simultaneously, switching from one to another, in order to save time (and money for airtime) when the computer is loading. In that sense, they keep open various ad sites, proxy lists, translation machines and search engines, as well as e-mail boxes and chat rooms.

Scammers do not only scam, of course. Apart from scamming, which might nonetheless take most of their online time,[13] they also use the internet for 'private issues', be it communication with relatives or friends, abroad or in Cameroon, online friendships or dating acquaintances, or browsing on sites of interest to them. Some stated that they would try to keep their private and business-related communications and activities separate, for example, with separate e-mail and messenger chat accounts, and even reserving certain time slots for each.[14]

---

13 Scammers can spend several hours a day (and night) in cyber cafés. Among those I met, some indicated they spent from 3-4 up to 7-8 hours online on a daily basis.

14 Even though scamming practices are illegal, the activities are performed relatively open in Bamenda. In that sense, the issue was not as sensitive as one might expect: it was generally not difficult to contact and talk to scammers in the field, provided I was transparent and explained my intentions. Having the confidence of a few people involved in scamming practices meant having easier access to their peers. Nevertheless, there was a difference between informal conversations and more 'formal interviews', where the confidence was more difficult to win. Overall, scamming was a very popular issue in both everyday narratives and people's normative statements about ICT.

SCAMMING PRACTICES AND SOCIAL SPACE IN PUBLIC CYBER CAFÉS

Public cyber cafés are viewed with suspicion by many people, especially by those who hardly ever enter them and are themselves not well versed in using the internet. The spaces of the cyber cafés are often linked to scamming and non-conformity with social values in general, as expressed in different popular discourses. The scamming business in fact produces social spaces and can be seen as one of the main reasons why the density of cyber cafés in Bamenda can be considered exceptional, with still more cyber cafés emerging in more recent times, since scamming practices have become widely popular in Bamenda since mid of the first decade of the new millenium.[15] Thus, in general, such media spaces change the local sphere: cyber cafés are very visible in the city-scape, usually indicated by eye-catching signboards and clearly marked entrances. The 'scammers' have become the main customers for many cyber cafés, and they also have certain standards and expectations regarding technology and equipment. This development leads to pressure on cyber café-owners to update their hardware and software and invest more in quicker lines, which means, in their provider-connection, higher bandwidths, and so on. In this sense also the cyber cafés' interior and operational procedures are adapted to the needs and habits of their customers. One example of this is the so-called 'night browsing',[16] which has recently become very popular and is related to the increasing competition among the numerous cyber cafés. This opportunity is mainly taken up by scammers, as they prefer to communicate in real time and thus

---

15 One question is why Bamenda is so intimately related to the scamming business and has such a density of cyber cafés compared to other cities. One reason might be that the prevailing internet language is English, as well as its proximity to the Nigerian border, where scamming practices first appeared. It could also be due to the economic marginalization of the town, which has few job opportunities for young people, as well as the rather high level of education in the Northwest Province. However, I cannot go more deeply into this issue in this chapter.

16 For security reasons, cyber cafés are closed and are locked from inside after regular opening hours, at about 9 or 10 pm, when there is a certain minimum number of 'night browsers', and only opened again at 6 am next morning. Of course, airtime is cheaper during these night hours.

during the waking hours of their potential customers, which is at night in, for example, the USA.

Of course public cyber cafés are spaces for young people in general and for other practices other than scamming (cf. Burrell 2009), but there are many cyber cafés which do rely mainly on scamming customers, especially in the outer parts of the city.[17] In public cyber cafés, where there are many scammers, to a certain extent they form inclusive groups of friends who know each other and come there every day. Especially in cyber cafés with a high percentage of scammer clients, commonality, sociality and the sense of togetherness seem to be important: the cyber café is not only a working space, it also serves as a platform, a stage, a space of interaction, a kind of 'parallel social space' (cf. Simone 2005) where performance, presenting oneself within and as a group, is important. Consequently, it might be noisy in such cyber cafés at times, with people discussing things and talking to each other, making phone calls and loudly commenting on their activities, sometimes also playing music in the background. This can in such cases lead to other people who are not scamming avoiding specific cyber cafés because they prefer a calmer working environment, and some might even feel threatened by the presence of the scammers. Similarly the scammers often also meet outside the cyber cafés,[18] in other spaces and settings such as bars, clubs or other meeting places for young people, and for different activities in common, such as drinking beer, listening to music, dancing, 'having fun' or related to their 'work', such as collectively picking up money that has been sent to them by 'their dupes'.[19]

---

17 In the city centre and along the main business streets, there are some cyber cafés where fewer scammers are to be found: these cyber cafés have a higher turnover of customers, who pass by to check their e-mail boxes. Furthermore, whether a cyber café attracts many scammer customers or not depends on the quality of services and on the policies of the owner and employees. The fact that these cyber cafés, where there are mainly scammers, are more in the outer areas thus does not mean that these practices are hidden. Scammers usually do not fear to be seen entering a certain cyber café.

18 Thereby they build permeable social groups, mixing up with youth who are not scamming.

19 'Dupes', 'to be duped' or 'scammed': references to scam victims, also called 'mugu'.

Despite the importance of commonality among groups of scammers, however, interpersonal trust often seems to have its limits. Even though scammers exchange technological tricks and share information to a certain extent within a group, in the cyber café, on the phone, or online in e-mail or chat communications there seems to be a certain distrust towards others, even among 'friends'. Especially if one has had success in pursuing a business contact, one might hide this information from others until the 'profit is realized': It is very common for scammers to spy on other scammers and to try to 'snatch away' their businesses and clients. 'Spying out' the scam work of other scammers is mainly done by putting spy-ware on computers in order to be able to enter somebody's e-mail box.[20] In that sense, scammers might fear the environment of a cyber café, where they do not have knowledge of peer internet users, of the maintenance of computers or of the practices of updating anti-spy-ware.[21] Learning from each other is common, but mainly on a very informal level. Most of the scammers stated that they learned by doing, through 'trial and error', as well as by asking friends for advice when they had a specific problem or question. Nevertheless, specializations exist regarding 'animals' that are sold (e.g. only English Bulldogs, or Yorkshire Terriers), regarding countries and languages (e.g. somebody is only posting ads in Spanish). Furthermore, specialization in the sense of collaboration might exist when somebody is especially well versed in a certain setting, for example, providing others with the latest proxy lists (to change IP addresses), or creating the internet sites and fake documents that scammers need for their practices.[22] Payment for such preliminary work and services usually depends on the successful outcome of a certain business transaction.

---

20 The public cyber café, which is perceived as a public space, is probably not seen as an adequate working place when it comes to highly organized scammers, who go beyond the level of 'small-scale' scamming; they are said to prefer working at home.
21 I witnessed that, because of these anxieties, scammers might shift as whole group to a new cyber café and 'occupy' that new space as a group.
22 As is also often done by non-scammers.

Figure 3: Interiors of cyber cafés

Source: photo by the author

'LIFE-STYLE', STATUS, AND CONSPICUOUS CONSUMPTION AMONG 'SCAMMERS'

In local narratives, the notion of 'the scammer' has become a buzz-word and an epitome of what some people value as negative, as illegitimate and opposing morality in society. Accordingly, young media users (whether scammers or not) in this setting – and even outside of the space of the cyber cafés – are associated with particular characteristics and attributes, contributing to the general 'criminalization of youth'. As a result, many people think they are able to identify scammers from their outer appearance and conduct. The negative attributes that are ascribed to scammers might be based on similar negative attributes related to the new media, and could be further enhanced by the emergence of a separate social space, the public cyber café. Furthermore, such negative attributes are fuelled by the scammer's appearance in a group in public and the dynamics of group conduct, as already described. They are also related to scammers' styles, as an expression of conspicuous consumption, pointing to their stance regarding a 'global consumer culture' or 'global youth culture',[23] though these styles are not confined to scammers. In this setting, emulating a 'global youth cul-

---

23 Social youth movements often emulate the powerful, emphasizing the access to riches in the Western world and ambiguities related to the danger of seduction through wealth, without regard of social norms, as e.g. witchcraft associations in the region (Argenti 2007: 15).

ture' is related to identification with certain lifestyles and local interpretations of such lifestyles, represented by certain fashion styles. Most often, this consists in displaying 'luxury items' such as watches, gold necklaces and fancy mobile phones, as well as branded clothing (fake or 'real'). Overall, this is often a matter of emulating the 'Gangsta style' of famous (black) US Hiphop stars such as 50cent, Snoop Dog, Notorious BIG and Tupac, as well as various Nigerian stars and other examples (cf. Malaquais 2001; Bucholtz 2002). Also the 'Rastafari style' is very popular among certain youths, which involves wearing dreadlocks, caps and jewellery in Rastafarian colours, and images of Bob Marley. Such displays of styles are also related to age group and gender[24] and tied to a certain conduct, such as handshakes, ways of walking, talking and verbal expressions, music and dance. In this way these young people (boys and men) also separate themselves from other groups who display their 'success'[25] in other ways. Also, behaviour forms a part of displaying: scammers are generally described as behaving 'irresponsibly' and in opposition to social rules of morality, politeness and respect to other people. In popular narratives, scammers are referred to as indulging in 'rough' and 'excited' conduct, such as shouting, fighting, drinking and smoking, going to night clubs, having irresponsible sexual relationships and showing disrespect to elders.

Of course, young people who express a certain lifestyle in such ways may only form relatively small groups, but they are highly visible in the urban area and they contribute greatly to forming the image of young people as being opposed to society and its norms of morality, as 'irresponsible people' (cf. Jua 2003; Argenti 2007; Rydin and Sjöberg 2008). Lifestyles in the sense of displaying wealth that is related to the symbols of an individualized, 'irresponsible' and egoistic way of life[26] can promote feelings of aversion and jealousy among other members of society.

---

24 To a certain extent, such orientations through styles are also pursued by girls and young women. Nevertheless, scamming is an almost exclusively male business.
25 As e.g. 'traditional authorities', or those with a good education and jobs in the government administration, as well as genuine business men.
26 As is also conveyed by images in film, video, TV and other popular media, which is related on the one hand to an abundance of wealth and a pleasant life-

Style (cf. Giddens 1991) relates to expressions of belonging to a group and demonstrates the potential of the individual. In fact, displaying wealth and acquiring status among one's peers in youth's life-worlds, and in particular in these alternative spaces, are an important aspect, among scammers in particular. Displaying wealth has to do with showing one's potential to others: when one has made money, it is announced and the news spread in bars and places where young people meet: who has made money, how much and by what means?[27] Similarly, the 'successful' invite their friends and let them participate in their success. Also the act of 'chopping' or eating the money can itself sometimes be performed in very expressive ways, related to showing immediate generosity (Malaquais 2001; Bucholtz 2002; Simone 2005).[28] Such displays of spending for others in the sense of displaying status symbols put the individual who is spending in a better position, at least temporarily. This is also expressed in calling him 'the boss', and by exclamations as: 'You are the boss' as a way of expressing one's appreciation.

However, there seem to be crucial differences between being a regular provider for one's family in the sense of continuous investments over longer periods of time, which might in return enhance a long-term appreciation and consolidation of one's status among related groups of people, and demonstrations of status among groups of scammers. In the latter case it rather seems to be about maintaining a momentum, a more transient situation, regarding the very irregular and unreliable sources of 'income', the way the money is said to be used instantly ('in one night only'), the nature of the monetary investment or spending ('having fun'), regarding the group of people one is spending for (friends, though they can change easily), and also regarding the resulting appreciation and honour, which might only last for a short period of time and is easily shifted on to others instead. Of

---

style, but on the other hand also to a certain decadence in the West and the corruption of moral values, social ties and solidarity.

27 E.g. stories like a particular friend has just picked up 1.2 million CFA from Western Union, having sold a German shepherd dog to a 'dupe' in Germany, and many other similar stories.

28 I was told stories of scammers who poured money over people in night clubs, and I witnessed scenes when scammers were dancing collectively, their hands full of money and showing their full purses.

course, being one of the few who are in a position to celebrate success more often, or regularly, one can build on a reputation for being 'a good scammer', and thus enhance and solidify one's status within this group of people and even beyond it. This is also expressed in circulating stories about one or other 'notorious scammer' in town, and calling one another by nicknames, related most often to images of success in this field, such as highlighting their economic viability, their mastery of technology (internet, computer), their status, or in general 'global references' that point to one's potential in one way or the other.

Scammers' ways of displaying wealth, which are often referred to as 'extravagance', seem to enhance the impression that they do not spend money wisely. They only think of themselves and spend money on status symbols and pleasure, 'chop it themselves', instead of using it for their family's most important concerns. They are said to spend money in an irresponsible and morally deplorable way, for 'useless' activities such as going to nightclubs, drinking and smoking, as well as 'to show off' to their peers by spending money on them or by acquiring status symbols related to their style. Furthermore, money is 'chopped' and spent carelessly and instantaneously'', without having a plan or thinking of the future or an investment that could enhance one's life situation and perspectives. In that sense scammers are said to 'misuse money', and their handling of it has become the epitome of 'chopping the money', diametrically opposed to ideals of redistribution or accumulation. Finally, the money they use is acquired in an illegal and objectionable manner, by duping others, instead of through honest hard work, ignoring the negative implications for their life prospects. Related to these attributes of the scammer such as the non-observance of moral duties, their short-term and pleasure-oriented way of thinking, their pursuit of an illegal business, scammers are thus seen as an embodiment of 'irresponsibility', and the image of 'success' that they display is seen as merely a matter of conspicuous consumption not leading to social recognition. Concern about such corrupting developments does relate to scamming as a burden and an illness: 'This scamming destroys our society' (Divine 13 August 2009), in the sense that it destroys social cohesion and relations of trust in families as well as business relations, and 'demoralizes youth'. 'It has a great effect on our young people. They infect their friends with the scammer virus' (Adolf 17 October 2008), as well as damaging the reputations of Cameroon and Cameroonians in the world: 'Kenya is famous for its wildlife, Cameroon for scamming' (Peter 02 December 2008).

'MISUSING MONEY' AND THE DANGERS OF ILL-GOTTEN WEALTH

As we have seen, scammers are regarded as irresponsible people in popular narratives since they spend money for irresponsible purposes and not in a morally approved way. In this sense, non-conformity is also related to the attributes of 'scamming money', or money achieved by illegal practices such as scamming, 'ill-gotten wealth', similar as people's connotations of the 'wealth of the rulers', which is accumulated by morally dubious practices related to a corrupt system. It is said that such money has a kind of negative quality and 'can never do anything good'. Their practices of acquiring wealth, but also money itself, that is 'stained' are often said to be influenced by occult forces or *nyongo* (practices related to witchcraft) (cf. Nyamnjoh 2005; Malaquais 2001; Geschiere 1997), and can drive scammers into difficulties or even death. Related to this are stories about scammers who had agreed to conditions with people in the internet (on occult and dangerous sites), but could not fulfil them and subsequently went mad or died.[29]

Scamming is an irregular and unreliable business, as one can never know if, when and how much income one will earn within a certain period of time. Scammers are thus said to live from hand to mouth, 'chopping the money' instantly and ending up with nothing the next day. Of course, this situation does not differ much from the experiences of others who are trying to survive by making other kinds of business. However, regarding the scammers, this has the connotation that they are not determined to act in this way, as they could make a lot of money at once. 'Greed' is one of the major issues in stories for why scammers get into such 'difficulties': they

---

29 For example, someone receives a huge sum of money from such an occult source, with the condition that he spends it all in one day, but without spending it on other people, such as family and friends. As he could not spend this money under these conditions, he died.

might become involved in occultism because they cannot get enough money,[30] or also because the 'business is not moving'. This is related to ideas about how scammers spend money: instantaneously and carelessly 'chopping it in one night only', and also the importance of status symbols among their groups of peers. In that sense, they constantly need more money in order to maintain their level of livelihood and this kind of lifestyle: 'they've got used to having money' (Clement 31 August 2009). In that sense they have become 'slaves to this scamming money', dependent on money, on illegal means to acquire it, as is also expressed in the saying that a scammer could hardly stop scamming once having started it.[31] Thus, nor can they think wisely or heed advice or warnings seriously that they could be spoiling their future. Similarly, some people also pointed to the deplorable fact that many scammers give up scholarly education or do not enter professional training due to their scamming activities. Therefore, they would prevent themselves from obtaining 'real success', a job, migrating abroad and fulfilling their dreams in the long run; in short, they would waste the chance ever to become a 'responsible person' and lead a 'responsible life'.

The reason why they seem not to be in a position to handle the money, in the sense of spending it reasonably and even saving for more difficult times, seems, many people felt, to lie in the very nature of how the financial means are acquired. 'Scamming money' is seen as 'fast money'; it is not acquired in long strenuous hours of work: 'When you work hard for your money, you will automatically spend it carefully. But when you make "fast money", and a lot of it at once, you cannot handle it' (Ernest 11 August 2009). This was also sometimes related to 'their young age' by some people, in the sense that when young people who did not have money before suddenly obtain a huge amount of money, they will be overwhelmed by it. This is also seen as the inversion of notions of success, gain and income related to age and position: 'one cannot deal with money responsibly when one is not yet a responsible person' (Ernest 11 August 2009). Related to the

---

30 This is also reflected in the colloquial expression, 'having a long throat'. Greed and sometimes involvement with occult forces are also attributed to 'big men', whether in the fields of politics or business.

31 In that sense, it was said that if they were not successful in scamming anymore, having completed neither an education nor a profession, they would easily slip into other criminal activities and become thieves and robbers.

nature of work, 'hard work' is related to honest work, which should ideally lead to a success that comes gradually, but has long-term connotations. In that sense, however, it is considered hardly possible in Cameroon for anyone to climb the social ladder through hard and honest work alone (cf. Jua 2003; Nyamnjoh 2005), due to a lack of jobs in general, the distribution of job opportunities depending on bribery and connections, and the hampering of businesses through infrastructure and taxation-related disadvantages.[32] Such possibilities and the appreciation of 'hard and honest work' are related more to opportunities abroad, as a place where such ideals are still valid. Referring to the 'scammers' money' being acquired by immoral practices and in unjust ways, some people stated: 'It is not fair that they are making money like this, and we [who are honest] are still struggling' (Miranda 13 July 2009). Being used to 'make fast money' means that scammers did not want to 'work hard' or be patient until their work comes to fruition: 'They are lazy people and do not like to work hard for their money' (Divine 13 August 2009). In this sense, scamming is not seen as 'a job'; it is not considered 'work', regarded as a continuous effort in order to achieve something, and also, as somebody stated appropriately: 'Work is when you give and you are given something [a salary] in return, but you cannot speak of work when you get paid without giving anything' (Claudia 22 July 2009).

'SCAMMING' AND LEGITIMACIES: DIFFERENTIATING VIEWS FROM 'WITHIN'

So far I have mainly referred to popular discourses and narratives about scammers. When talking to the scammers themselves, they, of course, have a more differentiated picture of themselves and their peers, their motivations and ideas. But they also orient their discourses about being scammers and the scamming business clearly to the social discourses about legitima-

---

32 In fact, also related to the scamming business itself, it would not be possible if it did not take place within a system of corruption and bribery. Police and even people related to money-transfer institutes and banks also seem to profit from the scamming business. Several scammers said that they had been to prison and released when they paid, and in general they cultivate good relations to the police.

cies. Nevertheless, scammers do not necessarily correspond to the images that are attributed to them. Some said that they deliberately do not want to evoke the impression that they are scammers. In that sense, the importance of reaching out for a certain lifestyle as expressed in status symbols such as dress, mobile phones (in a few cases even cars) and conduct, as 'having fun', dancing, drinking and taking girls out, is very much dependent on the individuals' life situation and conditions, as well as on social relations and integration in peer groups.[33] Related to the idea that scammers 'make a lot of money', statements also pointed to the fact that the scamming business is not easy, incomes are very irregular and uncertain, and the work sometimes does not pay, taking into account the expenditure for airtime in cyber cafés. Regarding the notion of 'work', some stated that they consider themselves to be 'working hard', and said they were struggling for everyday survival.

Regarding the impact the scamming business has on education, especially formal education, many had interrupted school or just had O-levels or A-levels; in general, studying in combination with scamming was said to be difficult. Thus they often pointed to unfavourable conditions, and not only to voluntarily giving up education. Regarding the sense of reciprocity and responsibility, for example, towards one's family and juniors, many people who were involved in scamming practices seemed in fact to contribute to their family's incomes, even though their family often seemed unaware of where the money was coming from. In some cases people stated that their parents were ignorant, while in other cases they had serious problems with at least one parent. For most, a certain independence in financial terms and avoiding parental control seemed to be important. As somebody stated: 'I don't know whether they suspect, but they [the parents] never ask me what I am doing' (Bryant 10 July 2009). Some rented a place on their own or lived together with age mates. Apart from the family, some emphasized the importance of having friends and the pleasure of sharing something with them, when available, in a reciprocal sense. Also, as some stated, they were aware that for outsiders it looked as if they were spending their money irre-

---

33 E.g., what individual preferences does someone have, how successful is somebody in the business, is one living with friends or together with younger siblings for whom one feels responsible, or even in one's parents' compound? Similarly, probably, many 'scammers' spend their money on everyday needs rather than on status symbols and pleasure.

sponsibly for pleasure alone, but outsiders did not know what percentage was spent on it or whether the rest of the money was being used in order to pay school fees for younger siblings, or to invest in setting up another business, and so on. Regarding the illegal nature of their business, moral issues were looked on in very different ways, depending on the individual. Some downplayed moral concerns and excused their activities with arguments as 'The white man has also duped us for so long', or more often: 'If you lose money so easily, you seem to have enough of it', and: 'They are greedy,[34] that is why they are duped' (Elvis 31 July 2009). Some also raised the issue of a 'professional desensitization' with respect to lying, cheating and duping people: 'One gets used to it with time'. Or: 'It changes you a lot: you become harder' (Jack 01 August 2008). Others told me that they would 'ask the lord for forgiveness every day', and that they would really like to have an alternative if they had a chance: 'It is not good, what I am doing, I cannot consider it as a job' (Augustus 15 July 2009). Some were indeed trying to start another business or to concentrate on education.[35] And regarding all the stories about occult issues that scammers are involved in, and also related to circulating rumours and stories of scammers who had died mysteriously,[36] people referred to it in different ways. For many, occult forces were an issue and seen as a threat, showing that the internet was a dangerous and insecure place.

Many people who were not scammers themselves but were in daily interaction with people involved in scamming activities, such as internet-literate young people who also spent much time in cyber cafés, as well as employees in cyber cafés, not only made negative statements about the scammers and their business, but also said that they had friends and ac-

---

34 Going for cheap or the cheapest offers or ads and not being sensitized regarding warnings on ad sites related to cheap ads.
35 I was able to talk to one scammer who had stopped scamming and gone to Douala to work in a computer repair business instead. Another person had applied for studies abroad and said he regretted not having started studying but scamming instead after school.
36 Like one story of a young man who was a scammer and who died in a car crash when I was in the field. I heard several versions of this story, and several reasons were given by the people telling these stories as to why the circumstances of this car crash were related to occult forces.

quaintances among them. Some said that they could not blame them, as: 'It is tempting going into it, due to a lack of alternatives' (Jan 17 November 2008). Some others, however, said they blamed them especially because they were internet savvy and had not recognized the internet's potential regarding other opportunities. In summary, we have seen that individual motivations and life histories differ and are full of ambivalences and contesting views: in such ways, scamming practices can sometimes even be used in the sense of pursuing ideals of social solidarity, as well as accumulation and the will to take over responsibility in society. Thus, being a scammer is not a fixed, but rather a transient condition, despite phrases like 'once a scammer, always a scammer'. In that sense, such discourses point to a contested realm in which the negotiation and re-evaluation of ideals is taking place.

SCAMMERS, BUSHFALLERS AND THE DEPLOYMENT OF SPACE: SOME ANALOGIES

Interestingly, popular narratives and imaginaries about scammers do have a kind of analogy in the notion of the 'bushfaller'. A 'bushfaller' is somebody who has gone abroad but has ongoing relations with 'home'. 'Bushfalling' (cf. Jua 2003: 22f.; Nyamnjoh 2005) is associated with 'going to the bush to hunt and returning with game'. Discourses related to scammers and bushfallers have certain similarities regarding the displaying of wealth and style which point to narratives of irresponsible ways of spending money for oneself and for prestige goods, and in this sense, not meeting the moral prerequisites of reciprocity.

In this context, one important aspect which contributes to negative connotations regarding scammers and bushfallers alike is that the circumstances in which wealth is accumulated are not transparent. How wealth is acquired to a certain extent remains a 'mystery' to outsiders, due to a lack of know-how about the internet and certain ideas of 'a life abroad'. Regarding the opacity related to these 'spaces', similarly, ideals of morality and social and cultural norms seem to be endangered in these realms. Related to the narratives of being irresponsible, regarding scammers and bushfallers alike, the 'life abroad' as well as the internet are also linked to 'negative influences', in the sense that those involved can easily be distracted and carried away by greed and new ideas of the individual enhancement of lifestyle. Scammers, but also to a certain extent bushfallers, are said to contribute to 'negative developments', to the corruption of morality and decadence in society related to social transformation.[37] Similarly, notions that carry a kind of moral ideal, such as 'hard work', which renders wealth legitimate, cannot easily be attributed to accumulation in these spaces, as it is not visible and not imaginable. As a representation of an 'opaque way of accumulating wealth', scamming practices, like the ways in which bushfallers achieve success, are often related to practices of *nyongo* or witchcraft as a prevalent threat and a manipulation of interpersonal social relationships (Nyamnjoh 2005: 248; Jua 2003; Ndjio 2006). This term is also used as an explanation for a perceived loss of solidarity in society, as well as for global and local inequalities (Malaquais 2001: 33). As Goheen (1996: 146) states: 'An individual who uses wealth for purely egoistic goals, one who has a "closed hand", who hoards and accumulates, is apt to be accused of witchcraft'.

Images of the bushfaller and scammer are admired and rejected[38] at the same time: on the one hand, 'they made it', on the other hand, they seem to oppose moral values, and even to employ dangerous forces. Basically, these ambivalences point to spaces that offer both opportunities and dangers. There are even more similarities that link images of scammers and bushfallers, or practices of scamming and bushfalling, in the sense that both take place in a translocal and even transnational space: Ndjio (2008), Malaquais (2001) and Smith (2007) also hint in that direction, pointing out that fraudulent practices are increasingly extended to foreign countries (Ndjio 2008:13), related to establishing and maintaining contacts online, with business partners as well as potential 'clients' or fraud victims. Furthermore, regarding the imaginaries, the scamming practices are very much influenced by images of 'greener pastures', of 'also having a share', that are

---

37 In certain settings, scammers and bushfallers can even be seen as competing: there are many stories about veritable combats between scammers and bushfallers in nightclubs around Christmas and New Year, a time when bushfallers return 'home' to spend their holidays, and when scammers and bushfallers alike try to surpass each other in order to show their economic worth.

38 Of course, the image of the scammer and his 'immoral business' of scamming, is much more morally condemned in popular narratives than the bushfaller.

related to migration and 'a life abroad'. Nevertheless, scamming does not seem to be a substitute for migration, but a temporal strategy to 'survive': most of these young people still dream of going abroad. But meanwhile, through scamming, it seems easier to enter a realm of potentiality, pointing to success, as migration has become more and more difficult.

Figure 4: Interior and wall painting in cyber café

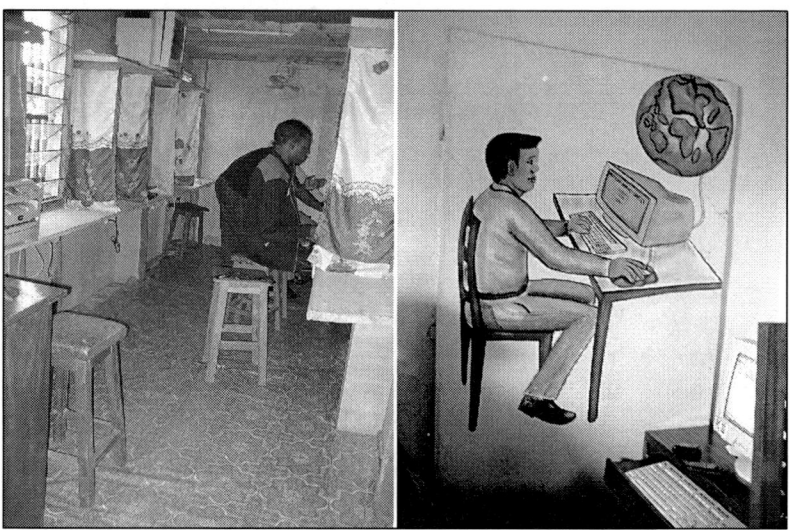

Source: Photo by the author

'SCAMMING WILL NOT DIE OUT':
CONCLUSION AND OUTLOOK

> ... Poverty no good at all, no
> Na im make I join internet
> Overscamming no be thief, it is just a game, everybody dey play em
> If any white man fall mugu, I go internet oh, I go scam em
> I go chop your Euro, I go take your money and disappear,
> 419 is just a game, you are the loser, I am the scammer ...
> ANOTHER EXCERPT FROM DJ SKIPPER, I GO CHOP YOUR EURO, BAMENDA

The original song, 'I go chop your dollar', has been called the 'anthem of 419 scammers'.[39] The song's text relates to the difficult economic situation in Cameroon and the reaching out for opportunities, as expressed in the line: 'Poverty no good at all, no...na im make I join internet'. Especially when young people have examples of peers who 'are in the business', they might well be tempted to become involved due to the lack of alternatives. The line 'Overscamming no be thief, it is just a game, everybody dey play em'[40] points to this, as well as opportunities to negotiate identity, the virtual space of the internet, and thus the abstraction that can be made regarding actions in this space: social interactions are mediated, the 'dupes' are distant, and actions do not seem to be as momentous and substantial as in face-to-face interactions with someone who is physically present. 'If any white man fall mugu (victims of scam), I go internet oh, I go scam em', is addressing the possibility to 'dupe' the 'white man', which points to the quick and in a sense 'creative' appropriation and taking over of new technologies among youth, but it has also the connotation 'of beating the whites with their own weapons',[41] in the sense of taking advantage of the internet as a virtual space and transactions in their own way, and to prove that one is

---

39 In 2007 Nkem Owoh, the author of the original song, had himself been arrested and accused of lottery fraud and immigration violations, but was later released (http://en.wikipedia.org/wiki/Nkem_Owoh) (accessed 15 January 2010).
40 'It is not the same thing as robbery, we do not hurt people physically' (Derrick 18 August 2009).
41 'It is their (the whites') fault that they got used buying and selling in the internet' (Jack 01 August 2009).

'cleverer' than them: 'You are the loser, I am the scammer'. Related to 'Dollar or Euro', this points to the potentiality of the 'Western world' and related images as 'greener pastures', and to the internet as a means to reach out to this world. Thus, it also relates to respective historical and current inequalities: the line 'I go chop your Euro' expresses, full of relish, that the scammer is eating the money of the white man in the sense of inverting global power relations, and as a kind of a new opportunity for social mobility.[42] As I have tried to argue in this chapter, scamming practices might work as a strategy to enter an alternative realm, promising access to wealth, success and status with to some extent transformed references: they thus reflect youths' 'economic and social dreams of success and nightmares of failure' (Diouf 2003: 11).

The realm of new media offers opportunities to avoid the 'gatekeepers' of power to a certain extent, which points to a negotiation of power relations, on both the local and national levels, regarding age, hierarchies and the predatory practices of those in power, symbolically even up to the global level. However, local notions of morality serve as a background and basis for such negotiating processes and discourses in an atmosphere of an ambivalent anxiety regarding status derived from the accumulation of wealth and power, characterized by admiration and rejection alike. In this sense, as we have seen in this chapter, the notion of 'chopping money' can be used as an allegation that those who do so are misusing power and opposing morality, and as well to define and negotiate moral legitimacies and to provide an expression of protest. The scamming business, as also expressed by scammers themselves, can only lead to the satisfaction of desires related to conspicuous consumption and a certain recognition among competitive peer groups. Its 'success' is limited to a certain social space and also time, as it is designated as a 'youth practice' integrated into youth's lifeworlds: the need to 'become responsible' is always referred to as an issue by scammers themselves. Thus, the practice of scamming is not accorded the potentiality of social recognition, but rather seen as a transient opportunity to deploy an alternative space of opportunities and to fulfil immediate desires, partly as an expression of protest against 'those who chop' in society (i.e. the powerful and the wealthy). Even though in local narratives

---

42 See a good discussion of the song's text on this site: http://akin.blogcity.com/igochopyourdollars.htm (accessed 15 January 2010).

bushfallers are also accused of not observing moral legitimacies, in the case of the scammers this also relates to the nature of the accumulation, which is already designated as not meeting the precepts of responsibility and social adulthood, whereas migration ventures are credited with the possibility of achieving 'real success' and becoming a 'responsible person' and a 'big man'.

In accordance with statements that 'the scamming business has become harder', one might predict that the business would decline further, as awareness of scamming related to the internet, ad sites and media in general is apparently increasing. Furthermore, efforts are on the way in, for example, Nigeria to enforce the fight against cyber crime (in collaboration with Microsoft in 2009; cf. Apter 2005), and in Cameroon advances have been made in identifying mobile phone users by a policy of registering SIM cards introduced by the end of 2009. In general, as Ndjio puts it, the 'whitization' of scam victims has made western governments start 'real political, administrative and juridical offensives against the méchant African criminals who have become the nightmare for many western governments and financial institutions trapped into the nets of West African economy of fraud and hoodwinking' (Ndjio 2008: 15, 19).

But of course, there will be always ways and opportunities to pursue dreams of a better life. In that sense, as some people expressed it, scamming will probably never die out as long as young people are searching for opportunities to make a living. These malpractices of scamming have only become possible through the accessibility of space transcending communication and information media, as the internet and mobile phone, which offer opportunities to come into contact with potential business partners (or scam victims) worldwide, access online advertising, buying and selling, and easy transnational money transfers. The internet can be seen as a media where illusions can easily be created and where the true identities of people can be obscured, where fraudulent business practices can therefore easily be performed. Glickman (2005: 471) points out that scamming practices take advantage of the prevailing insecurity of the internet. However, the emergence of scamming practices cannot be seen solely as born out of a situation of constraints and exclusion from the world market (Warnier 1993), or solely attributed to the characteristics of media like the internet: this would mean failing to account for the complexity of the situation and prevailing conditions, which are multifaceted and related to 'spheres of the negotiation' of notions of 'success' and 'responsibility', between the accumulation of wealth and the moral predicaments involved in taking over responsibility for others, between individuality and solidarity, emancipation and submission, redistribution and the desire to take part in a global consumer culture. A statement by one interviewee sees the scamming phenomena as an outcome of negotiating processes on several levels:

"One does not become a scammer because one wants to become one. You are becoming one in a more indirect manner: by going to the internet with the aim to inform yourself about whatever opportunity, going abroad, work, education, looking for greener pastures. By doing this, you get ideas how you could make money and you see others who do it, and are successfully doing it." (Derrick 19 August 2009)

REFERENCES

Apter, Andrew H. 2005. *The Pan-African Nation*. Chicago: University of Chicago.

Argenti, Nicolas. 2007. *The Intestines of the State. Youth, Violence, and belated Histories in the Cameroon Grassfields*. Chicago: University of Chicago.

Bayart, Jean-Francois. (1979) 1985. *L'état au Cameroun*. Paris: Fondation Nationale des Sciences Politiques.

---. 1993. *The State in Africa: The Politics of the Belly*. New York: Longman.

Bayart, Jean-Francois, Stephen Ellis and Beatrice Hibou (eds.). 1999. *The Criminalization of the State in Africa*. Bloomington: Indiana University.

Bucholtz, Mary. 2002. 'Youth and Cultural Practice', *Annual Review of Anthropology*, 31: 525-552.

Burrell, Jenna. 2009. 'Could Connectivity replace mobility? An Analysis of Internet Café Use Patterns in Accra, Ghana'. In: Inge Brinkman, Mirjam De Brujin and Francis Nyamnjoh (eds.). *Mobile Phones. The New Talking Drums of Everyday Africa*. Bamenda: Langaa: 151-170.

Diouf, Mamadou. 2003. 'Engaging Postcolonial Cultures: African Youth and Public Space', *African Studies Review*, 46(2): 1-12.

Geschiere, Peter. 1997. *The Modernity of Witchcraft. Politics and the Occult in Postcolonial Africa*. Charlottesville: University of Virginia.

Giddens, Anthony. 1991. *Modernity and Self-Identity. Self and Society in the late Modern Age*. Cambridge: Polity.

Glickman, Harvey. 2005. 'The Nigerian' "419" Advance fee Scams: Prank or Peril?', *Canadian Journal of African Studies/Revue Canadienne d'Études Africaines*, 39(3): 460-89.

Goheen, Miriam. 1996. *Men own the Fields, Women own the Crops. Gender and Power in the Cameroon Grassfields*. Madison: University of Wisconsin.

Jua, Nantang Ben. 2003. 'Differential Responses to Disappearing Pathways: Redefining Possibility among Cameroon Youths', *African Studies Review*, 46(2): 12-36.

Jua, Nantang Ben and Piet Konings. 2004. 'Occupation of Public Space Anglophone Nationalism in Cameroon', *Cahiers d'Etudes africaines*, 175(3): 609-633.

Macamo, Elisio and Dieter Neubert. 2008. 'The New and Its Temptations: Products of Modernity and their Impact on Social Change in Africa'. In: Afe, Adogame, Magnus Echtler and Ulf Vierke (eds.). *Unpacking the New*. Berlin: Lit : 271-304.

Malaquais, Dominique. 2001. 'Arts de feyre au Cameroun', *Politique Africaine*, 82: 101-18.

Mbembe, Achille. 2001. *On the Postcolony*. Berkeley: University of California.

Ndjio, Basile. 2008. *Cameroonian Feymen and Nigerian '419' Scammers: Two examples of Africa's 'Reinvention' of the Global Capitalism*. ASC working paper. Leiden: African Studies Centre.

---. 2006. *Feymania: New Wealth, Magic Money and Power in Contemporary Cameroon*. PhD dissertation. Amsterdam: University of Amsterdam.

Nyamnjoh, Francis. 2005. 'Images of Nyongo amongst Bamenda Grassfielders in Whiteman Kontri', *Citizenship Studies,* 9(3): 241-269.

Rydin, Ingegerd & Sjöberg, Ulrika. 2008. *Mediated Crossroads. Identity, Youth Culture and Ethnicity. Theoretical and Methodological Challenges*. Göteborg: Nordicom.

Simone, Abdoumaliq. 2005. 'Urban Circulation and the Everyday Politics of African Urban Youth: The Case of Douala, Cameroon', *International Journal of Urban and Regional Research*, 29(3): 516-532.

Smith, Daniel Jordan. 2007. *A Culture of Corruption: Everyday Deception and Popular Discontent in Nigeria*. Princeton: Princeton University.

Warnier, Jean-Pierre. 1993. *L'esprit d'entreprise au Cameroun*. Paris: Karthala.

---. 1996. 'Rebellion, Defection and the Position of Male Cadets: a Neglected Category'. In: Fowler, Ian and David Zeitlyn (eds.). *African Crossroads. Intersections between History and Anthropology in Cameroon*. Oxford: Berghahn: 115-124.

INTERNET SITES (JANUARY 2011)

http://en.wikipedia.org/wiki/Nkem_Owoh
http://www.scamorama.com/
http://spamlinks.net/scams-advancefee-419.htm
http://www.fraudwatchers.org/
http://arstechnica.com/tech-policy/news/2009/10/nigeria-actually-arrests-shuts-down-online-scammers.ars
http://news.bbc.co.uk/2/hi/8322316.stm

Women and Magic in Dakar

Rural Immigrants Coping with Urban Uncertainties

AMBER GEMMEKE

INTRODUCTION

At about half past five in the afternoon my interpreter Aminata and I arrive at a marabout's place.[1] At this time she usually wraps up her work for the day and urges the rest of her clients to go home. Three clients are still present in her waiting room. The marabout, hidden behind a curtain, is speaking so loud that Aminata and I can follow the conversation she has with her clients. The first client is a young woman, around twenty years old, wearing jeans and a tight top. The marabout tells her that her fiancé will propose marriage very soon. Smiling and visibly relieved, the young woman leaves the building. The second is a young woman in her late twenties dressed in

---

1   The term 'marabout', often used by francophone West Africans and by western scholars, can refer equally to men and women, to imams or prayer leaders, teachers, scholars, preachers, saints, religious ceremony leaders and leaders of Muslim brotherhoods, as well as to any type of specialist in esoteric knowledge, producers of amulets, and diviners (*cf.* Graw 2005: 28-29 and Soares 2005: 30). Even a diviner and healer without specific knowledge of the Islamic literary corpus, Islamic esoteric practices, or written Arabic is often referred to as *marabout* or addressed as the equivalent *serigne* (Wolof), *thierno* (Fulani) or *mooroo* (Mandinka) (*cf.* Dilley 2004; Evans Pritchard 1949; Monteil 1980 and Triaud 1997).

an elegant *boubou* [robe], along with her young son. The marabout tells her that she has a problem with her husband, but that everything will be solved. The third is a woman in her thirties, well dressed in a *boubou*, jewelry, and heavily perfumed. The marabout says she sees in her divination session that her co-wife is jealous of her, and that she should give sugar as alms. She adds that the woman should follow her treatments to solve the problems with the co-wife. That evening, Aminata tells me:

"You saw today at that marabout's place what the secret of marabouts is. They know what women's problems are. They all follow the same pattern: first they put your mind at ease, so that you are really relieved, and then they tell you what almsgiving you have to do or which treatment you have to follow in order to solve the problems with your fiancé, your husband, your co-wife, or your mother-in-law."
(Conversation on 20 May 2006)

The three clients and the marabout's reaction to them are quite representative for marabouts' work in Dakar. Marabouts deal daily with gendered issues at the heart of Senegalese society: polygamy, female celibacy, infertility and the emigration of men leaving their wives and children behind.[2] These issues seem to be magnified in Dakar, where the majority of its residents are first or second generation migrants from rural areas fighting in a fiercely competitive environment for housing, jobs and – especially women – for suitable marriage partners. Marabouts play an important role in this urban environment where opportunities and insecurities abound and interrelate. They offer divination sessions for insight into the thoughts and intentions of family members, spouses and neighbours. Their spells should make landlords forget to collect the rent, superiors and colleagues secure jobs, and co-wives insane, leave the house, or even die. In attending to these issues, marabouts play an ambiguous role. On the one hand, they offer tools for containing and expressing feelings of fear, anxiety, frustration, and jealousy. They also, on the other hand, produce these feelings.

Based upon fieldwork in an outskirt of Dakar, Parcelles Assainies, this chapter explores visiting marabouts as a female migrants' coping strategy

---

2   The official term for a marriage system in which a man can marry more than one wife is *polygyny*. Because of the widespread use of the term polygamy, however, I have opted for the latter term in this article.

in a newly constructed urban life world. All clients and marabouts featuring in this chapter are first generation migrants from rural areas, settled more or less permanently in Parcelles Assainies. Here, I lived among women for whom the services of marabouts formed an integral part of their lives. Aminata and Coumba (my two hostesses), Fatou (the maid next door) and two co-wives in a neighbouring household not only regularly discussed rumours on marabouts' work circulating in the neighbourhood, they all consulted a marabout themselves at some point during my stay. In this descriptive article, their stories will help to illustrate the popularity of marabouts among women in Parcelles Assainies.

PARCELLES ASSAINIES

From the 1980s onwards, Dakar has exploded with population growth, largely due to massive rural-urban migration.[3] The continuing droughts in the 1970s, the economic crises of the 1980s, and the 50 per cent devaluation of the FCFA in 1994 devastated household economies. This unprecedented economic crisis was exacerbated by the vicious effects of structural adjustment programs: high unemployment among people with skills and education, and increasing poverty in the cities as well as in the countryside fuelled social discontent and Casamance separatist movements (Hesseling 2002: 1425). While economic crises have been leaving rural areas deserted, Dakar – where each square kilometre is populated with 4,145 inhabitants – is overflowing.[4] A third of these residents are first generation rural migrants, the overwhelming majority of them living in Dakar's sprawling outskirts.

---

3   Rural-urban migration within Senegal as well as migration abroad began much earlier than the 1980s. Already in the 1930s, Senegalese from the Casamance and from the Fouta Toro, especially Manjak, Serakhole, and Soninke, were working as labourers in France and in Dakar. See Manchuelle (2004) for a study on early migration of Soninke to Europe.
4   These data are reported in the Census of 2002. In comparison, the population density in the countryside varies from 10 inhabitants per square kilometre in the region of Tambacounda to 214 at the most in the Diourbel region (DPS).

Dakar's outskirts spread from the Cap Vert peninsula well into the mainland. Parcelles Assainies ('Cleansed Plots') is situated between these outskirts on the east, bounded by the populous neighbourhood of Grand Yoff to the south, by the sea to the north, and by the fishing village of Yoff to the west. Relatively new, Parcelles was built specially for the overflow of the populous neighbourhoods of central Dakar Fass, Le Plateau, Rebeuss, and Médina, as well as for future rural migrants. The neighbourhood is a prestigious project of the World Bank, begun in 1970 and completed in 1980.[5] Today, Parcelles Assainies mainly attracts businessmen, middlemanagement government employees, skilled labourers and rural migrants (Fall 2005: 77).

Parcelles resembles a gigantic excavation site. In contrast to the traffic, which is in a permanent jam that seems to tighten a little more every day, the real estate market in Parcelles Assaines is in constant movement. Apartment complexes are built; floors are added and then disassembled and built up again with amazing speed. Due to the overwhelming demand, the real estate market is extremely profitable. The 18-21 law of 1981 protecting tenants from price rises is not enforced (*Le Quotidien* November 16, 2003). Rooms and apartments are thus expensive and tenants unprotected. Landlords close down buildings or remove tenants at will. Furthermore, most buildings, being hastily built for an often absent émigré, are of poor quality and endangering their residents (*Le Soleil* December 11, 2003).

The typical building in Parcelles is built as a square surrounding a central patio. The buildings have one to four stories connected by stairs in the corners. Also in the corners are the bathrooms, consisting of a toilet and a space for washing, usually without running water. Tenants share these facilities. They cook on the galleries that surround each floor, usually on gas. On the ground floor, a water tap provides residents of the building with wa-

---

5   While nearby neighborhoods Pikine and Thiaroye are classified as 'pauvre' by sociologist Abdou Salam Fall, he classifies Unité 9 of Parcelles Assainies as a 'quartier moyen ou intermediaire' (2005: 50). Though the neighborhood was originally intended to provide the lower income categories with basic, but good and cheap housing, many of the beneficiaries sold their *parcelle* to Senegalese businessmen, thus driving up the prices (Piga 2002). Among the 285 plots assigned in Unité 9, for example, 185 have been sold by their owners (Fall 2005: 79).

ter paid for by the bucket. Residents have to carry the heavy buckets up the stairs each day. In a few buildings, a well instead of a tap provides water to the residents. In Parcelles, I visited several buildings where up to nine people shared a single room and had to take turns in sleeping. Upon entering such a building one sees people everywhere: cooking, cleaning, sleeping, playing, studying, grooming. Often animals are kept in the buildings as well, especially chickens, goats and sheep.

To cover the costs of living in Dakar, most new migrants have to get by in the informal *système D* – D for *débrouillard* 'savy' or 'a savy person' – which requires a different pace, language, attitude and dress than in the countryside.[6] Language, both in the literal sense (urban Wolof) as in the metaphoric sense (language as a means of pretence or a creator of false impressions), is used to show that one is integrated into and successful in urban life. Another important characteristic of successful urban life is dressing well, as appearance is noticed and commented upon continuously in Dakar.

The valorisation of physical beauty in Dakar – ubiquitously visible on the beaches and streets where people play sport and dance, sensually dressed – has been argued to be a reaction against the colonial ideal of intellectual success, intellect alone clearly not providing a stable job in crisis-ridden Senegal (Diouf 2002: 264; Harvard 2001: 63). Numerous studies have commented on the reactions of Dakarois, especially youth, to the crises of the 1980s and 1990s (Cruise O'Brien 1996; Diop *et al.* 2002; Havard 2001; Villalón 1999). The effects of Senegal's socioeconomic decline reached far beyond political disillusionment and underemployment. Migration from the countryside to the city - and from Dakar to Europe and the United States brought about cultural changes among the young, expressed in western dress, a focus on corporeal beauty and fitness, and urban language (Rabine 2002: 35). The obsession with appearance is more than just an affair of the young, however. Several names describe well dressed persons: *thiof* for a rich, handsome, and well dressed man, *diriyanke* for a rubenesque, well dressed, heavily perfumed and bejewelled woman of around thirty years of age or older, and *diskette* for a slim, trendy young woman dressed in 'western' style. According to the elegantly dressed women and

---

6 See also McLauhlin (2001). *Système D* is French slang, widely used in France, and, to a much lesser extent, in the Senegalese media.

men (of all ages) I met in Parcelles Assainies, dressing well meant a source of national pride (Senegal often said to have the most beautifully dressed people of West Africa), of dignity in the face of neighbors, as well as better access to jobs and marriage partners. Fall has described the female competition for men in Parcelles Assainies as: '*la bataille est vestimentaire*' (2005: 133). For women, beauty and seduction are – along with marabouts' services – important weapons in the competition for marriage partners.

Due to the relatively young marriage age for women (on average eighteen years), polygamy, and extremely rapid divorcee and widow remarriage (within less than a year on average), both married and unmarried women are in fierce competition with each other for the attention and support of men. In Parcelles Assainies, marabouts' waiting rooms are full of women seeking assistance in getting, and in keeping together, a marriage. Although men also frequently visit marabouts, women form the majority of the clientele of both male and female marabouts.

I could not use the hours I spent in the waiting areas of marabouts, waiting for the last client to leave, to talk with the clients. The atmosphere in a waiting area was always somewhat tense. Clients stared aimlessly, avoiding looking at other clients. They seemed to be looking inward. Even when coming with friends or family members, clients usually awaited their turn in silence. The answers to my questions were so short and so reluctantly given that I soon gave up asking questions in the waiting room altogether. The number of clients in the waiting rooms varied. The most popular marabout I visited had fifteen to twenty clients waiting during the four times I visited her. Others had five to ten clients waiting for them. As clients left, others would quickly fill up their seats. The consultations would normally not take long: most people came for divination sessions of only about ten minutes. More time consuming consultations took between fifteen minutes and an hour.

BEING A CO-WIFE

In the 1970s, several academics hypothesized that the institution of polygamy would be structurally incompatible with modernization and that along with the processes of urbanization and industrialization, polygamy would lose its salience as a social institution that had been viable in an agricultural mode of production (Goode 1970; Gough 1977). Statistics proved otherwise. As of the 1980s, academics realized that polygamy was not necessarily decreasing with urbanization and had on the contrary even increased in, for example, urban Zaire (now the Democratic Republic of the Congo, Clignet 1987; Lesthaeghe et al. 1989). The proportion of Senegalese polygamous marriages in urban areas is among the highest in Africa. According to a census in 1988, 40 per cent of married women in Dakar are in polygamous marriages. In Parcelles Assainies and in Yoff the number is higher: more than half of the married women aged thirty-five to thirty-nine, of every social layer, are in a polygamous marriage.[7]

In 1989 and 1990, IFAN-ORSTOM carried out an intensive study on the residential and marriage history of professionals in Dakar, based on 1,557 respondents. One of the aims of the study was to determine which factors contributed to polygamous marriage and which factors did not. The study proved several of the researchers' hypotheses to be wrong. In contrast to their expectations, a higher level of education, income and housing conditions did not correlate with a decrease in polygamy. In Dakar, highly educated men have the same rates of polygamy as illiterate men. Polygamous behaviour does not vary according to employment, type of lodging or ethnicity. Furthermore, the absence of children in a first marriage does not influence polygamous behaviour (Antoine and Naniteliamo 1996: 134).

According to Antoine and Naniteliamo, although women are opposed to polygamy, social pressure is such that unmarried women are prepared to enter into polygamous unions (ibid: 144). Public opposition of Senegalese women to polygamy is, however, not new. In 1979 Mariama Bâ wrote *Une si longue lettre* [Such a long Letter], a novel portraying two women whose husbands decide to take second wives. One divorces, and the other chooses not to divorce but to distance herself from her husband. Today, the novel is still regarded as one of Senegal's great literary successes. Women's rights activists continue to struggle against polygamy in Senegal, often targeting Islamic reformists (Sow 2003). Despite critique, however, polygamy is widespread, affecting almost every (extended) family in Senegal. It is fuelled mainly by social conventions of a young age of marriage for women, women being on average twelve years younger than their husbands, and the absence of celibacy promoting extremely rapid remarriage of divorcees

---

7   50,8 per cent (IFAN-ORSTOM 1995: 61).

and widows – on average within less than a year. The divorce rate increased by three times in the last twenty years, divorce thus being becoming commonplace (Dial 2008: 179). Since celibacy, especially for women, is not accepted, and since divorced women accept polygamous marriages even more readily due to social conventions, the high divorce rates seem to increase insecurity and competition among women for marriage partners.

In traditional Wolof society (as in all other societies in Senegal), the number of wives a man could marry was not limited. The elite could have as many as thirty wives. Islam reduced the number of wives to four but permitted men to have as many concubines among his slaves (*taraa*) as he could pay for. The abolition of slavery put an end to this type of union, but to this day the leaders of the politically and economically influential Senegalese Sufi brotherhoods, especially the Murid marabouts, have relations with more than four wives in a system of concubinage (Diop 1985: 184). Traditionally, a strict hierarchy existed between co-wives according to their chronology of marriage and the social status of their parents (Ly 1979: 111). In contrast to the traditional inequality among co-wives, Islam stressed the need for a husband to treat all wives equally in every respect. The disappearance of the Wolof (and other societies') monarchies has indeed diminished inequality among co-wives, but to this day the first wife enjoys special privileges and authority (Diop 1985: 188). In earlier days, co-wives worked together on the land and in the household. Today, the organization of a polygamous household is very much oriented towards the autonomy of the co-wives and their children (ibid: 199). Especially in urban Senegal, polygamous men strive to house their wives in separate houses, they themselves moving in between the houses (*cf.* Dial 2008).

Such housing arrangements are only possible for a small elite, however. In Parcelles Assainies, the vast majority of co-wives seem to live together. I will describe one such household to provide an example of women trying to cope with the situation by asking marabouts for support.

In this household, two wives originating from the region of Tambacounda and their seven children in the ages from four to seventeen shared three rooms. Their husband was in Spain since eight years, occasionally sending them money. The two women were in a precarious financial position, especially the second wife, whose children were not earning any money yet. One day, the second wife came to our house in distress to ask for some money. She said that it was the day for the other wife to cook a meal, but she had not cooked enough food. She did not share the food with the second wife and her children, even though the second wife had cooked for everyone the day before. Although it was almost time for dinner, the second wife's children had not yet had lunch.

The two wives did not speak with each other, and even some of the children did not speak with the children of the other wife. A relative of theirs told me that when the husband had been at home, the situation was even worse. The two women would then fight each other openly. Now, they were just not on speaking terms. According to this relative, the seventeen-year-old son of the first wife regularly threatened the other wife. 'The first wife has been afraid of the second wife ever since she hit her in an angry dispute. Now she turns to her son if she has a problem with her', she said. The fourteen-year-old daughter of the first wife had refused to go to school since the beginning of the new school year in October 2003, claiming that the second wife had 'maraboutéd' her to prevent her from concentrating on her schoolwork. The two women knew a large number of marabouts in Parcelles Assainies, helping me to arrange interviews with in total six of them. The women both told us they had met these marabouts through the mediation of friends and neighbours. For example, one of the marabouts was the neighbour of the owner of the bakery where the second wife had worked. At the time, her husband had forbidden her to use money that he sent to the family. She therefore started working at a bakery in Parcelles Assainies, and she told the owner her problems. The owner put her in touch with his marabout neighbour.

I never talked with the two women about their actual conversations with the marabouts. Aminata, my interpreter, warned me, however. 'This is not to be taken lightly', she said. 'These women are in a state of war. They are both visiting marabouts to make their co-wife leave the house.'

MOTHERS-IN-LAW

Financial problems and lack of space also seemed to create tensions in the household downstairs of the apartment I stayed in in Parcelles Assainies. This family lived on only a few square meters: with five adults and three children in two bedrooms and a living room. Apparently, both mother-in-law and daughter-in-law had used the services of marabouts to try to solve the tensions. The family came from the region of Sedhiou in the Casamance and was made up of a twenty-three-year-old woman, a thirty-year-old man, their three-year-old son, the man's mother, his aunt, two of his cousins (seven and nine years old), a maid, and three white sheep.

In Parcelles Assainies, many households have sheep. These sheep are tied up on the roof, under stairs, or in small wooden constructions on the street, and are kept to be slaughtered on festive occasions. They are also tension absorbers. It is believed that a white sheep protects its owners and generates peace in the household. A white sheep absorbs all jealousy from neighbors as well as any tensions that might arise in a family. Even (or maybe especially) in the houses of the better neighborhoods of Dakar that I visited, in Sacre Cœur and in Almadies, I often saw sheep kept for their powers of absorption.

Fights broke out regularly between the wife and the mother-in-law living downstairs. These fights usually had trivial starts: the mother-in-law and the wife would disagree over the clothes the child was wearing, or over the cleanliness of the bathroom. The fights usually took place during the day, when the husband was out of the house. From eight in the morning until around seven in the evening the husband was at work, repairing refrigerators. The wife took care of her son and helped the maid cook and clean. The mother-in-law spent most of her time sitting in front of the house, moving according to the shade, at a table loaded with vegetables that she sold to her neighbours.

In the middle of one night I awoke to the sound of doors slamming, objects breaking, and people screaming. The wife and the mother-in-law living downstairs were fighting again. Over the previous week, fights had disrupted the house several times, but now the situation seemed to be exploding. The mother called her own daughter to come and assist her, and the wife called her uncle. Most of the neighbours gathered, some to calm the two parties and to keep them apart, as they were hitting each other and throwing objects. Others had come simply to watch the show, sitting on hastily arranged plastic chairs, with cold drinks in their hands. To the audience's delight, the mother-in-law tripped over a stool and fell on the floor. Keeping her *pagne* together, she was even more furious as she stood up. The *chef de quartier* arrived, but he could not improve the situation. He took the side of the mother-in-law (to the discontent of most of the neighbors) instead of remaining impartial. Finally the wife, who was eight months pregnant, called a taxi and left with all her belongings, including her mattress, to stay with her uncle. The next day, the mother-in-law was happily cleaning the house. She was singing as she swept out her daughter-in-law's room. She said proudly that her marabout was obviously stronger than her daughter in-law's, and that she was now cleaning to make sure none of her enemy's amulets were left in the house.

Among neighbours, opinions on the reasons for the fights were divided. According to one woman, the problem was the mother-in-law's jealousy. 'This woman has been divorced herself, four times', she said. 'She cannot accept her son giving attention to anyone else but her, or anyone else giving attention to him.' According to a man, however, money was the main problem. Indeed, during the fights the mother-in-law had frequently accused the wife of not bringing any income into the family while she herself tried to make some money by selling vegetables.

Clearly, the position of women in households causes more tensions for them than for men. They live with their co-wives and mothers-in-law. The IFAN-ORSTOM study shows that most women, especially when their husbands are between the ages of twenty-five and thirty-four, live with family members of their husband (1991: 78). The majority of women live with their parents until the ages between fifteen and twenty-five. Most women older than sixty live in another household (their children's or a sibling's). Most men live with their parents until the age of twenty to thirty years. From age thirty-five until the end of their lives, the vast majority (around 80 per cent) of men are head of their household (ORSTOM 1995: 78). In Parcelles Assainies, precarious financial situations and limited space aggravate already existing tensions between family members.[8] Women, who have to deal on a day-to-day basis with the preparation of food and childcare, especially suffer from poverty.

---

8   This space is becoming more and more limited. According to the IFAN-ORSTOM study, in 1955, 29 per cent of households and 45 per cent of the population of Dakar lived with more than three people in one room. In 1989, the situation has worsened: 44 per cent of households and 54 per cent of the population now lived with more than three people in one room (1995: 50).

INFERTILITY

When we met, Aminata, my interpreter, who originated from the region of Tambacounda, had been married for five years without having any children with her husband. The couple actively sought treatment both at the hospital and among marabouts. Aminata told me she had consulted many marabouts in the first years of her marriage:

"If someone tells me to solve my problem [through the services of a marabout], I always say it is my husband's problem. I have a child. My husband is undergoing treatment in the hospital at the moment. But whatever I say, marabouts always insist that I have a jinn husband who is preventing me from getting pregnant again. I have never really believed that, but I've heard it so often now that it is difficult for me not to believe in a jinn husband." (Conversation on 23 October 2003)[9]

In Senegal in 1992, a married woman in Aminata's age group (thirty to thirty-four) had given birth, on average, to five live children (EDS-II 1992/93: 32). Statistics on infertility are difficult to find. Most studies are focused on fertility rates, oriented towards Africa's high fertility rates and high rates of population growth; moreover, they do not usually take into account the frequent problem of secondary infertility, that is, infertility after giving birth to one or two live children.[10] According to the EDS of 1992/93, however, 70 per cent of all women the research team approached said, like Aminata, that they wanted more children than they actually had (ibid: 73). The marabouts I spoke to in Parcelles Assainies named the wish to have children as the second most frequent problem among women (after 'problems in the household'). Children are of vital importance to women in Senegal. Women

---

9   In Dakar, the French translation often given for the word 'jinn' is *diable*. The term *diable* does not have the negative connotations of the English 'devil' but means rather a spirit that has all the characteristics of a living person, the only difference being that he or she is not visible. When a woman has problems in her relationships with men or in conceiving children, she is suspected to have a jinn husband who is jealous of her human husband and is preventing her from getting pregnant.

10 The studies of Viola Hörbst, working on both male and female infertility in Mali, are a notable exception (2006, 2008).

are perceived as adults only after they have given birth. Their marriage is not considered complete (or even justified) without a child. For a large part, children define the value and status of a woman. Furthermore, children are supposed to take care of their mothers in their old age.

Infertility is widely regarded as a woman's problem. Aminata already had a child from a previous relationship and two other pregnancies before her current marriage. 'It is because I have a child that my husband agreed to go to the hospital', Aminata said. 'Normally, a man cannot believe he might be infertile.' Women with infertility problems go to the hospital too. There are, however, several reasons for consulting a marabout. A marabout might be cheaper and less humiliating: a marabout will do no internal examinations (*cf.* Jaffré 1999). Interestingly, the practices of urban marabouts increasingly resemble the private clinics of formal health care; featuring waiting rooms, fixed working hours, appointment books and client files. For example, I visited with Aminata once the *Centre de l'Orientation et de Lumière* of marabout Chaibatal Hamdi Diouf. This marabout advertised cures for various problems including those caused by jinns as follows: '*la santé avec le Coran et les plantes*'. Aminata, after having seen his television advertisements in which radiant women assured that after years of infertility they had given birth helped by marabout Diouf, was convinced of this marabout's effectiveness. She was not the only one: the marabout's waiting area was filled with clients, being assigned a number, waiting for hours for their appointment.

CELIBACY

Besides tensions in the family and infertility, the third most frequently mentioned problem that women consult marabouts for, according to marabouts I interviewed in Parcelles Assainies, is the search for a suitable husband. The social convention that women should marry at a relatively young age and should be unmarried for as short a period as possible, leads to feelings of despair, anxiety, and incompleteness among unmarried women.

Coumba for example, Aminata's younger sister, had been actively looking for a suitable husband for almost three years when I met her. Still single at twenty-one, she compared herself frequently with married women younger than herself in the neighbourhood. After she had lived in Dakar with her older sister for a year, she decided to find a husband in her natal village of Maka Kolibantan. It would be better, she argued, to marry someone whose background and family she already knew. She prolonged her summer holidays in the village, ignoring her sister's wish for her to come back to Dakar. She stayed seven months in the village in total. Five men proposed to her in this period, all decent, financially stable men, as Coumba said. But each man had a flaw. One had two wives already. Another had a mean mother, Coumba said. A third was reportedly violent. She rejected all of them. Strangely enough, during this time her left foot started swelling. She went to see a marabout who told her someone had taken dust from her footprint to cast a spell on her, but he assured her that this person meant no harm. Nevertheless, Coumba was worried. Swelling of body parts is usually suspected to be caused by a marabout on behalf of his client. It is widely believed that *korte* (a disease borne by an insect or the wind) can harm someone even when the victim is a great distance away from the person who threw the *korte*. Maybe Coumba had insulted one of the suitors or his family, or his wives. However, a second person also told her not to worry. Without being asked, this woman diagnosed the swelling as marabout's work as well. After a week, Coumba's foot was normal again and she went back to Dakar.

In Dakar a married man soon took an interest in Coumba. Whereas in Maka Kolibantan Coumba had not consulted a marabout to find out if one of the five suitors would make a good husband, in Dakar she visited three marabouts to see if this new candidate would be a good husband for her. 'When you have known a man and his family all your life', she said, 'there is no need to go to a marabout to see if it will be a happy marriage. But if you don't know him, you should consult one' (Conversation on 12 November 2003). All three marabouts said Coumba would marry one day, but not this man. She declined his offer.

Coumba is actively looking for a husband without much interference from her parents or other relatives. This way of seeking a partner was not traditionally the practice of any of the ethnic groups in Senegal. In all groups daughters and sons were married very young, often promised to each other by their respective families long before puberty (Diop 1985: 97). The preferred type of marriage for all ethnic groups in Senegal is the cross-cousin marriage. Parallel cousin marriage was traditionally prohibited. The groom and his parents paid a bride price to the parents of the bride to help them find wives for their sons. Islam and – more importantly – economic development changed this system of marriage. The bride price, which was formerly used by the family of the bride for their sons' marriages, is now consumed by the bride and her parents. Correspondingly, the groom is nowadays largely responsible himself for amassing the bride price, without the help of his relatives. Rapid urbanization and monetarization of the bride price have resulted in two trends: first, the majority of young urban people now take their right to choose their own spouse for granted; and second, especially since the economic crisis of the 1980s, men are postponing marriage until after the age of thirty. Young men are typically unable to afford a bride price or a marriage ceremony, hence this delay (Augis 2002: 83; Silberschmidt 2001: 6).

Although Coumba hoped to be married soon, she took her time to find a husband. Her working older sister took good care of her. Not all girls in Parcelles Assainies are as protected as Coumba, however. In Parcelles Assainies, and in Dakar as a whole, many young rural girls work as domestic workers. In Dakar, the vast majority of households employ a domestic.[11] The domestics are mainly Diola, Manjak and Serer, originating from the Sine-Saloum and from the Casamance. They are typically unmarried and may be as young as eight years old. The girls come to Dakar on their own or with peers. From the 1950s, Dakar became the preferred centre for female migrants form the countryside who saw increasing opportunities to work as cooks, laundry-maids, and nursemaids. According to Michael Lambert, who did extensive research in western Casamance, the tradition of female migration started when the idea of a trousseau that women amass for themselves became current. Today, however, women primarily migrate in the hope of marrying a Dakarois (2002: 103). They have typically both a weak social network and a precarious financial situation, as the story of Fatou illustrates (*cf.* Delaunay 1994: 183).

Fatou, a Casamançaise neighbour in Parcelles Assainies, worked as a domestic. This twenty-three-year-old woman had come to Dakar to stay for

---

11 According to Diaw 1996: 'A Dakarois household would have to be extremely poor, and even then, not to have at least one *mbindaan* [maid]. The profession of maid occupies more than 88.000 people [...] It is a traditional practice in large families to borrow one or two girls from some of its members who are in need to assist them with household chores' (op cit. Wittmann 2003: 158).

a few months, leaving her three-year-old son in the care of her mother in her village in the Casamance. Fatou slept with her boyfriend in Pikine because (as she said) he gave her clothes. Always dressed in tight jeans, fashionable pointy shoes, revealing tops, and a cap like Christina Aguilera's, Fatou looked like a true *diskette*. 'Look what my boyfriend in Pikine gave me', Fatou said proudly, showing the blue cap; 'now I can look my best for my employer' (Conversation on 24 November 2003). She worked as a maid for a businessman whom she hoped to marry. The man was classified as a *thiof* by Coumba and Fatou: attractive and wealthy. The house he rented in Parcelles Assainies was big and well constructed and had a beautiful floor covering. He travelled frequently between Dakar and Touba, where he owned a house and where his wife lived. For a few months, it seemed that Fatou's employer actually had plans to marry her. He told her he loved her and even left his first wife, who (as he said to Fatou) did not take good enough care of him. Suddenly, however, he changed his mind. Within a week he married another young woman instead and threw Fatou out on the street, saying she had not cleaned the bathroom well enough. For several days Fatou came to our house to eat and slept in another neighbour's house at night. In this period, she told us that she consulted two marabouts in order to be reconciled with her former employer. Fatou did not see any results from her marabouts' efforts, and left for her village in distress.

Fatou's sleeping with her boyfriend for clothes is not unique. Sleeping with more or less permanent lovers for money and gifts is a recurrent activity in Parcelles Assainies (*cf.* Fall 2005; Augis 2001). Fatou used the gifts for herself. I heard several stories, however, in which the exchange of sexual relations for money and gifts was welcomed and encouraged by the young women's families as an important source of income. In the Senegalese media, considerable attention is given to this 'new' female sexuality. Newspaper articles display both fascination and fear with respect to this 'urban polyandry', presumably generated by the economic crisis of the 1980s (Biaya 2001: 79). The perceived problems of the loosening of social control over sexuality and the rising number of unmarried women are major subjects in Senegalese public debates. Runner-up in the presidential elections in 2000 and later Prime Minister Moustapha Niasse made the 'problem' of unmarried women an item on his agenda during his campaign. In Niasse's view, 'the phenomenon is a real plague that depraves our society.' According to him, 'delayed marriage leads to sexual freedom and all of its consequences, such as an increase in sexual transmitted diseases' (*Le Quotidien* May 5, 2000). The hotly debated morality of women's sexuality testifies of a public struggle for honesty, honour and values in changing urban contexts (*cf.* Perry 2005).

Diskettes like Fatou and Coumba fill up the waiting rooms of marabouts. Typically, about five young women from around fourteen to around thirty years of age would be occupying the benches and chairs when I came in. I witnessed the following consultation of a *diskette* visiting marabout Fanta:

A beautiful young woman in her early twenties comes to Fanta for a divination session. This is her first visit. She has heard about Fanta from her friends. She has remarkably fair skin, long straightened hair, and is dressed in tight jeans and a black, low-cut top. She speaks in a soft voice and moves with grace. Fanta shakes the forty cowry shells on a plate and gives about fifteen of the shells to the girl. The girl takes the shells and 200 FCFA in her hand and whispers her concern, inaudibly, with her mouth close to her hand. She throws the shells on the plate. Fanta looks at the cowry shells, shaking them again after every explanation she gives.

Girl: Yes, she lives in Grand Yoff.
Fanta: The man took the initiative, but his wife warned you not to start anything with her husband. She has already taken steps and offered alms to stop you seeing her husband. You have not seen this man for two, three days now.
Girl: That is true.
Fanta: You are wondering if you will ever see him again. If you give three white kola nuts as alms, he will call you. You are only thinking about the money you would like to get from him. But he is even considering marrying you.
Girl: Yes, that's what he said; but he also said that he is not at ease at the moment. He moves around a lot for his work. And there is his wife, who wants to break off this relationship. She is Bamana and her name is N.F.B.
Fanta: Give the alms and all will be well. I see a long life full of happiness, pleasure and money for you. All the problems that trouble your head will disappear. Are you planning to travel?
Girl: Yes, to Ziguinchor.
Fanta: Before you go, give one white kola nut and you will be safe.
Girl: Thanks a lot.

(Conversation on 29 November 2003)

After the session, Fanta told me that the woman's specifying the name of her lover's wife meant that she wanted Fanta to cast a spell on her. A name is necessary for any spell to be effective. Fanta emphasized that she had let the comment pass, because she does not want to cast bad spells on anybody. Instead, she had reassured the woman and predicted 'a life full of happiness, pleasure and money' for her. Fanta had also distracted her client from her issues with her lover's wife by changing the subject and asking about her travel plans instead. Nevertheless, the young woman looked disappointed as she thanked Fanta and left.

When I visited Fanta another day, the street was filled with music, white plastic chairs, big cooking pots, and with well dressed, excited women: a wedding. Fanta said that the mother of the bride had told her how she had arranged the marriage. Before going to France to visit a friend, she had gone to her to magically treat a picture of her daughter. As soon as the friend's son saw the picture, he fell in love with the daughter. His parents objected to the marriage, claiming that their son was marabouté, and feared that he was going to be used by the girl and her parents for money and a residence permit. They visited a marabout for a counter-attack, but that had not worked: the marriage was being celebrated that day. According to Fanta, the groom had already given one million FCFA as bride price and had promised another 250.000 FCFA and a visa for the young woman (Conversation on 20 December 2003).

Emigration of men from Senegal increased rapidly between 1980 and 1990. Women, although some do now migrate as well, largely remain in Senegal. Many do however aspire to marry an émigré in the hope of following him to the diaspora. The risks of being married to an émigré in Senegal are nevertheless high. Whatever the nature of a woman's problems with her husband or her in-laws, she occupies a significantly weaker position than a woman who lives with her husband. She has less access to information about her husband, social pressure on her husband from her relatives is less effective, and she cannot use her sexuality as a weapon in negotiations. A neighbor in Parcelles Assainies, for example, thirty-five years old, had not heard in seven years from her husband in Italy when I met her. She wanted a divorce before it was too late for her to have legal children with another man, but her husband's family, with whom she lived, refused to allow this.

For a woman married to a 'ghost,' visiting a marabout remains one of the few options to influence her husband.

A woman in her thirties was sitting on Fanta's bed as I came in one day. This client was clearly in distress: she was speaking with an edge of panic in her voice, gesticulating wildly. She explained that she is married as a third wife to a man living in France. 'His other two wives live in Mali, and I live in Parcelles Assainies. My husband was interested in me for a long time and after six years I finally agreed to marry him,' she said. From her wedding day on, however, she has suspected her husband's second wife of trying to *marabouter* her.

"My husband bought me some land [to build a house on] in Parcelles Assainies. But he suddenly changed his mind and says now that for as long as I do not bear him any children, I will not get the land. The second wife has said that she will do anything to prevent me from having children for as long as she has no children herself. Apparently she has been successful with her visits to marabouts." (Conversation on 20 January 2003)

At the time we spoke, her husband was not sending her any money. Fanta tried to comfort the woman. She acknowledged that this was a complex situation and explained that she would take care of it step by step. First, Fanta would make sure that the husband started sending money again. To this effect, she would prepare a potion for her client to wash herself with. The women in the room (Fanta, Fanta's sister and Aminata) were moved by the woman's story. Fanta's sister spoke about her own experience with a married man. Fanta and Aminata nodded seriously. Fanta turned to me: 'Do you see our problems here in Senegal? Polygamy is not a good thing!' Later, I met Fanta's client twice again in Fanta's room, again in distress as her relationship with her husband had not greatly improved.

IN THE WAITING ROOM

In the centre of Dakar, notably in Le Plateau where mostly expatriates and high government officials live, marabouts do not have waiting rooms. They receive their clients discreetly one at a time. An upper-class woman told me that marabouts for wealthier people do not seat their clients in a waiting room, as this causes embarrassment. This woman told me that when she had accompanied her aunt to such a marabout, a government minister had just left the house. For each category of clients, then, there is a category of marabouts.

The services of marabouts are of central importance to almost every Senegalese, regardless of where he or she lives. In Dakar's outskirts, however, problems relating to polygamy, infertility, female celibacy, and the emigration of men are magnified. Here rural women, in general, have more possibilities, freedom and economic independence than in their home villages. The urban environment brings, however, also new insecurities, competition, and precarious living conditions, as the stories in this article showed. Marrying and having (legal) children are the two most important goals in the life of virtually every Senegalese woman. Relationships between husbands and wives are, however, generally perceived as highly unpredictable and uncontrollable, and as a source of stress and fatigue for women (*cf.* Gemmeke 2006). The plight and duties of women in marriage is ubiquitous in popular music. In her popular song *Sey dou choix* [Marriage is not a choice], for example, Coumba Gawlo Seck, a young female singer, affirms that a happy marriage is not a choice but sheer luck.[12] While celibacy causes feelings of despair among women, within marriage, the majority of women compete with mistresses, co-wives, and mothers-in-law –often living day and night on a few square meters with their rivals. As one woman said:

"Here in Senegal, we live with masks on our faces. We are so used to pretending for the outside world that our family is perfect while we live with our biggest rivals. We live with our co-wives, with our half-brothers. Even of our husbands, who sleep in our beds, we know nothing. We do not know what they earn, and they do not know how much we earn. That's why marabouts are indispensable for us. They comfort us. They take away our fears so that we can become our normal, calm selves again. For example, I know a woman who doesn't care who her husband sleeps with or marries. A marabout once told her she would die as his only wife."[13]

---

12   Gawlo and Diego 2003 *Sey dou choix* (African Productions/ Melodie, France).
13   Anthropologist. Francis Nyamnjoh at the Codesria research institute in Dakar, was kind enough to let me listen to his interview on 6 October 2003 with this woman, a colleague of his.

Offering comfort and solace is indeed an important aspect of marabouts' work. In every consultation that I witnessed marabouts repeated several times that problems would be solved and wishes would be granted as long as the client followed their recommendations and treatments. Like Fanta, they assured their clients of a world full of 'happiness, pleasure and money'. In this way, the services of marabouts have the same function as white sheep: to absorb tension.

Marabouts furthermore offer, to use Soares' phrase (2004: 925), a 'home away from home'. While most new migrants try to adopt – as fast as possible – the dress, language, and streetwise attitude of the city (sneeringly calling those who adapt not fast enough *kaw-kaw*), marabouts present themselves as having only just arrived from the countryside. They speak Wolof, Dakar's lingua franca, poorly or not at all. They emphasize their regular contact, by phone and through travels, with their 'natal' village in the countryside. And they wear simple uni-coloured cotton *grand boubous* as opposed to vibrant colours or tight fitting and synthetic fabrics, which is highly remarkable in a city where fashion is taken extremely serious. Marabouts thus provide a connection to rural areas through language, dress, and artefacts that forms a source of power and identity for both them and their clients. The countryside is imagined, by marabouts and clients, in Dakar and abroad, in public media as well as in the private sphere, as a source of power and identity (Gemmeke 2007).

Since the 1970s, the notion of a progressive 'disenchantment', in Max Weber's words, became disputed. The former axiom of an increasing and irreversible 'secularist' modernity caused by urbanization and globalization was contested by empirical proof of the opposite (Casanova 2008). From the 1990s onward academics asserted that modern, urbanised societies not only constitute magic as their counterpoint but also create their own forms of magic (Comaroff and Comaroff 1993; Geschiere 1995, 1998; Pels 2003: 3). Whether or not urbanisation leads to an increase in consultation of the services of marabouts (such as divination and amulets) is a popular topic of conversation in Senegal. While the answer remains unclear, it is apparent that the topic of marabout consulting is discussed more openly in urban Senegal today than it was in the 1960s and 70s. In the decades following independence talking openly about consultations with marabouts was considered, at least by the Western-educated elite, backward and only relevant for the poor and the uneducated. During the last two decades, however, the esoteric craft of marabouts has been openly discussed on television, on the radio, and in newspapers. Even among the highly educated in Senegal it is no longer uncommon to express a belief in the esoteric powers of marabouts.[14]

Many of my interlocutors in Senegal were nostalgically reminiscent of the time when, according to them, marabouts 'genuinely tried to help their clients, asking only for symbolic payment', as one man put it. They believe that as of the 1980s, when Dakar began to overflow with rural migrants – including marabouts – in search of money, the profession of marabouts has monetarized rapidly. Urban marabouts are increasingly paid in cash (rather than in services or goods), esoteric services being their main sources of income instead of a side activity as is frequently the case in the countryside. A considerable number of marabouts have become aggressive entrepreneurs in Dakar, avidly looking for publicity (*cf.* Geschiere 2003: 167).

Modesty is one of the key criteria for reliability of marabouts and related to the Sufi concept of *baraka*: divine grace and/or blessing. *Baraka* is obtained through kinship, teachers, and exemplary behaviour. It is associated with knowledge, a strong personality, wealth and power (see also Cruise O'Brien and Coulon 1988 and Soares 2005). It encompasses the capacity to give blessings that protect against a wide variety of misfortunes (Bop 2005: 1113). Advertising oneself, be that in newspapers, on radio, or television, or in self-presentation, is considered as a sign of spiritual weakness, unauthenticity, and display of commercial greed instead of altruistic piety. A marabout is supposed to attract clients through his or her knowledge, piety, and exemplary modest behaviour, advertised by satisfied clients and by the grace of God. Despite negative attitudes towards advertisements, however, Senegalese marabouts are virtually everywhere in the public sphere. They not only advise leading politicians and sportsmen, but also appear in or host popular radio and television shows, often answering questions from the audience, praying for them, and giving them advice on *sacrifices*, alms-giving. They advertise on television, the radio, and in newspapers, such as

---

14 Ibrahima Thioub, historian at Université Cheikh Anta Diop, personal communication. Geschiere points out that in the years after independence in Cameroon talking about witchcraft was considered a hindrance to the young and 'modern' state (2003: 168).

for example marabout Chaibatal Hamdi Diouf of the *Centre de l'Orientation et de Lumière* mentioned above.

In the competitive chaos of Dakar, where people of all ages continuously have to find new houses, jobs and marriage partners, marabouts thus have an ambiguous role. On the one hand, they promise to be an anchor in the turmoil. On the other hand, the great majority of marabouts are, just like their clients, rural migrants in search of a livelihood for themselves and their families. Therefore, marabouts in Dakar are suspected of deliberately aggravating their clients' problems in order to create more work for themselves. Marabouts identify individuals or spirits as the source of problems and do not address the structural dimensions of gendered dilemmas like polygamy, nor provide long-term solutions to their clients' problems. They thus can manipulate and intensify tensions notably by accusing people close to their clients of trying to harm them. In doing so, marabouts form an integral part of the urban life-world of most people, and especially of most women, in Dakar.

REFERENCES

Antoine, Philippe and Jeanne Nanitelamio. 1996. 'Can Polygyny be avoided in Dakar?' In: Kathleen Sheldon (ed.). *Courtyards, Markets, City Streets: Urban Women in Africa*. Boulder: Westview: 129-150.

Augis, Erin. 2002. *Dakar's Sunnite Women. The Politics of Person*. Unpublished Dissertation, University of Chicago.

Bâ, Mariama. 1979. *Une si longue lettre*. Dakar: Nouvelles Éditions Africaines du Sénégal.

Biaya, Tshikala Kayembe. 2001. 'Les plaisirs de la ville: masculinité, sexualité et féminité à Dakar (1997-2000)', *African Studies Review*, 44(2): 71-85.

Bop, Codou. 2005. 'Roles and the Position of Women in Sufi Brotherhoods in Senegal', *Journal of the American Academy of Religion*, 73(4): 1099-1119.

Casanova, José. 2008. 'The Problem of Religion and the Anxieties of European Secular Democracy'. In: Gabriel Motzkin and Yochi Fischer (eds.). *Religion and Democracy in Contemporary Europe*. London: Alliance: 63-74.

Clignet, Remi. 1987. 'On dit que la polygamie est morte: vive la polygamie!' In: David Parkin and David Nyamwaya (eds.). *Transformations of African Marriage*. Manchester: Manchester University: 199-210.

Comaroff, John and Jean Comaroff (eds.). 1993. *Modernity and its Malcontents: Ritual and Power in Postcolonial Africa*. Chicago: University of Chigaco.

Cruise O'Brien, Donal B. 1996. 'A lost Generation? Youth Identity and State Decay in West Africa'. In: Richard Werbner and Terence Ranger (eds.). *Postcolonial identities in Africa*. London: Zed: 55-74.

Cruise O'Brien, Donal and Christian Coulon (eds.). 1988. *Charisma and brotherhood in African Islam*. Oxford: Clarendon.

Delaunay, Valérie. 1994. *L'entré en vie féconde. Expression démographique des mutations socio-économiquse d'un milieu rural sénégalais*. Paris: Centre Français sur la Population et le Développement CEPED.

Dial, Fatou Binetou. 2008. *Mariage et divorce à Dakar. Itinéraires féminins*. Paris: Karthala.

Dilley, Roy M. 2004. *Islamic and Caste Knowledge Practices among Haalpulaar'en in Senegal: Between Mosque and Termite mound*. Edinburgh: Edinburgh University.

Diop, Abdoulaye Bara. 1985. 'Jeunes filles et femmes de Dakar: conditions de vie et attitudes relatives à la famille, au mariage et à l'éducation sexuelle', *Bulletin de l'IFAN,* 44(1/2): 163-212.

Diouf, Mamadou. 2002. 'Des cultures urbaines entre traditions et mondialisation'. In: Momar-Coumba Diop (ed.). *Le Sénégal contemporain*. Paris: Karthala: 261-288.

Evans-Pritchard, Edward Evan. 1949. *The Sanusi of Cyrenaica*. Oxford: Clarendon.

Fall, Abdou Salam. 2005. *Bricoler pour survivre. Perceptions de la pauvreté dans l'agglomération urbaine de Dakar*. (PhD Thesis). Amsterdam: University of Amsterdam.

Gemmeke, Amber. 2007. 'The Map of Magic: Migrating Marabouts in Suburban Dakar'. In: Elisabeth Boesen and Laurence Marfaing (eds.). *Les nouveaux urbains dans l'espace Sahara-Sahel: un cosmopolitisme par le bas*. Paris: Karthala-ZMO: 233-257.

---. 2006. Hoe vind je een man in Dakar? En hoe houd je hem? *ZemZem. Tijdschrift over het Midden-Oosten, Noord-Afrika en islam*, 2(3): 72-77.

Geschiere, Peter L. 1995. *Sorcellerie et Politique. La viande des autres*. Paris: Karthala.
---. 2003. 'Witchcraft as the dark Side of Kinship', *Etnofoor* XV(1): 43-61.
Goode, William J. 1970. *World Revolution and Family Patterns*. New York: Collier Macmillan.
Gough, Harrison G. 1977. 'Further Validation of a Measure of Individual Modernity', *Journal of Personality Assessment*, 41(1): 49-57.
Graw, Knut. 2005. 'Culture of Hope in West Africa', *ISIM Review*, 16: 28-29.
Havard, Jean-François. 2001. 'Ethos "bul faale" et les nouvelles figures de la réussite au Sénégal', *Politique Africaine*, 82: 63-77.
Hesseling, Gerti. 2002. 'Senegal'. In: Herbert M. Kritzer (ed.). *Legal Systems of the World. A Political, Social, and Cultural Encyclopedia. Volume IV: S-Z*. Santa Barbara: ABC Clio: 1423-1432.
Hörbst, Viola. 2006. 'Infertility and InvitroFertilization in Bamako, Mali: Women's Experience, Avenues for Solution and Social Contexts Impacting on Gynaecological Consultations', *Curare*, 29(1): 35-46.
---. 2008. 'Focusing Male Infertility in Mali: Impacts on Gender Relations and Biomedical Practice in Bamako'. In: Jonathan Bockropp and Thomas Eich (eds.). *Muslim Medical Ethics: Theory and Practice*. Bloomington: University of Indiana: 118-137.
Jaffré, Yannick. 1999. 'Pharmacies des villes, pharmacies "par terre"'. In: Jean-Philip Olivier de Sardan (ed.). *Anthropologie de la santé*. Berlin: Lit: 63-70.
Lambert, Michael C. 2002. *Longing for exile. Migration and the Making of a Translocal Community in Senegal, West Africa*. Portsmouth: Heinemann.
Ron Lesthaeghe, Georgia Kaufmann and Dominique Meekers. 1989. 'The Nuptiality Regimes in Sub-Saharan Africa'. In: Ron Lesthaeghe (ed.). *Reproduction and Social Organization in Sub-Saharan Africa*. Berkeley: University of California: 238-337.
Manchuelle, François. 2004. *Les diasporas des travailleurs Soninké (1848-1960). Migrants volontaires*. Paris: Karthala.
McLaughlin, Fiona. 2001. 'Dakar Wolof and the Configuration of an Urban Identity', *Journal of African Cultural studies*, 14: 153-172.
Monteil, Vincent Mansour. 1980. *L'Islam noir: une religion à la conquête de l'Afrique*. Paris: Seuil.

Pels, Peter. 2003. 'Introduction: Magic and Modernity'. In: Birgit Meyer and Peter Pels (eds.). *Magic and Modernity Interfaces of Revelation and Concealment*. Stanford: Stanford University: 1-38.

Perry, Donna. 2005. 'Wolof Women, Economic Liberalization, and the Crisis of Masculinity in Rural Senegal', *Ethnology*, 44(3): 207-226.

Piga, Adriana. 2002. *Dakar et les ordres soufis. Processus socioculturels et développement urbain au Sénégal contemporain*. Paris: Harmattan.

Rabine, Leslie W. 2002. *The Global Circulation of African Fashion*. Oxford: Berg.

Silberschmidt, Margrethe. 2001. 'Disempowerment of Men in Rural and Urban East Africa: Implications for Male Identity and Sexual Behavior', *World Development*, 29(4): 657-671.

Soares, Benjamin F. 2005. *Islam and the Prayer Economy. History and Authority in a Malian Town*. Edinburgh: University of Edinburgh.

---. 2004. 'An African Muslim Saint and his Followers in France', *Journal of Ethnic and Migration Studies*, 30(5): 913-927.

Sow, Fatou. 2003. 'Fundamentalisms, Globalisation and Women's Human Rights in Senegal', *Gender & Development*, 11(1): 69 –76.

Triaud, Jean-Louis. 1997. 'Introduction'. In: David Robinson and Jean-Louis Triaud (eds.). *Le temps des marabouts: itinéraires et stratégies islamiques en Afrique occidental français, v. 1880-1960*. Paris: Karthala: 11-29.

Villalón, Leonardo. 1999. 'Generational Changes, Political Stagnation, and the Evolving Dynamics of Religion and Politics in Senegal', *Africa Today*, 46(3/4): 129-147.

Wittmann, Frank. 2003. 'Zur Ambivalenz des Populärjournalismus in Senegal. Strategische Aneignung und mediale Repräsentation der Hausmädchen', *Afrika Spektrum*, 38(2): 153-172.

REPORTS

Direction de la Prévision et de la Statistique 2002. *Projections de population du Sénégal issues du Recensement de 2002, Recensement générale de la population et de l'habitat-résultats provisoires*.

Ministère de l'Économie, des Finances et du Plan & Direction de la Prévision et de la Statistique 1992. *Recensement général de la population et de l'habitat de 1988. Rapport régional Dakar.*

'They behave as though they want to bring heaven down'
Some Narratives on the Visibility of Cameroonian Migrant Youths in Cameroon Urban Space

PRIMUS M. TAZANU

INTRODUCTION

It was common during my fieldwork in Buea, the capital of the South West Region of Cameroon, to hear negative and sometimes derogatory remarks about young migrants. Non-migrants between the ages of twenty to forty were discontented because of the consumerism, fashion, taste and leisure activities of these *bushfallers* of the same age range.

Even though studies on African and in particular Cameroonian youth are plentiful, there has not been much attention on urban commentary directed at Cameroonian *bushfallers*. One exception, however, is Bruno Riccio's (2005) study of Senegalese migrants who are also known as *modou modou*. He describes how non-migrant family members, outsiders and even the migrants themselves admire these unskilled *modou modou*, especially their skill at trading and saving money. Upon their return and visits to Senegal, they show off through their cars, big weddings and other symbols of success (Riccio 2005: 105). Studies of African and in particular Cameroonian youth have instead concentrated on detailed issues such as violence, identity, sexuality, and political and economic difficulties (Comaroff and Comaroff 1999; Diouf 2003; Nyamnjoh 2005a/b; Fokwang 2008;

Cruise O'Brien 1996; Jua 2003; Abbink 2005; Reynolds *et al*. 2008; Roth 2008; Weiss 2005). Concerns about youth disenchantment amidst political, economic and social uncertainties have concentrated on the slippery path to adulthood. Other literature has dealt generally with unachieved and underachieved desires to consume arising from the inability to pay or 'accelerated consumerism' that produces 'consumers without affordability and affordability without the typical signs of effort' (Nyamnjoh 2005a: 296)[1] or 'the will to consume' not matching 'the opportunity to earn' (Comaroff and Comaroff 1999: 293). Nyamnjoh further observes generally that ordinary citizens become frustrated with the provocative consumerism of the national and local elites, who are quite complacent about their lifestyles, which are achieved at the expense of the majority (Nyamnjoh 2004: 73). Comaroff and Comaroff (1999) detail how South African youths resort to violence and occultism in order to redress their economic malaise.

This vital literature reveals some dilemmas faced by a majority of youths in Cameroon as well as the main areas in which scholarship on them has focused on. Urban commentary on them could provide an additional theme to this scholarship. Their presence and visibility is so noticeable that it influences urban conversations in Cameroon in ways that need a deeper understanding. Studies on migrant African youths in African urban spaces could unravel plenty of knowledge that touches on issues like morality and identity claims, envy, jealousy, abuse of trust, suspicion, family and friendship conflicts, witchcraft, challenges to masculinity, violence and confrontation, sex, deception, mockery of migrants' achievements, consumerism, etc. This chapter touches on the themes of morality, consumerism and the mockery of achievements.

METHODOLOGY

The data presented in this chapter are based on five months of anthropological field research in Buea, Cameroon between September 2009 and Febru-

---

[1] Although not particularly dealing with Cameroonian youths per se, Nyamnjoh (2005) writes about sexual gratification strategies employed by men and women in order to sustain their consumption.

ary 2010.[2] Participant observation, in-depth face-to-face narrative interviews and group interviews were all used to ask non-migrant youths about their perceptions of visiting migrants. Questions and responses on these perceptions of migrants were parts of a broader interview framework dealing with the use and meaning of the new media (internet and mobile phones) in maintaining transnational relationships between Cameroonians. Even though I considered myself a Cameroonian who shared certain historical and cultural backgrounds with the participants, there were moments when this insider status became questionable. It turned out that I was seen more as a migrant than a researcher. Over time, I acquired identities as an investor, a driver, a money-lender, a potential husband, etc. These identities made it hard at times to identify myself solely with what I was supposed to be doing, namely fieldwork. Sticking to my mission often made people think I had changed or that I had become one of 'them', i.e. those migrants whose mentalities have been tainted by European values. I was considered to be one of the few who have succeeded (Abbink 2005: 23), which often subjected me to hurtful comments made by people quite close to me. My status as a migrant led people to assume that I was snobbish (I was snubbed many times), noisy, excited, immoral and depraved. Cameroonian migrants are canonically perceived in this way.

Many people were nonetheless interested in talking to me about migration, business plans, education, the possibilities of helping them or someone they knew to travel abroad, etc. These encounters in the field made me identify myself as an insider or outsider depending on the context of interaction. I easily acquired access to research participants as an insider (see also Ganga and Scott 2006), but I had problems in developing trust and rapport in certain circumstances because of some of the problems mentioned above. I was constantly conscious that my migration experience could influence the way I perceived interviewees' narratives. Though there was much reflexivity and self-questioning regarding some of the assumptions

---

2 Certain perceptions are also informed by six months of fieldwork among Cameroonians in Freiburg, Germany. Both periods of fieldwork formed part of my PhD studies on new media and transnational social ties. I am grateful to the VW Foundation funded project 'Passages of Culture', which examines the role of the media in Africa. The project links universities in Africa (Cameroon, Nigeria and South Africa) and Europe (Switzerland and Germany).

about being a migrant, I still believe this chapter is not bias-free (cf. Wiles 2008: 121-122). I have selected interviews that deal specifically with perceptions of visiting migrants from the forty-eight interviews conducted on experiences of using the mobile phone and internet to maintain transnational social ties. The interpretation and analysis of the data are based on transcribed interviews, informal conversations and notes from field observations specifically concerned with remarks on the visibility of migrants. Migrants are more or less presented as a homogenous category in this chapter; the general comments directed at them often do not take into account their different social attributes such as migration status, educational achievement, socio-economic background etc.

THE VISIBILITY OF MIGRANT YOUTHS

Upon return to Cameroon, many migrant youths live in an urban area such as Buea, the provincial capital of the South West Region of the country, which has a population of about 90,000 inhabitants. Before the establishment of a university in the early 1990s, Buea was mainly an administrative and agricultural town. It has good access in terms of transport and communication. This research was carried out in the neighbourhood of Molyko, which serves as the main entrance into Buea. Molyko is characterized by high mobility of people coming in and out of the town. Students make up the bulk of its population, but there are also teachers, the unemployed, the underemployed, petty traders, hawkers, peasants, roadside sellers, those 'surviving' and those 'not doing anything' (Archambault 2009: 2). Many people in Molyko do not have a regular job and often supplement their incomes through networks of acquaintances or moving back and forth to the rural areas, where most of their parents and relatives live.[3] Some young men have found unstable employment as middlemen in landed property, car sales etc. There is a wide array of other unregistered jobs, such as the 'document chasers' who get around the administrative bureaucracy through their connections and ability to bribe the right person in order to obtain the right or fake documents for anyone who employs their services. There are

---

3   For more about the vital rural-urban connection in Cameroon, see Geschiere and Gugler (1998); Ouden (1987); Eckert (1999); Yenshu (2008).

dokimen (*dokiman* as singular), specialists in making forged documents. There are also internet scammers who profit from 'stupid rich whites who prefer puppies to starving human beings'.[4] This list of sources of income is not exhaustive, as in any urban area, but they indicate some of the survival strategies of young people in Molyko. In fact, many of them live a life of 'compromise', as indicated in their readiness to switch to a different (better) job if the chance arises, a situation comparable to barbers in Arusha, Tanzania (Weiss 2005: 107). This wide array of livelihood strategies in the Cameroonian urban space reveals the uncertainties but also the creativity, resilience and ability of Cameroonian urban youths in surviving economic hardship.

Molyko is split down by a road that doubles as the main street.[5] Businesses line the road on both sides. The combination of these businesses and business or social-related activities, the heavy presence and movement of people on foot and in cars, engender an urban life-world of contracted space by rendering the road busy and narrow. This narrow space offers a chance for people to note easily what is going on – what new car (with either a foreign number plate or a chassis number) drives past, where the car goes to, where the owner of the car lives, where he spends his free time etc. This narrow space also offers a chance for people to notice certain traits that are usually associated with migrants, such as playing loud music in cars, drinking from one bar to another, having a 'fresh' body colour and a peculiar way of dressing, talking, topics of discussion and other visible signs of success.

Being 'fresh' deserves further commentary, as this goes beyond the desirable pale body colour and the positive appreciation of fat and bulk, which could also be associated with better living standards, comfort and even beauty. Being 'fresh' suggests newness, rarity and the absence of the daily problems such as unemployment, underemployment and the general desire for economic independence.

---

4 These are the words of an internet café owner, who has connections with scammers. Jua (2003) details different employment and livelihood ventures that Cameroonian youths practice as a survival strategy in the wake of the economic crisis and the difficult pathway to adulthood.

5 There are also streets that branch off from this main road but are less accessible by car.

Figure 1: Molyko is separated in the middle by a road that doubles as the main street

Source: photo by the author

This aside, Molyko displays the mixed characteristics of an urban and a rural area alike. It claims its urban character from its populations and diverse economic activities. Its rural character reveals itself when seen from the angle that anonymity, which is usually associated with urbanism, is generally lacking, especially along the roadside. In fact, businesses along the roadside often also function as spaces of sociality and even relaxation, since it can be hard at times to distinguish business from social relations (see also Slater and Kwami 2005: 12). At such drinking spots, restaurants, hotel verandas, telephone call points (popularly known as call boxes), computer documentation services, internet cafés, retail shops, barber shops and hair salons (just to name a few) act as 'venue[s] for conversation' and 'places to wait, to watch [and] to talk' (Weiss 2005: 109).

It is within this bustling life-world that many migrant youths find themselves. They are often distinguishable from other youths, as they are apparently better off economically, as indicated in their spending habits. Many of them also own and drive cars, one great asset that testifies that someone has been to Europe, North America or increasingly to the Middle East, South East Asia or South Africa. It is also within this very space that many of them are making investments in the form of constructing houses. For example, it is partly thanks to migrants that Buea has expanded into the neighbourhood of Bomaka, which is just about a kilometre or so from Molyko. Many migrants own houses and landed property in this vicinity. This presence and the achievements of the migrants markedly contrast with the lives of their non-migrant compatriots, who often consider themselves to have been 'left behind' (Glick-Schiller 2004: 462). It is common in Molyko to hear negative and bitter remarks about migrants, especially around December, when these *bushfallers* visit Cameroon mainly to spend Christmas or get married. Narratives about their moral uprightness and success, and also the consequences of them sharing the same urban space with non-migrants, are issues that deserve attention.

REMARKS ON MORALITY AND CONSUMERISM[6]

In urban Cameroon, the general image of a *bushfaller* is male, despite the fact that there are also female *bushfallers*. It is on this basis that maleness and masculinity run through the narratives of the non-migrants. Even in Moses' interview below, the female migrants' visibility is identified only in comparison to that of the men.[7] The popular urban perception is that migrants should desist from displaying success. Such perception further indicts women who are considered as more spoilt than men if they display achievement from abroad. This is perhaps because a 'good' woman is expected to be reserved (see also Drotbohm 2010: 58). In any case, the male migrants are more conspicuous mainly because the proportion of Cameroonian migrant men who often visit Cameroon (in terms of frequency and number) is much greater than their female compatriots. Female migrants

---

6 Morality here is treated more in terms of doing the 'right' or the 'wrong' thing that is either socially approved or disapproved. It is not used in the religious sense.

7 The names used in this article are fictitious in order to respect the privacy of participants.

are less visible than men, according to Moses, whose masculinity is threatened by these supposedly economically independent women:

"Female bushfallers are very secretive. Maybe it is because they do not see anything to gain from men since they are rich [...]. They also live with their families, unlike men, who do not have much restriction in moving [around...]. The girls have more attachment to the family, but boys have more attachment to friends. Boys go to the village, give gifts to their parents and then leave." (21 October 2009)

The masculine imagery that frequently appears in the narratives on the migrants paints a picture of an excited, spoilt and noisy lecher driving a flashy car. The three interview excerpts below with youths in Molyko confirm this perception. Theo is a 35-year-old shop owner who has aspirations of going abroad in the future through the help of his migrant brother, who has been living in Sweden (illegally) for a year (before November 2009). He resorted to doing business because he could not find a job after graduating from a professional school. The second quotation is drawn from an interview with Janet, a 33-year-old university graduate who now sells clothes and jewellery. She tried unsuccessfully to obtain employment in the public service through writing public competitive exams. Theo's and Janet's businesses are both located along the main street in Molyko. Ken is a born-again Christian studying at the University of Buea. He has a brother who often visits Cameroon. They have no difficulties in profiling a migrant youth, as they respectively say:

"[...] you find them around snacks and bars. They behave as though they want to bring heaven down. They make noise, talk and the way they spend money proves this [...]. I wonder if these people have permanent investments such as houses because those cars can crash beyond repairs on the road and they could be costing a lot of money. I would prefer to invest my money if I were a *bushfaller*." (02 November 2009)

"For example, when they come here, they deceive young girls and behave like rascals. There are some who come with their cars and put the music so loud that they disturb the environment. I do not think they put high volumes in the cars when they are in Europe." (12 October 2009)

"Since *bushfallers* often consider Cameroonians left behind as inferior people, there is always the tendency that they get the luxurious cars with tainted screens. They just want to show that they are tough guys in the country. Most of them carry two girls behind [in the back seat of] their cars and loiter around to show that they are more than the people left behind." (03 December 2009)

Only on very few occasions do non-migrant youths make distinctions between the female and male migrants, the educated and uneducated, or even the 'good' and 'bad' migrant. There are generally two categories: the good and the bad *bushfallers*, but they move on to talk in detail about the bad ones, who are usually seen as representing migrants in general. In his study of perceptions of migrants in Senegal, Bruno Riccio observes that the commentary directed at them is in part a cultural production of consciousness i.e. the awareness of their presence in Senegalese physical and social space (Riccio 2005: 100). In the life-world of Buea, part of this consciousness has been the tendency to identify the migrants' 'abnormality'. The point here is that there is a high predisposition to define migrants' behaviour as 'abnormal'. Whether the descriptions of the *bushfallers* are real or imagined, the responses above uncover a certain consciousness of social inequality that exists between migrants and non-migrants.[8] Non-migrants often contrast themselves with migrants, who are strongly associated with wealth, comfort, well-being, knowledge and experience (Tazanu 2010: 87-88).[9] However, these non-migrants typically (and ideally) profess to distance themselves from the 'abnormal' but successful migrants.

---

8 Nearly all interviewees expressed the wish to go abroad, citing the notion that migration confers greater social status on them. At the same time, it indicates progress and a pathway to independence. It is a sort of 'moving up', in the words of Steven Vertovec (2009: 75) or the conversion of (supposed) economic capital into symbolic capital (prestige) (Ong 1999: 89-93). Ong's book is about Chinese struggling to acquire a higher social status. My chapter, on the other hand, deals with the social status attributed to migrants back home in Cameroon. What links the two is the fact that the migrants have a higher social status than non-migrants.

9 Many migrants in Freiburg, Germany, who have been to Cameroon said they felt uncomfortable that they are granted higher status simply because they have migrated. In reality the higher status accorded to them is just an illusion because

Remarks on migrants usually target their achievements, appearance, music, cars, money, residence, consumption choices etc. It seems as if everything about them is wrong. A deeper interpretation of these comments could be seen from the perspective of non-migrants' current life experiences, feelings of entrapment and also threat (for example, challenges to one's masculinity – the inability to drive around with girls too!). Maybe it is the feeling of being intimidated that makes non-migrant youths want their migrant cohort to bear disproportionately the accusation that in postcolonial Africa youths are 'dangerous, criminal, decadent and given to a sexuality that is unrestrained and threatening to the whole society' (Diouf 2003: 4). Mamadou Diouf (2003) writes that African youths have lost their position as the hope of the future, which was the optimistic view that politicians portrayed of young Africans in the period immediately following independence. Non-migrant youths thus unconsciously embrace the political elite's discourse (youth as non-conformist) to describe the migrant youths. The present context does not invoke talk about this 'lost generation' (Cruise O'Brien, 1996) or disenchanted youths, but shows that non-migrant youths often raise concerns about the decency of visiting Cameroonian migrants of the same age range when they find themselves in the same urban life-world in Cameroon.

It is worth stressing that the independence and freedom of returning youths, who live in hotels, travel enormously, share drinks, drive in cars, (some of them) have sex with many girls, etc. subjects them to scrutiny and even jealousy.[10] Some remarks directed at them question their consumerism in part because it is considered provocative to display success amidst poverty. This often raises questions about their moral uprightness. Francis Nyamnjoh (2005b) has observed that visiting migrant youths' displays of

---

they may not be rich and are often considered an underclass in the host country. Many of them wished to be respected according to their age and as human beings, not because of their migration status.

10 While in the field, I saw bushfallers exhibit certain lifestyles that non-migrants often accuse them of. In what looks like a transitional period in Cameroon during visits, the bushfallers tend to spend a lot of money and display an unsettled life. They appear always to be on the move and in a hurry. When asked where they live, the bushfallers say 'I deh everywhere' (I'm everywhere), 'just around,' 'Kumba and Limbe' (names of towns they simultaneously live in!), etc.

success come alongside feelings of victimhood for the non-migrant. In short, the non-migrant youths do not find it comfortable that young people (of the same age range) come so close to them and indulge in life-styles that are usually associated with people in wealthier countries or the socially isolated local elite. Migrant life-style displays, coupled with media that portray 'unimaginable wealth and wellbeing that are now easily imagined (and instantaneously mediated) and therefore all the more painfully unattainable' (Weiss 2005: 119), do in fact breed a mixture of envy and scorn (Riccio 2005: 112). One of the many responses to the discomfort and unease in accepting that they share the same urban space with successful youths has been the invention or redefinition of what Cameroon is. Cameroon is usually portrayed as a non-dynamic place where authentic moral culture is located. Such claims of moral cultural authenticities easily point accusing fingers at migrants who are believed to have overstepped moral boundaries. It is thus no surprise to hear Janet claiming that migrant youths are half-baked Cameroonians influenced by a foreign liberal, immoral and care-free culture, which is also to blame for promoting deviation from what could be termed 'Cameroonian culture':

"In Cameroon, there is a particular way people expect you to dress, while in Europe, as I heard, nobody cares if you dress half-naked. If someone dresses like that, it is as if the person is not well cultured [...]. I am not too mobile because I sit in my shop the whole day. I see them passing with their luxurious cars and they play their music in very high tones. They dress with their chests out; some with very large chains, which is not just common in Cameroon. Usually, the people I see dressing this way are Cameroonians, but they have stayed in Europe or America." (12 October 2009)

Janet pays attention to migrants' material possessions, their 'uncultured' and annoying displays of visibility. Evidently, she pities their inability to adjust to 'Cameroonian culture.' Her comments are not an exception, but part of the general perception of migrants. Of particular interest is the accusation of the West as the source of corruption and potential unconformity of the visiting migrant youths. Deviancy is constructed by making reference to the West, while Cameroon becomes the focal point of authenticity. 'Negative' observations on dressing codes, high volume music in cars, large chains and being 'half-naked' all point to threats resulting from the encroachment from outside forces under the banners of freedom and consumerism. In fact, many remarks on the migrants have an anti-consumerist thrust and are thus an indirect protest against a (selected) 'Western' way of life from which many non-migrants profess to distant themselves. There is a particular concern that consumerism has made enormous inroads into urban Cameroon, where the desire of youths to consume far outstrips their ability to pay (Nyamnjoh 2005a; Comaroff and Comaroff 1999; Weiss 2005). The allure of consumerism comes too close, but only a few people of their generation can easily afford to pay.

It is evident from their narratives that most non-migrants youths have become cynical with regards to restricted means of consumption. Others are defiant and question the consumerist activities of migrants such as staying in hotels and eating at expensive restaurants. They will rather spend the money on their families unlike the bushfallers who 'waste' money. In this life-world, the consumption choices of migrant youths thus spark contestations over what to do with money – invest for the future and in the family, as opposed to ephemeral extravagance. The setting of priorities on how to use money is comparable to Bourdieu's (2002) suggestion that working-class people perceive the expenditure of the upper classes as extravagance. Working-class people might engage in some consumption, but not 'without a painful sense of wasting money' (Bourdieu 2002: 374). They might also tend to regard the expenditure of the upper classes as 'crazy' because there are 'so many things that come first' which are in fact a 'necessity' (Bourdieu 2002: 375). 'Necessity' is nevertheless subjective, but the presence of migrant youths with the ability to spend much more than the local standard breeds envy, scorn and even conflict with other youths in the same age range.

Quite prominent in these anti-consumerist voices are claims of ideal local values, including the desire to maintain pride and dignity. Many non-migrant youths stressed that they still upheld their pride and dignity, despite not being as successful as the migrants. This was often in conformity with a cultural belief which claims that these values are better than material objects, although this is purely an ideal type of thinking. For example, many people said defiantly: 'It is not all about money', 'Going to Europe is not my priority'. Or: 'What am I going to do there (Europe)?' only to wish suddenly that they were migrants who worked, had accumulated some money, had sent remittances home and were independent like other migrants. Such remarks on retaining one's dignity, unlike consumerist migrants, are in fact a way to question the civility of the migrants, who are considered as behaving badly. Worth noting is the observation that remarks on the morality of migrants do not reflect reality all the time. There are non-migrants who engage in similar public consumerist behaviour but are disregarded or receive less public indictment than do the migrants (Archambault 2009: 4).[11] There is usually a demarcation with regards to who receives the greater negative comments in this urban setting.

What is interesting in these judgments of migrants is the observation that non-migrants often (obviously) position themselves favourably (see also Drotbohm 2010: 54).[12] One could go further and say that migrants are seen as people who 'desecrate' and 'make immoral' the life-world of Buea, which is ideally calm, peaceful and chaste in the absence of these migrants. I turn to a remark that appeared before concerning *bushfallers* and girls. The young men often painfully commented that the *bushfallers* carry girls in their cars and outdo them (non-migrants) as far as spending on these girls is concerned.[13] To them, their masculinity is being challenged. They are aware that it is hard to catch up with the *bushfallers*. Riccio (2005: 111-112) voices similar concerns in Senegal, where the presence of migrants not only makes life uncomfortable for non-migrant youths of their generation, it also provokes these non-migrants into trying to catch up (though they often fail). Besides challenges to masculinity, the girls (especially those in the university) in Molyko are more concerned with these boys deceiving them and the fear of being abandoned. To them, trust is either abused or stands

---

11 One migrant on holiday contested the generally bad reputation that migrants are sexually obsessed. He mentioned that the rich unfaithful married non-migrants should receive greater indictment than the unmarried sexually promiscuous migrants (in an interview on 5 November 2009).

12 This is comparable to Gluckman's (1963) observation that gossipers 'consider themselves higher in status' when they talk about people because they want 'to put those whom they consider lower in their proper place' (Gluckmann 1963: 309).

13 It is common in Cameroon for girls/women to be supported materially and financially by their male partners. One disgruntled young man said that they (non-migrants) have very thin chances of getting the choicest girls in the presence of bushfallers. They might succeed only through telling lies and making fake promises to the girls (in a conversation on 6 January 2010).

the test of being abused. It is commonsense knowledge nowadays in Molyko that these girls should be smart and only involve themselves halfheartedly in any relationship with the *bushfallers*. In any case, non-migrants often present themselves as potential losers (though with dignity). The migrants' presence could thus be a source of discomfort in continuously reminding the non-migrants of their 'junior' status in this urban world. The challenges and pressure of being in the same life-world with migrants are so enormous that many non-migrants have resorted to questioning migrants' visibility. They do this through mockery of the migrants and their supposed success.

MOCKING MIGRANTS AND THEIR SUCCESS

Popular opinion in Cameroon concerning migration and migrants is that these *bushfallers* must succeed abroad. The success is judged in many instances by looking at their material possessions. It was common to hear participants express disappointment that their migrant friend, brother or relative has not invested in Cameroon or that he had not sent any cars (yet).[14] They indeed ridiculed these migrants for being failures and for not being smart enough in snatching opportunities. In many of these comments, the migrant's source of success was never questioned; after all, abroad is believed to be ridden with opportunities of economic advancement to the extent that even the lowly educated migrants also succeed. They also display visible signs and symbols of success when they visit Cameroon.[15]

---

14 Though such standards may vary, people often stress the material aspects of success such as cars, having a piece of land or a house or having accumulated money for subsequent investment. When asked what she perceives of a migrant who is not extravagant, one participant had this to say: 'I will say you are a broke bushfaller if you do not go around in a car. You are supposed to go around in a car to prove that you are a bushfaller. You can rent a car if you do not have one. You have the money. Why should you walk?' (in an interview on 27 November 2009).

15 This perception somehow works in favour of the migrants, who are not subject to accusations of earning their money through witchcraft. People are interested in knowing the source of sudden success or wealth in Cameroon. On average,

Figure 2: Success is often linked to the outside world in Cameroon urban areas. In this photo, people are promised of a better life in USA if they play the American immigration lottery.

Source: photo by the author

This, however, does not mean that the jobs they do and the opportunity costs of success are not subject to scrutiny. A mock commentary has evolved around what the migrants are believed to be doing abroad. There was the constant reiteration that migrants never disclose what jobs they do and that they are secretive about doing such jobs abroad. This concern should not be erroneously interpreted as sympathy or worry that these migrants do rejected or 'odd' jobs. The comments are geared towards puncturing the migrants' pride for doing these jobs, telling them that they (who are

---

migrants return to Cameroon and display success after three years staying abroad, which is a very short time in Cameroon for employed people to show visible signs of success. Witchcraft practices and occultism may be used to explain sudden success in Cameroon. See, for example, Nyamnjoh (2005b); Ouden (1987); Ardener *et al.* (1960).

left behind) know the humiliation that these migrants go through abroad, as expressed in the words of Anasta, whose studies are partly supported by her step-sister in the United States. She defends her sister for doing 'odd' jobs as a student, but says generally that migrants' working lives are shrouded in concealment, deceit and secrecy:

"[Migrants] don't usually tell us the work they do because what they do [out] there are mean jobs. They are ashamed to tell us that they are cleaning toilets or taking care of old people. In fact, they are really ashamed. It is like, they would lose their pride if they revealed to us that they do these jobs. They may tell only their best or closest friend that they do odd jobs. They may also tell their friends not to tell anyone that they do such jobs. It is also to these friends that they may reveal the way they suffer in Europe." (13 December 2009)

This sort of mock commentary demonstrates non-migrants' willingness to ridicule the migrants by reminding them of their disgrace abroad. They should neither boast nor display conspicuous consumption in Buea because their hard lives abroad are widely known about! This is a call for modesty and an appeal to the *bushfallers* not to be unnecessarily arrogant or noisy as they presently are because such excitement is absent from their daily lives abroad. In some way, this is related to gossip as analysed by Max Gluckman (1963) and Robert Paine (1967). According to Gluckman (1963), gossiping is used to maintain the interest of the social group. For Robert Paine, gossiping is used as 'a device intended to forward and protect individual interest' to the detriment of others (Paine 1967: 278). The interest here is perhaps to make the migrants feel bad, meaning that the remarks and gossip purveyed in this urban setting are strategies of mockery aimed at deflating the migrants. The goal could also be that the non-migrants want to feel better about themselves and their life situations which are often evaluated negatively and seen as not satisfying in the presence of *bushfallers*. After spending time and conversing about abroad and success, many non-migrant youths wish they could do such jobs (temporarily) if they were to go abroad. At hand is the observation that the success of Cameroonians who have gone abroad is subject to degrading remarks and even jealousy, especially when these migrants share the same urban space with the non-migrants. Conversely, many non-migrant youths do not hesitate to date the migrants or engage in public consumption with them if they have a chance, for 'no bi man just get for take yi own?' ('Isn't it just a matter of snatching a piece for yourself?').¹⁶ This element of deceit and contradiction in turn subjects non-migrants' morals to question and also cast doubts on any sense of morality they might claim for themselves. Mercy is a high-school student who does not pardon migrants for doing 'odd' jobs. She ridicules 'odd' jobbers, but does not hesitate to enjoy her brother's money, earned through such jobs in Switzerland, where he currently studies. In her narratives, abroad is seen as a smooth place where a migrant can easily get a job:

"It is a bad thing if you have a degree in your hand and do odd jobs in another man's country. You went there to further your studies. Instead of furthering your studies, you demean yourself […] and do odd jobs [...]. I have enjoyed my brother's money. I felt good spending his money. We felt good in the family. He was generous. He gave drinks to all his friends and everyone was happy." (03 December 2009)

Deception of this nature was prevalent in derogatory remarks directed at migrants. Digressing a little from this is the observation that Buea is not only an arena where the display of visible success acquired abroad is locally condemned, but a space that brings the 'outside' – symbolised by acquisition, accumulation, success and consumerism – to touch on the 'inside', which is often seen in terms of a lack of opportunity and restricted consumerism. In this context, the same urban life-world generates different meanings and experiences, depending on whether one is a migrant or non-migrant youth. To the migrants, Buea offers the space to spend time relaxing before returning abroad. It is also a space where they feel at home. Buea offers the opportunity to try out new adventures and perhaps to venture into the life-styles they witnessed in earlier migrants before migrating, thereby reproducing the image that non-migrants have of migrants. In this respect, migrant youths are not necessarily inspecting home with a view to a final

---

16 The words of one female participant, who says that feasting with the immoral migrants is a means of obtaining free drinks. However, she does not sleep with the migrants because they are 'wayward' and 'use girls'. It is interesting to notice the way the girls are presented in these narratives. At some point they are seen as smart girls who are capable of humbling the mighty but lecherous migrants. At another point, their agency is neglected and they are seen as desperate girls who are 'used' and 'dumped'.

return, nor measuring their success against those who have not migrated (cf. Duval 2004: 63). To them, the urban space in Buea offers them a chance to display success, if only temporarily and periodically. This, however, has different interpretations and meanings to the non-migrant youths who may (mis-)interpret the migrants' visible success as a provocation or as the failure to observe the expected modesty.[17] To them, the migrant youths exaggerate happiness in the form of displaying success. For their part, the non-migrant youths see the urban world as a place where they struggle for survival but are periodically reminded of these struggles by the 'provocative' migrants who display success.[18]

Among the many mock commentaries is the constant quest to trace the authenticity of the goods consumed by the migrants (while they are in Cameroon), as well as the 'cleanness' of the migrants' money. In certain settings within Cameroon, the most desirable goods should come directly from abroad (mainly Europe, the USA and Japan). This scaling could mean that a migrant is looked down on if he buys certain items in Cameroon. Related to this authenticity of the sources of goods is the belief that some migrants are conmen who deceive Europeans (Riccio 2005: 109; Jua 2003) or sell illegal drugs, which means that their money is unclean or inauthentic and therefore subject to disparagement. As far as the authenticity of consumer items is concerned, migrants could be mocked if they drive cars that are bought or rented from Doula (Cameroon). These cars might be considered less genuine than those imported directly from abroad by the migrants themselves. This point was reiterated by Paul, who is usually suspicious and mistrustful of migrants, the more so because his migrant cousins and

---

17 Interviews with returning youths, as well as those Cameroonians in Germany who have visited Cameroon, reveals that these migrants are living a 'normal' life in Cameroon. There are issues of different interpretations of public visibility. The greatest guess is that the non-migrants are inclined to be defensive regarding already held views about migrants, while the migrants may not be adjusting to the realities on the ground. In fact, they have moved and experienced life abroad. Their life back home is partially influenced by their experiences of abroad.

18 As noted before, many non-migrant youths did not have a job; those who had a job were ready to switch to a better job if it came up. This reveals the uncertainty in their economic situation.

uncles never display success when they visit Cameroon. He constantly complained that his cousins and uncles do not share their success, despite being in Britain for a very long time. According to him, his uncles and cousins are either being deceitful by presenting themselves as poor in order to dampen down expectations of support from Paul, or they might be living a dubious life abroad.[19]

"I have heard a lot of bizarre things about them [i.e. migrants]. I have heard some of them rent cars from Douala in order to display here. This is to deceive people that these cars belong to them. I have heard some of them are conmen, some are scammers, some are drug dealers, etc. I am even sceptical about this paternal family of mine. I suspect something is wrong, but I cannot actually pinpoint it. With all the rumours and what we see, I cannot really trust them." (11 January 2010)

The huge attention or awareness of migrants in Buea is very interesting in that they are talked about even in their absence. It was common for non-migrants to confront the invisible migrant, and sometimes defiantly. One such act of defiance capitalizes on the fact that some migrants are illegal or have low education, with a direct connotation that they are a nuisance. They form the bulk of the excited migrant youths playing loud music in cars and thus polluting the life-world of Buea. This perception is typical of those non-migrant youths who have attended higher education. They are quite critical, if not bitter, of the success of those migrants with just basic or secondary school education. According to them, migrants with low education are upstarts appropriating life standards that do not tie in with their education. These accounts often associate economic achievement with academic credentials, which unfortunately is never like that. Such viewpoints, geared at deflating the achievements of migrants, may incorporate mockery that ranges from their desperate strategies to stay abroad (e.g. getting married to an old, fat or rejected European woman) and harsh conditions in staying abroad (sleeping under the bridge, con-artistry, doing illegal and low-paid jobs and running away from the host country's immigration police).[20] These

---

19 A 'good' migrant in Cameroon is often believed to be the one who shares his success.
20 One participant, an unemployed 38-year-old 'struggler', makes interesting and even contradictory remarks about going abroad, which in fact is directed against

narratives of defiance often downplay the fact that low-educated or even illegal migrants could find a smooth path to success while abroad. The point I am making here is that non-migrant youths are inclined to seek justifications, information and evidence that helps them to deflate the prestige of migrant youths. They are keen to reiterate their point that migrants go through hard times while abroad, even though they display success and happiness back home. The display and question of migrants' success is important in urban Cameroon considering perceptions that surround success. There was a general wish that migrants share their achievement. This is given further consideration in the next segment of the chapter.

MIGRANTS' SELECTED EXPERIENCES OF SHARING AN URBAN LIFE-WORLD WITH NON-MIGRANTS

The opinions of Adeline and Lucy below suggest that many non-migrants desire the attention of migrants in one way or the other. Unlike the 23-year-old Lucy, 28-year-old Adeline neither has migrant friends nor family members. As a woman with village roots, she is often expected to be generous to everyone when she visits the village. She does not feel at ease about this and considers it as annoying. Conversely, she has expectations of generalised hand-outs (just like Lucy) from migrants in Molyko. Excerpts from their interviews paint a broad picture on these generalized expectations from migrants. They stress the point that migrants keep success to themselves. Adeline is a part-time nursery school teacher. Her income is not enough. For this reason, she depends on food from her mother's farm in the village. Lucy moves back and forth to the village and does not have a stable income. She spends some time as a typist in a documentation shop. They have the following comments respectively about tight-fisted migrants:

> the migrant: 'I do not have any zeal to travel to Europe... It is this situation that makes people to sleep under bridges, run from the police and also live a hard life. As foreigners, you never get certain jobs except the rejected ones.... I can go there for studies or business or job. I do not want to go there with fake papers and escape when I see a policeman coming' (in an interview on 10 January 2010).

"But we find in a nutshell that they do not really want to share [...]. They only make you to know [that] they have. And you actually see that they have. They spend money and move around with women, but they do not give things out. This means they just amass the wealth for themselves." (27 November 2009)

"[...] we expect something [money] from them when they come back, but you don't really see what they have gone [out] there to work or what they have worked [...]. Some come around and flatter people [...]. They come and brag that they have worked for money, but you do not see the money." (30 September 2009)

Buea is replete with countless opinions of this nature. There are personal disappointments and rumours of greedy *bushfallers* who ignore the presumed rules of generosity by either refusing or not realising that they could share in the success acquired abroad. This general 'outcry' might tempt one to conclude that it is the obligation of the migrants to share their successes with whomever they meet.[21] One begins to question why there are such expectations from the migrants, whereas successful non-migrants around Buea are not subjected to similar expectations. Why do migrant youths suddenly become a source of attention in this setting to the extent that they are (subtly) expected to share their success? Is it because of the illusion that migrants earn their money without much struggle or even freely while abroad?[22] Whatever the case, this perception of *bushfallers* as successful but greedy Cameroonians partially contributes to certain negative experiences that they encounter while visiting Cameroon. Interviews in Freiburg reveal that *bushfallers* usually do not feel safe when they are in Cameroon. The knowledge that their success is a source of jealousy often encourages many of them to take precautionary steps to avoid being exploited, robbed or even beaten. The following paragraphs gloss over some of the reasons for security concerns, a security measure taken by a migrant, as well as a

---

21 Interestingly, the non-migrants may rejoice and mock a migrant for not being prudent if he spends his money on the people back home and becomes desperate. Few people would offer to help him (as is expected the other way round).
22 When conducting interviews in Freiburg, many Cameroonians mentioned (painfully) that their non-migrant friends and family back in Cameroon believe that they pluck money from trees or that they pick money up from along the street.

futile strategy employed by some non-migrants in order to partake in the success of their 'tight-fisted' migrant friends.

Stories of migrant youths being attacked by armed robbers abound in Buea and partly explain why most of these youths prefer to stay in hotels that have security guards. Gabriel, a 28-year-old newly married student from Sweden who returned to spend Christmas with his family, recounts his ordeal during a robbery targeting him in their family home on New Year's Eve (2010):

"We were in my room watching movies up till 2.30 am when we finally slept [...]. Something strange happened around 3.30 am. In my sleep, I felt like there was someone in my room. I woke up and saw two young boys, one masked with a cutlass, but the other did not cover his face. I asked who they were, and they threatened to cut me into pieces if I opened my mouth [...]. They took my laptop, my camera, phone and wallet that contained about 250,000 FRS. I was from the bank [to collect money] that same evening [...]. I was very happy since they did not wound or harm any of us because another gang killed a young business man in Molyko one week after and went away with huge sums of money."[23] (05 February 2010)

The armed youngsters who had probably been monitoring him were never traced. From this experience, we see that *bushfallers* could at times become victims of what appears to be success in the eyes of non-migrants. The robbery of the migrant could be interpreted far beyond the mere extortion of migrants' property. One way of looking at this is to situate the act within the broader socio-economic and political disenchantment of African youths, who may once in a while use violence to achieve their goals (Abbink 2005; Cruise O'Brien 1996, 2003). In this respect, one could suggest that the robbery of migrants is 'an instrument of income redistribution' (Comaroff and Comaroff 1999: 289). They either share their success or are forced to do so by armed robbers who seem to be silently posing the question: 'What are

---

23 There is controversy as to whether the young businessman was killed as an act of revenge or whether he was killed by people interested in his goods and money. Some people reported that nothing was taken from his shop. However, the murdered man returned from abroad at some point, and it was rumoured that he had started his business with money earned from abroad. There were also many reports of migrants being robbed or assaulted in other towns in December 2009.

you doing with all that money?' (Cf. Bourdieu 2002: 374-375.) Using forcible means to extract the achievements of migrants also demonstrates that the 'mighty' migrants are vulnerable too: they can be humiliated, made to go down on their knees and rendered powerless when they visit Cameroon. Youths who use violence to achieve their goals could in fact be reclaiming their territory, i.e. telling the migrant youths that they no longer belong to Buea. The brutal seizure of migrants' valuable possessions indirectly questions their (assumed) consumerism and lifestyle, or even the wish to render them incapable of returning to Europe or North America, where most of them live. There is often the mockery that most migrants buy only one-way tickets to Cameroon and won't be able to return to their host countries if they do not sell the merchandise that they have brought along. Cars and electronic gadgets top the list. Stealing all their valuable and, most of all, saleable belongings could be an attempt to make sure that they cannot afford their return flights and hopefully fall back to the same level as the disenchanted robbers. It could be a means to strip them of their migrant status.

Assaults and threats (either real or imagined) against migrants have led some of them very concerned about safety and security, whether physical or spiritual, even before they leave for Cameroon. Security concerns not only encourage some of them to prefer to stay in hotels, but also to seek spiritual intercession by consulting diviners in order to protect themselves from jealous friends and relatives, who might appear surreptitiously and cast a spell on them at any time is this urban world. A few migrant youths have made it a routine to head directly to the diviner after landing at the airport in Cameroon. They do not announce their presence in the country unless they have spiritually fortified themselves against witchcraft attack.[24] Others are very concerned with what and where they should drink or eat and from whom. There are some who are concerned about who they visit and where they visit. Furthermore, others wear amulets, avoid certain friends and relatives, do not stay in one particular place for long, etc. These are measures that certain visiting migrants take in order to avoid injury, poisoning or even death. One such migrant whom I met in Buea was Clovis. His fear of witchcraft was rife and partly contributed to his vagabond-like life-style. He rarely spent a long time in one place for fear of being noticed. He be-

---

24 A few migrants in Freiburg, as well as some visiting migrants whom I met in Cameroon during my fieldwork, confirmed this.

lieved that his jealous friends and family members could render him incapable of returning to Norway, where he lives.[25] He never informs anyone but his parents and wife that he is visiting Cameroon. It is the same when he leaves. Clovis' concern is to leave no trace as he travels from Norway to Cameroon. The fact that he lives such a sneaky life-style, even after visiting Cameroon many times over the years, tells how seriously he considers the threat from witchcraft. It should be noted, however, that it is such constant movement from one place to another that contributes in reproducing the observation that migrants are extravagant.

Aside from these uncomfortable experiences, some migrants whom I met in Buea said that there is a tendency for their friends to take advantage of them, thanks to the fact that they no longer live in Cameroon. All of them reported that their friends offer to play the middleman role, such as selling the migrants' car or electronic gadgets, offer them a piece of land or even look for girls for the 'sexually obsessed migrant'. These non-migrants would naturally present the situation as though it is for the benefit of the migrant. But the reality is that they could be exploiting or wishing to exploit their migrant friends. I met Kevin in Buea during my fieldwork (December 2009). He had been living in Denmark for close to five years as a student and has kept ties with his friends and family by sending remittances and making phone calls. He realized that his friends were becoming frustrated because he could not take them out every day for free drinks while on his visit to Cameroon. They found a way to extort money from him by offering him University of Buea girls:[26]

"Some of them tell me that they have beautiful girls on offer. They know they can easily manipulate me if they give me a girl. They can easily extract money for me. For me it is no problem because I am not interested. I tell them that it is not what I am here for." (05 November 2009)

---

25 Similar concerns for spiritual protection were mentioned in Freiburg among Cameroonian migrants who have visited Cameroon. Some of the migrants who had not remitted money to friends and family actually avoided some of these people who (potentially) could bewitch them.

26 There is a belief that bushfallers have a special love for Buea University girls, perhaps because these girls have a higher social status than other girls in Molyko.

He is not the 'real' *bushfaller*, his friends would conclude. They had intended to benefit from a *bushfaller* who was believed to be a sex addict. Unfortunately, this belief in migrants' sex addiction did not hold for Kevin.

This list of the consequences of sharing the same urban space is not exhaustive. The intention of this section has been to demonstrate that there is a tendency for migrant youths to be exploited or a wish to exploit them in one way or the other when they share the same urban space with non-migrant youths. Additionally, their concern for security is not unfounded. Their visibility provides an opportunity for some of their non-migrant contemporaries to seek 'justice' through opportunistic behaviour. They are bent on 'snatching' their own piece of success acquired abroad, but displayed at home since the *bushfallers* 'do not want to share' what they have 'amassed' abroad.

Conclusion

In his article entitled 'Urban life-worlds in Motion: In Africa and Beyond' (2010), Hans Peter Hahn emphasizes that migrants within and across the borders of the nation-state have an impact on the lifestyle and dynamics of African cities. He further says that there is a need to examine and account biographies of the different actors in the urban setting in order to understand life-worlds in African cities (Hahn 2010: 115,118). Cameroon urban life-worlds do not escape such observations. Non-migrants' comments directed at Cameroonian *bushfallers* in fact answer one of Hahn's call that we account for the perceptions, experiences and expectations of the urban dwellers. This case has used non-migrants' remarks to demonstrate that the urban life-world in Cameroon is partly characterised by unfulfilled expectations and disappointments.

The aim of this chapter has been to highlight derogatory remarks directed at Cameroonian migrant youths in the urban life-world of Buea when they visit and share such space with their non-migrant cohorts. The chapter has focused on the issue of the consciousness of inequality, especially in terms of social status and abilities or inabilities to consume. This consciousness of inequality is widely stressed when the migrant youths display the success and achievement they have acquired abroad. In the face of what could be considered as threat to 'Cameroonian culture', non-migrant youths stress the ideal form of behaviour, not directly, but by subtly detailing the negative or unwelcome attitudes and activities of migrants, who are seen as immoral and depraved, as indicated by their excitement, music, cars, mode of dressing, spending habits and insensitivity to modesty. Such consumerism and the presence of the 'greedy' migrants are considered a provocation in a place where (it is believed) morality and generosity prevail. Non-migrant youths who engage in similar activities as the migrants either go unnoticed or are overlooked. Basically, there is a conflict of consumerism here that is fuelled by illusions and imaginations of success and achievement. The visible presence in terms of the material evaluation of migrants provokes anti-consumerist feelings, not necessarily because the non-migrants are anti-consumerists, but because it is hard for them to meet their desires to consume. The urban life-world thus becomes a playground where success and disenchantment clash, fuelled by the realities of migration and the visible material success that comes from migrating. Non-migrants, however, have found strategies to dampen down migrant youths' status and success. In this way, they have developed self-soothing strategies by making degrading remarks and mocking the success and achievements of the migrants. Conversely, many youths who mock the migrants actually benefit from the *bushfallers*, and many also wish to go abroad. One cannot but conclude that the negative remarks directed at the migrants have an element of jealousy. Moreover, the perception of the migrants as successful but greedy youths has in part contributed to attempts to redistribute their success either forcibly or through 'soft' means. Migrants too are taking necessary physical and spiritual precautions to keep jealous friends and family at bay.

REFERENCES

Abbink, Jon. 2005. 'Being Young in Africa: the Politics of Despair and Renewal'. In: Jon Abbink and Ineke van Kessel (eds.). *Vanguard or Vandals: Youth Politics and Conflict in Africa.* London: Brill: 1-34.

Archambault, Julie S. 2009. 'Being Cool or being Good: Researching Mobile Phones in Mozambique', *Anthropology Matters*, 11(2): 1-9.

Ardener, Edwin, Shirley Ardener and W. A. Warmington. 1960. *Plantation and Village in the Cameroons: Some Economic and Social Studies.* Oxford: Oxford University.

Bourdieu, Pierre. 2002. *Distinction: A Social Critique of the Judgment of Taste.* London: Routledge.

Comaroff, Jean and John L. Comaroff. 1999. 'Occult Economies and the Violence of Abstraction: Notes from the South African Postcolony', *American Ethnologist,* 26(20): 279-303.

Cruise O'Brien, Donal B. 1996. 'A Lost Generation? Youth Identity and State Decay in West Africa'. In: Terence Ranger and Richard Werbner (eds.). *Postcolonial Identities in Africa.* London: Zed: 55-74.

---. 2003. *Symbolic Confrontations: Muslims Imagining the State in Africa.* London: Hurst.

Diouf, Mamadou. 2003. 'Engaging Postcolonial Cultures: African Youth and Public Space', *African Studies Review,* 6(1): 1-12.

Drotbohm, Heike. 2010. 'Gossip and Social Control Across the Seas: Targeting Gender, Resource Inequalities and Support in Cape Verdean Transnational Families', *African and Black Diaspora,* 3: 51-68.

Duval, David Timothy. 2004. 'Linking Return Visits and Return Migration among Commonwealth Eastern Caribbean Migrants in Toronto', *Global Networks,* 4(4): 51-67.

Eckert, Andreas. 1999. 'African Rural Entrepreneurs and Labor in the Cameroon Littoral', *The Journal of African History,* 40(1): 109-126.

Fokwang, Jude T. D. 2008. *Being young in Old Town: Youth Subjectivities and Associational Life in Bamenda.* PhD Thesis, Graduate Department of Anthropology, University of Toronto.

Ganga, Deianira and Sam Scott. 2006. 'Cultural "Insiders" and the Issue of Positionality in Qualitative Migration Research: Moving "Across" and Moving "Along" Researcher-Participant Divides', *Forum: Qualitative Social Research* 7, 3. http://www.qualitative-research.net/index.php/fqs/article/view/134/290 (accessed 11 March 2010).

Geschiere, Peter and Josef Gugler. 1998. 'Introduction: The Urban-Rural Connection: Changing Issues of Belonging and Identification', *Africa,* 68(3): 309-319.

Glick-Schiller, Nina. 2004. 'Transnationality'. In: David Nugent and Joan Vincent (eds.). *A Companion to the Anthropology of Politic.* London: Blackwell: 448-467.

Gluckman, Max. 1963. 'Gossip and Scandal', *Current Anthropology*, 4(3): 307-316.
Hahn, Hans Peter (2010), Urban Life-Worlds in Motion: In Africa and Beyond, *Africa Spectrum* 45(3): 115-129.
Jua, Ben N. 2003. 'Differential Responses to Disappearing Transitional Pathways: Redefining Possibility Among Cameroonian Youths', *African Studies Review*, 46(2): 13-36.
Nyamnjoh, Francis B. 2005a. 'Fishing in Troubled Waters: Disquettes and Thiofs in Dakar', *Africa* 75(3): 295-324.
---. 2005b. 'Images of Nyongo amongst Bamenda Grassfielders in Whiteman Kontri', *Citizenship Studies*, 9(3): 241-269.
---. 2004. 'Global and Local Trends in Media Ownership and Control: Implications for Cultural Creativity in Africa'. In: Wim Van Binsbergen and Rijk Van Dijk (eds.). *Situating Globality: An African Agency in the Appropriation of Global Culture*. Leiden: Brill: 57-89.
Ong, Aiwa. 1999. *Flexible Citizenship: The Cultural Logics of Transnationality*. Durham: Duke University.
Ouden, Jan H. B. 1987. 'In Search of Personal Mobility: Changing Interpersonal Relations in Two Bamileke Chiefdoms, Cameroon', *Africa*, 57(1): 3-27.
Paine, Robert. 1967. 'What is Gossip About? An Alternative Hypothesis', *Man (N.S.)*, 2(2): 278-285.
Reynolds, Susan, Erdmute Alber and Sjaak Van der Geest. 2008. 'Generational Connections and Conflicts in Africa: an Introduction'. In: Erdmute Alber, Sjaak van der Geest and Susan Reynolds (eds.). *Generations in Africa, Connections and Conflicts*. Berlin: Lit: 1-23.
Riccio, Bruno. 2005. 'Talking about Migration. Some Ethnographic Notes on the Ambivalent Representation of Migrants in Contemporary Senegal', *Vienna Journal of African Studies* 8(5): 99-118.
Roth, Claudia. 2008. '"Shameful!" The Inverted Intergenerational Contract in Bobo-Dioulasso, Burkina Faso'. In: Erdmute Alber, Sjaak van der Geest and Susan Reynolds (eds.). *Generations in Africa, Connections and Conflicts*. Berlin: Lit: 47-69.
Slater, Don and Janet Kwami. 2005. *Embeddedness and Escape: Internet and Mobile Phone use as Poverty Reduction Strategies in Ghana*. Information Society and Research Group (ISRG). Working Paper. London: UCL.

Tazanu, Primus. 2010. 'Border Transgression and the Reordering of Social Relations: The Case of Cameroonian Migrants in Germany', *Freiburger Universitätsblätter*, 188: 81-92.

Vertovec, Steven. 2009. *Transnationalism (Key Ideas)*. New York: Routledge.

Weiss, Brad. 2005. 'The Barber in Pain: Consciousness, Affliction and Alterity in Urban East Africa'. In: Filip de Boeck and Alcinda Honwana (eds.). *Makers and Breakers: Children and Youth in Postcolonial Africa*. Trenton: Africa World Press: 102-120.

Wiles, Janine. 2008. 'Sense of Home in a Transnational Social Space: New Zealanders in London', *Global Networks* 8(1): 116-137.

Yenshu, Emmanuel. 2008. 'On the Viability of Associational Life in Traditional Society and Home-Based Associations'. In: Emmanuel Yenshu (ed.). *Civil Society and the Search for Development Alternatives in Cameroon*. Dakar: Codesria: 95-124.

Movements into Emotions

Kinetic Tactics, Commotion and Conviviality among Traffic Vendors in Accra

GABRIEL KLAEGER

> 'What is kinetic is affective, or potentially affective'
> SHEETS-JOHNSTONE 1999: 259

On a recent visit to Ghana I came across an article in the local BUSINESS & FINANCIAL TIMES (BFT) with the title *Agony of a street hawker* (5 August 2009). The columnist describes his encounter with a young man, Kwesi, one of the many 'poverty stricken youth [who] adopt all sorts of survival strategies to cater for the needs of their families or to generally improve their own standard of living'. Kwesi had been selling dog chains in the streets of Accra for more than a year. His 'daily ordeal' was marked by the physical challenges of chasing moving vehicles, the risk of being knocked down by 'reckless and aggressive' drivers, and the constant fear of harassment by the metropolitan authorities. According to the reporter, the 'hardship, misery and calamity' that struck Kwesi and his hawker colleagues on Accra's streets 'bear testimony of the vulnerable in society' whose predicament demonstrates 'how poverty has become almost intractable in our society'.

To my surprise, the article was published in the BFT's special edition entitled *LifeStyle* where it featured alongside articles dedicated to fashion, health, fitness, dating, celebrities and other aspects of 'fun & entertainment'. Among buoyant lifestyle issues, the pitiful account on the 'plight of the poor' in the country's capital seemed out of place. Yet, presumably it is the 'agony', vulnerability and precarious livelihood of street hawkers that socially privileged writers and readers of this newspaper perceive as fundamental to hawkers' lifestyle, which sharply contrasts with the lifestyle cherished by educated, well-off and otherwise privileged Ghanaian urbanites. The hawkers' lifestyle is seen to be marked by an incessant struggle for mere survival, if not for a better life, in which hawkers use creative coping mechanisms or survival strategies.

My account of hawkers working along the Ofankor road in northern Accra is concerned less with lifestyle than with life-world. The distinction is important to my attempt to provide an ethnographic glimpse into the lived everyday of Ofankor's hawkers. This focus allows me to move beyond mere description of the commonly noted struggles and strategies for economic survival and to shift perspective. To gain an understanding of hawking and street vending, it is certainly necessary to take into account the socio-economic and spatial conditions of these so-called 'informal' economic activities (Hart 1973) that are embedded in a specific urban, political and regulatory landscape and marked by various constraints such as institutional harassment.[1] Yet these economic considerations grasp only parts of the texture of the phenomenon at hand. They can easily neglect how hawkers' lived everyday both produces and is markedly shaped by practices and experiences as ways of inhabiting the world (Merleau-Ponty 1962; Ingold 2000; de Certeau 1984). Appraising this life-world requires an exploration of hawkers' everyday practices and experiences as bodily-sensory and emotive forms of engagement with their immediate, often risky environment, and not just as elements of calculated livelihood strategies.

Following Brad Weiss, hawkers' implication in and confronting their daily work on streets and in city traffic can be viewed as 'processes of *engagement* as they are culturally constituted' (Weiss 1996: 3; original emphasis). This view of engagement 'neatly captures the sense of reciprocal interchange between persons and the world that is entailed in any activity' (ibid.). It sheds light on hawkers' implication in their work environment: how they engage and appropriate the road, vehicular traffic and multiple

---

1 See Brown (2006b); Brown *et al.* (2010) or Hansen and Vaa (2004) for accounts on 'street economy' and livelihood strategies as part of informal sector activities.

users through intricate movements, differential speeds and tangible hazards. At the same time, it allows me to demonstrate how they become continuously *appropriated* by the features of this world and, most particularly, emotionally engaged by it. I will show that what emerges from these engagements are distinctive, at times ambivalent forms of corporeality, emotionality and sociality, framed by a life-world that is incessantly moving.[2]

STREET VENDORS: STRIKINGLY PRESENT, GROSSLY NEGLECTED

In his foreword to the edited volume entitled *Street Entrepreneurs* (Cross and Morales 2007), Ray Bromley notes that despite being 'one of the world's oldest and most widespread occupation' (xv), street vending has never received much scholarly attention. Its significance has been underrated by scholars who view it as unimportant, destined to disappear, or parasitic: an occupation that was 'unworthy of serious study because it had no future' (ibid.: xvi). Much more popular as a field of study, especially in the 1960s and 1970s, has been the analysis of marketplace trade: an 'economic anthropological laboratory of social interaction and commercial behaviour' that was considered more authentic, traditional and worthy of study (ibid.). Even when the concept of formal and informal sector emerged (Hart 1973), the numerous case studies on small-scale occupations mainly served the purpose of illustrating features of the overall economic system. Again, the focus was on the more 'productive' small-scale occupations rather than on street vendors (one exception being Bromley 1978). Only in recent years has the 'street economy' phenomenon been explored more systematically, mostly by scholars in geography, economics, development or urban planning.[3]

The same development can be observed in the study of street vending, hawking and peddling in African urban settings. For Ghana, for instance,

---

2   I greatly appreciate the comments and suggestions that Kurt Beck, Richard Fardon, Hans Peter Hahn, Kristin Kastner and Michael Stasik provided on several versions of this paper.
3   See, for instance, the edited volumes by Brown (2006b) and Cross and Morales (2007) and the most recent review by Brown *et al.* (2010).

social scientists, including anthropologists, have produced quite a number of studies on markets, traders, market women and on the so-called informal sector more generally.[4] Strikingly, not a single anthropological account exists of the prominent and much debated phenomenon of street vending in the country's urban centres like Accra and Kumasi.[5] My previous research in Ghana is proof of the same kind of neglect. During my ethnographic fieldwork on the Accra-Kumasi Road (AKR), I took a strong interest in the quotidian activities of small-scale entrepreneurs found on and alongside that road, yet, street vendors were not central to my research agenda – despite their pervasive presence in my field, in particular when joining commercial minibus drivers and their passengers on regular journeys to and from Accra.[6]

In Ghana's capital, street vendors work in public and often contested spaces in ways that are probably found alike in all major African cities. The informal trading activities of vendors who, tentatively defined, operate either from a stationary position or while walking around as hawkers[7], usually take them to bus terminals (or lorry stations), permanent markets, car parks and public buildings. By occupying pavements, entrances and streets, they compete with other city dwellers, disturb the flow of city traffic and pedestrians, add to congestion, and are therefore commonly perceived as (and regularly blamed for) creating major nuisance and 'filth' in the city's public sphere. As a result, street vendors in the Accra Metropolitan Area (AMA) have in recent years been targeted repeatedly by local au-

---

4 Some of the contributions are Attah *et al.* (1996); Clark (1994); Clark and Manuh (1991); Gough *et al.* (2003); Hart (1970, 1973); Robertson (1983, 1984).

5 The recent non-anthropological works on Ghana are Asiedu and Agyei-Mensah (2008); King (2006); Lyon (2003, 2007); Overå (2007); Quayson (2010); Yankson (2000) and Yankson (2007).

6 I carried out 13 months of ethnographic fieldwork on and alongside the Accra-Kumasi road in 2006-07. In this article, I draw from my occasional encounters with Ofankor's traffic vendors in early 2007 and in August 2009. I also raise desiderata for further research on hawkers and vendors in African urban centres.

7 In Ghana, non-stationary and roaming vendors are usually referred to as 'hawkers'. See Asiedu and Agyei-Mensah (2008: 193) and Brown (2006a: 8) for attempts to classify and label different modes of street vending; Quayson (2010: 76) uses the terms 'itinerant' and 'stationary vendors'.

thorities in their plans to 'decongest' the city. However, attempts to ban the activities of street traders and hawkers, to evict them from streets and public places and to relocate them to newly created markets have proven ineffective (Asiedu 2008: 199). In March 2007, I observed how the clampdown on vendors was particularly strong in the run-up to the fiftieth anniversary of Ghana's independence. As part of the 'cleanup exercise' instigated to improve the image (and reputation) of the city hosting the continent's first Golden Jubilee celebration, the infamous AMA task force, popularly known as *aaba eei* ('raiders'; Asiedu 2008: 199), managed to chase all vendors from the pavements around the notoriously busy Kwame Nkrumah Circle and in the central business district (Makola and Kantamanto markets). Yet this enforced cleanliness of Accra's streets was only temporary; thanks to inconsistent policies and enforcement, the vendors had soon regained the streets.

A particular variation of street vending, explored in the remainder of this article, consists in the activities of vendors who are prominent at the capital's major highway junctions and on particular road sections. Hoping to find customers passing in city traffic, these roadside hawkers, or 'traffic vendors' (DAILY GRAPHIC 2008), operate where (and at specific times of the day when) vehicles are slowed down or made to stop by traffic lights or heavy traffic.[8] They also gather where bottlenecks are formed on arterial roads, for instance where the Accra-Winneba Road traverses Kasoa, or where the first section of the Accra-Kumasi Road (also known as the Nsawam Road) winds through Ofankor, the last suburb of Accra's northwestern periphery.

TRAFFIC, TRAVELLERS AND TRADING IN OFANKOR

Traffic at Ofankor is notoriously heavy, particularly at rush hour. One reason is the suburb's position as the gateway to Accra, where regional, long-distance and even international motor traffic descends from the dual-carriageway or, in the opposite direction, where motorists are desperate to

---

8   For example, at the Kanda High Road/Achimota Road intersection, or along Liberation Road (Akuafo Circle) and Osu's Oxford Street (see Asiedu and Agyei-Mensah 2008; Quayson 2010).

escape the crowded city. The junction at Ofankor, with its bus stops, adds local vehicles to the heavy through traffic. There used to be a police checkpoint at Ofankor, locally known as 'Barrier', that further slowed traffic flow. It was removed in early 2007 at the commencement of road construction works that now prove equally, if not more, disruptive. The Ofankor road section continues to be referred to as 'Barrier', a metaphor for the constant presence of slow-moving, often congested traffic that attracts an impressive number of roadside hawkers.[9]

The traffic hawkers and vendors at 'Barrier' consist predominantly of young men and women, some of them minors, but most in their early and mid-twenties, and all very energetic and agile in their eager attempts to make a living through selling in urban traffic. They mingle and at times cooperate with senior female vendors, who are more settled both in terms of their age and work experience, and because they work seated at tables where their stock is displayed, often under a sunshade, yet still only a few steps from passing vehicles and customers (see Figure 1).

Conversing with Adwoa, the local ɔhemmaa ('market queen'; see Clark 2010; Lyon 2007), and with Rose, her colleague at the neighbouring stand, I learned why many in Ofankor had chosen to work, some for many years, on this particular road section. What makes the place 'good', they say, is its status as 'no-man's land'. Unlike streets and pavements in the city centre, the Ofankor road is not controlled by the metropolitan authorities and their task force; the common NO HAWKING signboards are completely absent. They do not need to seek any permit to set up a 'table-top' business and are never harassed; neither do they have to pay any tax or fees to a landowner: 'Anyone can come, no one can be sacked.' Another advantage is the heavy traffic that brings new potential customers, and its slowness (even standstill), which makes it easier to attend to travellers: advertising goods and exchanging them against cash through open vehicle windows.[10]

---

9   The number of vendors (approx. 50-80 in 2007) started decreasing in early 2009 when heavy construction works for a multi-lane flyover resumed at Ofankor and made vending increasingly difficult.

10 The DAILY GRAPHIC (2008) noted that it is '[traffic vendors'] prayer that the traffic jam will never ease because that is when they espect [sic] good sales'.

*Figure 1: The ɔhemmaa ('market queen'),
one of the senior bread sellers in Ofankor*

Source: photo by the author, 2009

Ofankor's vendors do not just engage with the regular traffic flows and slows by taking tactical advantage, but also move attune with the *differential movements* and speeds of stop-go traffic in ways that I will explore below.[11] Furthermore, vendors engage with the *sales opportunities* generated by the stop-go traffic, i.e. the arrival, waiting and (re)departure of vehicles and travellers that create needs and desires for travel-related consumption goods. Vendors are adequately equipped for this demand and offer an adapted range of items similar to the one found among traders at lorry stations and other transport hubs.[12] For instance, vendors sell refreshments for

---

11 See Beckmann (2004) on the occurrence of fastness/slowness, speed/inertia and mobility/immobility in the context of road traffic; see Rosa (2009) on the simultaneousness of differential speeds, as well as Tomlinson (2007) and Merriman (2007) on the perception and relativity of speed.

12 Time in transit, the stage of the journey and destination orientation, all producing a specific market, also explain why an estimated 80 per cent of all goods are sold in outbound traffic, i.e. to travellers who will be on the road for some time and are travelling to places where urban consumer goods are highly valued,

passengers who have been (or may be still) stuck in city traffic, or who arrive in the capital after long trips. They vocally tout snacks, through open car windows, to those embarking on long journeys on the AKR. Apart from items for immediate consumption in transit, they have goods that travellers take along as supplies for their homes, or as presents, to be distributed to people who regularly ask for such presents when travellers arrive. Some goods are advertised for this, such as when biscuit sellers shout '*Nkola wo fie!*' (literally: 'Children are at home'), meant to remind passengers to buy sweets for the children who are waiting at home.[13]

A popular commodity and travel present is bread. It is usually available in one form or the other at most inland destinations, but this bread – bread from the city – is special. It ranges from sugar bread, tea bread, butter bread and chocolate bread to bread sticks, which hawkers at 'Barrier' are best known for. The bread brand most cherished by travellers is labelled *CHRIST IN YOU*; it is produced by a nearby bakery of the same name and advertised by simply shouting '*CHRIST! CHRIST!*'. Hawkers get their daily stock of bread directly from that bakery or from its delivery van that comes to Ofankor twice a day. The still warm loaves are stored in wooden cases and covered with sheets (see Figure 2); later, they are packed in transparent plastic bags and either displayed on the tables of the senior female vendors or, as I shall describe in more detail, carried around for sale by the younger hawkers.

---

whereas travellers in inbound traffic proof to be less important customers in need of basic snacks only.

13 Apart from refreshments and travel snacks (water sachets, ice cream, pies, plantain chips, biscuits, chewing gum, etc.), hawkers also offer newspapers, phone credit, mirrors, dusters and many other items to arriving travellers. Items such as dog chains, seat cushions or footballs can only be sold in very slow-moving traffic, or to travellers who pull over: selling these items requires more time since customers need to have a proper look and then start bargaining as their prices, unlike the ones for food, are not fixed.

Figure 2: Packing and storing fresh bread loaves

Source: photo by the author, 2009

ENGAGING WITH TRAFFIC: RELOCATING, RUSHING AND CHASING CARS

Before I became acquainted with young bread sellers, I had assumed that they would not have time to chat with me since, from my initial impression as a customer in a moving minibus, their work appeared both stressful and absorbing. Yet standing by the roadside with a few of them, I realized that they were not only happy for any distractions, but regularly took time to relax, hang out and even sit down. Occasionally, though, my informants would suddenly disappear – rushing off without warning to attend to a decelerating vehicle carrying potential customers.

Speed matters, hawkers in Ofankor claim. According to Steven, a 25-year-old bread seller with whom I became friends during fieldwork, the speed of traffic determines – at least to some extent – how much he is able to sell, or how quickly he can sell his daily stock of bread. Business is better when there is both high traffic volume and, often as a result of this, slower cruising speed. The absence of traffic – meaning only few and comparatively fast vehicles – is disadvantageous and is referred to as a 'slow market', or 'slow business'. Interestingly, Steven and his mates argue that halting traffic or, even worse, a complete standstill, often turns out to be just as unprofitable and 'slow'. In their experience, travellers who get stuck in traffic jams – producing heat, dust, sweat and increasing annoyance inside the immobile vehicles – tend to be reluctant to buy the products offered to them because 'they are unhappy'. Hawkers agree the best circumstances for their selling, which makes traffic 'good', occur when vehicles are 'not too fast and not too slow' – a statement that may sound vague, but in fact reveals the close attention they pay to differential speeds and their implications.

Younger, moving vendors show, both verbally and through their corporeal-kinetic performances, that the success of their sales equally depends on their embodied efforts to engage with traffic by adjusting themselves to varying vehicle speeds. These efforts increase in response to a 'slow market', prompted by too fast or too slow vehicles. One tactic is to move *with* traffic: Hawkers settle at and, if necessary, relocate themselves to road sections and where congestions and tailbacks occur more regularly than elsewhere, such as spots where road works are underway or potholes are growing bigger. Moving with traffic also obliges their *continuous repositioning*, while selling, in rhythm with the dynamics of traffic volume and the continuous shifting of tailbacks. This becomes particularly necessary after vendors have been running alongside vehicles (see below) and end up at the point where vehicles accelerate again, which then requires them to move against the flow of traffic.

Another tactic is to swiftly move *towards* traffic or, in the hawkers' own terms, to try 'rushing'. This involves running towards cars, often pushing other vendors aside, and dealing with customers quickly enough to exchange money and goods through the open windows of moving vehicles before the drivers (who are often in a rush themselves) speed off. There is a 'need for speed', to use Neil Carrier's (2005) terms, to compete with other hawkers and sell successfully, despite the often restricted time frame for business transactions. Rushing is also seen as an enticement to persuade travellers to buy bread, which is thought particularly necessary when customers are stuck in traffic. Turning up quickly at standing vehicles, holding up bread loaves in front of travellers' eyes and at times even pushing them inside is a persuasive sales pitch.[14]

The most challenging and hazardous tactic to engage with more speedy vehicles is to move *alongside* traffic. 'Chasing cars', as traffic vendors say, fulfils the same entrepreneurial purpose as 'rushing', namely competition and advertisement (indeed, rushing often leads into chasing). 'You have to run, you have to chase the car', Steven explained, 'because if you don't chase the car, nobody will come and buy the bread. Even if the person [potential customer] hasn't called you, you just go fast – you run and show the bread to the person.' At the same time, chasing stands for the indispensable 'dromocentric'[15] practice and the distinct bodily attempt of keeping up with moving vehicles' speed through sprinting off, running zigzag, overtaking other hawkers or clutching the body of the car one has chosen to chase (Figure 3 and 5).

The brisk business of traffic vending thus unfolds as a dynamic interplay between the varying movements of vehicles and the tactical and corporeal movements of vendors with, towards and alongside traffic. Through their kinetic engagement, i.e. 'body movement as dynamically embodied action' (Farnell 1999: 341), vendors become part and parcel of what emerges as a workplace in motion. It requires corporeal skilfulness, swiftness and endurance at work, coupled with sensory agility, in particular visual and aural alertness. My interlocutors by the roadside demonstrate that they are alert to traffic developments and 'read the road', as commercial drivers often put it, when they describe how they grasped the movements, manoeuvres and constantly shifting vehicular flows. They equally need to be alert to the signs that emanate from passing travellers, Steven explains. What is crucial, for instance, is to watch out carefully for the 'looks' (i.e.

---

14 This sales pitch is equally employed by hawkers at bus stops or lorry station whose swift attending to arriving and potentially soon departing vehicles is not simply about competition and limited time, but about advertising and encouraging travellers to buy their products.

15 'Dromocentric' is my attempt to denote both people's concern with and their practices involving speed in the sense of rapidity, a term which is derived from the Greek *dromos* (running, race, race course). *Dromos* is used in a similar vein by Paul Virilio (1986) who coined the terms 'dromology' (the science of speed) and 'dromocracy' (the condition of modernity with its every-increasing speed).

eye movements) of travellers, as looks may reveal whether people are searching for goods and intend to buy. Looks are often paired with more or less unmistakable gestures and signs (e.g. pulling money out of the pocket, waving with a note) and vocal signals (e.g. making sibilant sounds, shouting '*brodo wura*', meaning 'bread seller'). For hawkers endowed with 'skilled vision' (Grasseni 2007) and sensory attentiveness (Ingold 2000), these signs and signals tell them incessantly whether it is a moment to move, rush, run or just relax.

Figure 3: Chasing cars and customers

Source: photo by the author, 2007

ACCIDENTS, RISKY MANOEUVRES AND COLLECTIVE EMOTIONS

The Ofankor vendors' workplace in motion[16] manifests itself with a number of challenges and constraints that are the subject of discussion both by themselves and by broader publics. Vendors generally complain about the impact of weather on their activities. Rain may not only spoil their bread, but some of the young female bread sellers say they feel cold and easily fall sick during the rainy season. In the dry season, there is the opposite problem of standing and running under a scorching sun for the whole day. Steven claims that it made his eyes turn unhealthily yellow: 'They look like the eyes of a smoker, but it's all because of the wind, the dust, the car smoke.' When construction works resumed along the Ofankor road, rainfall turned the scarified road surface into slippery mud, while drought produced irritating dust that left rusty-red laterite stains on vendors' clothes.

Accidents are another concern, though not all say they fear them. Ofankor is a notorious black spot on the accident-ridden AKR, and the bread sellers I talked to vividly recalled several fatal car crashes that had occurred there prior to my fieldwork. A trace of one remained – a disturbingly mangled mass of metal that could hardly be recognised as the remains of a passenger car. It had been wrecked by a tipper truck whose brakes had failed while descending from the new flyover towards the Ofankor junction, instantly killing all the car passengers. According to residents, some pedestrians and a bus station porter had also been victims of accidents in recent times. While some blamed technical failure, overloading and so-called 'overspeeding' on the AKR for these incidents, others mentioned spiritual beings and other invisible forces as alternative (or additional) source (see Klaeger 2009). They were made manifest in a huge cleansing ritual that I witnessed on the Ofankor road on a busy Saturday afternoon in November 2006 (see Figure 4). It was performed by officials from the local chief's palace and some ritual experts (*akomfo*). According to the chief whom I visited afterwards, the sacrificial killing of animals and pouring of libation

---

16 It could also be described as a 'moving market', incorporating both the movements of vendors and customers. See Gewald's historical account of travellers as customers en route, as 'the market [which] walked its way to the villages along the line of travel' (Gewald 2009: 45).

in the middle of the road was meant to appease a local deity called *Olila* and to exorcise the spirits (or 'souls') of people who had died in recent accidents.[17] Through this, the ritual was believed to prevent further accidents and protect those living and working on and alongside the busy through road. A different view was taken by a charismatic church at Ofankor, the *Mount Zion Action and Power Ministry*. One of its pastors told me that his church had heard about the fatal accidents that they believed had been caused by demons and other 'powers', and not by gods or spirits, as the 'traditionalists' believed. In accordance with their duty, as Christians, to assist those who were 'suffering' from the actions of such 'powers', some church members and pastors decided to hold a prayer session at the roadside with the vendors.

Figure 4: Cleansing ritual on the Ofankor road

Source: photo by the author, 2006

The bread sellers I had met after these events supported both the road ritual and the protective prayers. 'We all want the accidents to stop', some told me, meaning that they were concerned about physical hazards emanating

---

17 Further motives that contributed to the staging of this ritual event cannot be explored here due to the limited scope of this article.

not only from accidents as such, but from the particular manoeuvres of drivers. Standing with bread sellers by the roadside, we regularly needed to take evasive action when a vehicle suddenly swerved or drove onto the pavement. The driver, in most cases a commercial minibus (*trotro*) driver, had either decided to stop in order for passengers to board or alight, or to overtake using the edge of the road occupied by the vendors. '*Kwasia!* You fool!' they would shout at drivers whom they labelled as 'careless', or something less polite in their shock and anger. Commercial drivers are perceived by my interlocutors to undertake risky (and illegal) overtaking because they have become impatient with slow-moving traffic at Ofankor and worried about losing time and money on the road. Steven explained that these drivers follow the *kɔ ntɛm, bra ntɛm* principle, meaning that they have to (literally) 'go fast, come fast' in order to increase their daily earnings.[18]

Drivers' need for speed, and their impatient rushing, not only leads to overtaking (as an attempt 'to beat time', as bus drivers say), but also to unduly rapid acceleration. 'They are in a hurry', Steven explained. 'They will not wait until you have finished selling to the passengers. But as soon as they get the chance, they accelerate.' Then the vendors have to start chasing and end up in the way of vehicles approaching quickly from behind, which bears the risk of being hit or colliding with other vendors. Apart from being physically menaced by passing road users, vendors claim they are treated in derogatory, even abusive ways. Drivers shout at them when irritated by their interfering with the traffic flow, or when they clutch the window frames of the vehicles. 'But what else should you do?' one bread seller retorted, 'you *have* to hold the car to sell!' Passengers regularly insult them when they do not perform efficiently and fail to exchange money, bread and plastic bags in time before the driver speeds off.[19] Some travellers call vendors to their windows, make them run along with them, then do not buy from them, 'but all this so that they can laugh at you'. What Steven hates

---

18 The mentioned 'overspeeding' of drivers, regularly seen as part of drivers' attempts to save time and make money on the AKR, is hardly a problem in Ofankor; it affects much more those roadside vendors who sell fruits and vegetables on the open road where excessive speeding is possible.
19 Vendors are thus caught in some kind of love-hate relationship with commercial drivers as they bring both potential customers and dangers.

most are drivers of heavy trucks who he suspects blow their horn loudly simply to scare vendors and chase them off the road.

As a visitor to the roadside, or when passing through as a *trotro* passenger, I was witness to many instances when drivers' careless and impatient manoeuvres caused commotion. The bread sellers' angry gestures, shouts of indignation and insults are expressions of their moral condemnation and blaming of drivers' acts, but also of their emotions triggered by tangibly (and often very suddenly) sensing dangers. Risky movements evoke 'frustration-aggression' (Katz 1999: 22) that manifests itself in commotion by the roadside and in vendors' outcries. What is more, these moments lead to concerted emotions, to ritualised expression of 'collective emotions' (Durkheim 1995) producing a particular sense of community: the (mostly temporary) feeling of belonging to a true *Schicksalsgemeinschaft*, i.e. a community of fate whose members are collectively exposed to the hazardous manoeuvres of drivers.[20] Its members' being 'at risk' is equivalent to 'being sinned against, being vulnerable to the events caused by others' (Douglas 1992: 28). This sense of shared vulnerability is not just entangled with emotions, blame and moral condemnation of rushing drivers who are reprimanded for their 'immoral impatience'. It is also reinforced during instances such as the road ritual or public prayers described above, both of which addressed and underlined the sellers' communal need for protection in an environment imbued with dangers, both visible and invisible.

CRITICAL CORPOREALITY, COMMOTION AND CONVIVIALITY

Meanwhile, the fleeting forms of sociality that I encountered among Ofankor's bread sellers do not only emerge alongside with their – often emotive – engagement with exogenous constraints such as vehicular movements. Emotionality and sociality also emerge through their very own corporeal practices and kinetic performances. Part of them is the hour-long standing and tiring running: 'It is not easy. You have to suffer before you gain.' Vendors frequently lament that it affects their feet, legs and the waist, espe-

---

20 See Klaeger (2009: 220-21) on how this community feeling regularly emerges among public transport passengers.

cially at the beginning, and makes them 'hard' when they stay in the vending business for a while; some say they take painkillers for their aching bodies. Steven and his mates usually rest after having sold about fifteen to twenty loaves; then they hang out for a while with others a bit further away from traffic, occasionally sitting down at a colleague's bread table. While resting and socialising, one of the female and middle-aged bread sellers told me, laughingly, that running is particularly bad for women: 'It makes us open up "below", if you know what I mean…, so that our husbands become unhappy in bed! Some even accuse us and say that we have boyfriends.'

Besides bodily aches, so much rushing and chasing increases the likelihood of falls and collisions. Some vendors seem eager to jostle others, to push and pull while running, which is why hawkers regularly fall to insulting each other. Especially among younger and more dynamic sellers, tempers can be heated by competition. I have seen vendors get into proper fights when one of them had lost a sale to a swifter and more aggressive colleague. In this and many other instances, vendors' movements are suffused with aroused emotions, anger and frustration.

The sellers nonetheless take pleasure in their work. 'We run after the cars with joy!' one bread seller told me, explaining that their joy is triggered by the monetary rewards that result from their bodily effort. Joy and joviality may emerge as reactions to the movements themselves. For instance, vendors regularly joke about how strenuous their work is, or laugh (at times nervously) about the awkward task of chasing cars while simultaneously gesticulating with bread, shouting and bargaining. Laughter is often an effect of the ambiguity of their lived experience, of being subject to, and participating in the production of, a risky and dangerous environment (cf. Roitman and Mbembe 1995: 351). Sometimes, vendors do embark on risky manoeuvres merely for the fun and thrill of it. They find sensual pleasure from engaging in 'edgework' (Lyng 2005, 2008), i.e. voluntary risk-taking that is perceived as a source of positive emotions and embodied pleasures. Aesthetic arousal may also be experienced by the *observer* of movements. One vendor described her keen running as a 'show' – not meant in the sense of a staged performance for mere entertainment, but as bodily efforts revealing her uninhibited enthusiasm that naturally attracts recognition and admiration by others. These bodily efforts are regularly applauded, laughed at and mimicked by vendor colleagues and lead to what could be called 'convivial commotion'. Steven also recounted how his friends often tease him and suggest that he must have gone for *juju* when they see that he has been fast and successful. At the same time, vendors also mock their comical movements, or their mishaps of losing bread, money or a slipper while running. 'If you don't take care and you fall down, they will laugh at you and say "you don't know how to run!"' someone explained. Some even display a sense of *Schadenfreude* and laugh spitefully when seeing how others are unsuccessful, fail or fall while chasing cars.

Figure 5: Keen movements alongside speedy vehicles

Source: photo by the author, 2007

Hawkers' often strenuous movements appear to trigger an affective space for humour, self-irony, parody, mockery and spitefulness. Their expressions of joviality provide a glimpse into the sensory and emotional experience of running (Ingold and Vergunst 2008; Lee and Ingold 2006), confirming Sheet-Johnstone's assertion that affectivity is tied to the tactile-kinaesthetic body, and that motion and emotion are dynamically congruent (1999: 269). It is for this reason that Ofankor's vendors and hawkers apprehend the road and the socio-economic environment in which they operate as a genuinely 'moving' life-world: moving not just with regard to the flows and speeds of vehicles and customers and to the vendors' *corporeal and kinetic* ways of engaging with (and becoming engaged by) these movements, but also with regard to their *emotive* engagement with the movements of drivers, their colleagues and their own. Yet hawkers' expressions of joviality, together with anger, aggression and frustration noted earlier, regularly unfold in commotion, especially in the face of tangible risks, as well as in conviviality, both imbued with a sense of shared vulnerability, solidarity and collegiality. Commotion and conviviality thus have consolidating potential. Not only do they confirm the plight of vendors as a *Schicksalsgemeinschaft*, or concerned community. They also cement their apprehension of roadside vending as a shared and collective engagement with a life-world in which vehicular movements, kinetic tactics, corporeality and emotionality become entangled.

CONCLUSION AND PERSPECTIVES

"[What do] space and place, both given natural environment and socially and technically constructed environment, do to our mode of moving [?] How does a place influence the form of acceleration, and how do places and artefacts interact in the complex interplay of motion [...]? How do places affect our modes of moving, and how do we perceive place and space by moving?" (Bergmann 2008: 24)[21]

Shedding light on Ofankor's traffic vendors' life-world, in this article, was an opportunity to reveal how people working by the roadside engage with the stop-and-go of travellers and traffic. I have shown, at first, that they engage with the desires and demands for travel-related goods, which is created by travellers' arriving, halting and (re)departing, by stocking what is desired. Then I explored how vendors also engage with the differential movements, speeds and vehicular volume of stop-and-go traffic by attuning themselves to them with their own kinetic tactics such as relocating, rushing and chasing. This exploration thus gave insight into some of the processes of reciprocal interchange between traffic vendors and the features of their moving workplace, such as their tangibly corporeal and emotional

---

21 See Casey (1996), Feld and Basso (1996) and Ingold's work (e.g. 2000) on 'senses of place' and the perception of the environment through movements.

ways of both engaging *with* and becoming engaged and appropriated *by* these features.

Many forms of engagements and appropriations, however, remain untouched in this article meant as a first step towards a more extensive anthropological exploration of traffic vendors' urban life-world. The present account is an invitation to address, for instance, how the roadside community of vendors engages and interacts with the community of travellers in creative ways. One aspect is the vendors' attempts not only to adapt their range of items to an allegedly given demand, but to actively create (if not manipulate) demands and desires for consumption among passing travellers. This occurs through vendors' occasional introduction of new, often not travel-related consumer goods, and goes hand in hand with vendors' creative attempts to push travellers' propensity to buy, including the advertisement of goods through skilful modes of communication. *Creativity* and *manipulation* also play a part in vendors' handling of differential vehicle flows and speeds that they do not merely adapt to kinetically, but that they actively influence. At least, drivers, passengers and other road observers regularly ask themselves whether vendors and hawkers are (in parts) to blame for traffic jams, and at times accuse them of manipulating the traffic. This hints at the need for giving more serious consideration to how travellers perceive traffic vendors while on the move. Most apparent is irritation and disdain with regard to vendors' activities, but admiration and praise is sometimes expressed – and then only very briefly – for their brisk and successful manoeuvres.

The *ephemeral and fleeting manner* of encounters and interactions provides further ground for a timely analysis of the socialities that seem to continuously (re)emerge not only between travellers and traffic vendors, but also between roadside and travel communities more generally on and along major roads, in Ghana and beyond. For instance, swiftness and brevity mark the ways in which the quality of goods is checked, how prices and orders are communicated, and notions of trust or deceit are assessed and negotiated between both parties – usually with only a very few and brisk manoeuvres, gestures, words or looks. This form of business interaction within limited time frame may tentatively be labelled as 'instant trade', where all principles and practices of market exchange are creatively converged, yet also condensed, in one brief instant.[22] The phenomenon that something usually complex, regulated and thus potentially demanding now occurs in a rather quick and condensed way (e.g. instant trade, fleeting sociability, sudden anger, quarrels en passant, ephemeral attribution of blame, etc.) can be seen as intrinsically linked to road users' creative and adaptive engagement with the potentials, yet also constraints, of transport technology, road infrastructure, mobility and movements. Investigating the idiosyncratic *temporalities* of encounters, interactions, practices and other forms of sociality does not only contribute to the anthropological study of roads, a rather neglected field in African studies.[23] It also connects with theoretical, and at times rather sweeping, approaches to speed (Tomlinson 2007), rhythms (Lefebvre 2004) and related phenomena such as acceleration (Rosa and Scheuerman 2009), instantaneous time (Urry 2009; or immediacy, Tomlinson 2007) or suddenness (Sheets-Johnstone 1999) that have come under only limited ethnographic scrutiny so far.

In this context, the ways in which time and speed-related processes alongside the road give rise to *social distinctions and hierarchical orders* form another desideratum for research. One such distinction arises where some traffic vendors are required to rush and chase more than others. Newcomers on the roadside and very young bread sellers in Ofankor, for instance, are likely not to engage with moving traffic at all; they fulfil simple and stationary tasks and help out at the bread stands of the senior women. In contrast, the more experienced youths are the most active with rushing and chasing, usually more than those in their late twenties and early thirties (mostly female) who run only occasionally, often because they maintain a small table with stocks by the roadside. Again, senior bread sellers such as Adwoa, the *ɔhemmaa*, and her age mates hardly ever move: they are busy

---

22 'Instant trade' structurally resembles 'instant sacrifice', a notion that is apparently used in Nigeria to describe the act of (rather accidently) running over an animal on the road, an act which may be seen as fulfilling the same sacrificial purpose as the killing of the animal does in a more elaborate ritual. I am grateful to Richard Kuba for hinting at this parallel during the DGV conference (Frankfurt, 2009).

23 For an overview of relevant contributions see Gewald *et al.* (2009) and Klaeger (2009); a comprehensive overview of the anthropology of roads more generally is provided by Dalakoglou (2010).

managing their larger stock of bread, collecting money and supervising their helpers and employees. At the most, they would get up and walk towards vehicles purposely stopping in front of their stalls to buy from them. Varying degrees of dromocentric engagement with customer-vehicles thus appear to both reflect and reproduce certain distinctions and hierarchies among vendors – all obviously linked to age, gender, experience, status as well as to fitness and risk-taking. The socio-kinetic order among traffic vendors, perpetuated by the specific context that the informal work and social-economic environment provide, is indicative of their latitude for *social mobility*, an issue that I have not dealt with in this article. Clearly intertwined with corporeal-kinetic practices and habitus, social mobility by the roadside is proof of the fact, once again, that the life-world of traffic vendors cannot be but intrinsically in motion.

REFERENCES

Asiedu, Alex B. and Samuel Agyei-Mensah. 2008. 'Traders on the run: Activities of street vendors in the Accra Metropolitan Area, Ghana', *Norsk Geografisk Tidsskrift - Norwegian Journal of Geography*, 62(3): 191-202.

Attah, Memunatu, Nana Apt and Margaret Grieco. 1996. 'Expected to earn, constrained to trade: Trading a customary role for Ghanaian women'. In: Margaret Grieco, Nana Apt and Jeff Turner (eds.). *At Christmas and on Rainy Days: Transport, Travel and the Female Traders of Accra.* Aldershot: Avebury: 3-18.

Beckmann, Jörg. 2004. 'Mobility and Safety', *Theory Culture & Society*, 21(4/5): 81-100.

Bergmann, Sigurd. 2008. 'The beauty of speed or the discovery of slowness – Why do we need to rethink mobility?' In: Sigurd Bergmann and Tore Sager (eds.). *The Ethics of Mobilities: Rethinking Place, Exclusion, Freedom and Environment*, Aldershot: Ashgate: 13-24.

Business & Financial Times (BFT) 2009. 'Agony of a street hawker'. 5 August 2009.

Bromley, Ray. 1978. 'Organization, Regulation and Exploitation in the So-Called "Urban Informal Sector": The Street Traders of Cali, Colombia', *World Development*, 6: 1161-1172.

Brown, Alison. 2006a. 'Challenging street livelihoods'. In: Alison Brown (ed.). *Contested Space: Street Trading, Public Space and Livelihoods in Developing Cities.* Rugby: Practical Action Publishing: 3-16.
---. (ed.). 2006b. *Contested Space: Street Trading, Public Space and Livelihoods in Developing Cities.* Rugby: Practical Action Publishing.
Brown, Alison, Michal Lyons and Ibrahima Dankoco. 2010. 'Street Traders and the Emerging Spaces for Urban Voice and Citizenship in African Cities', *Urban Studies*, 47(3): 666-683.
Carrier, Neil. 2005. 'The Need for Speed: Contrasting Timeframes in the Social Life of Kenyan Miraa', *Africa*, 75(4): 539-558.
Casey, Edward S. 1996. 'How to get from Space to Place in a Fairly Short Stretch of Time. Phenomenological Prologomena'. In: Steven Feld and Keith H. Basso (eds.). *Senses of Place*. Santa Fe: School of American Research: 13-52.
Clark, Gracia. 1994. *Onions are my 'Husband: Survival and Accumulation by West African Women.* Chicago: University of Chicago.
---. 2010. 'Gender Fictions and Gender Tensions Involving "Traditional" Asante Market Women', *African Studies Quarterly*, 11(2/3): 43-66.
Clark, Gracia, and Takyiwa Manuh. 1991. 'Women Traders in Ghana and the Structural Adjustment Programe'. In: Christina Gladwin (ed.). *Structural Adjustment and African Women Farmers.* Gainsville, FL: University of Florida: 217-236.
Cross, John C. and Alfonso Morales (eds.). 2007. *Street Entrepreneurs: People, Place and Politics in Local and Global Perspective.* London: Routledge.
Daily Graphic. 2008. '"Traffic vendors live dangerously but..."'. http://www.modernghana.com/newsthread1/176691/1/ (accessed 20 August 2010).
Dalakoglou, Dimitris. 2010. 'The Road: An Ethnography of the Albanian–Greek Cross-Border Motorway', *American Ethnologist*, 73(1): 132-149.
de Certeau, Michel. 1984. *The Practice of Everyday life.* Translated by Steven Rendall. Berkeley: University of California.
Douglas, Mary. 1992. *Risk and Blame: Essays in Cultural Theory.* London: Routledge.
Durkheim, Emile. 1995. *The Elementary Forms of Religious Life.* Translated by Karen E. Fields. New York: Free Press.

Farnell, Brenda. 1999. 'Moving Bodies, Acting Selves', *Annual Review of Anthropology*, 28: 341-373.
Feld, Steven, and Keith H. Basso. 1996. 'Introduction'. In: (eds.) *Senses of Place*. Santa Fe: School of American Research: 3-13.
Gewald, Jan-Bart. 2009. 'People, Mines and Cars: Towards a Revision of Zambian History, 1890-1930'. In: Jan-Bart Gewald, Sabine Luning and Klaas van Walraven (eds.). *The Speed of Change. Motor Vehicles and People in Africa, 1890-2000*. Leiden: Brill: 21-47.
Gewald, Jan-Bart, Sabine Luning and Klaas van Walraven. 2009. 'Motor vehicles and people in Africa: An Introduction'. In: Jan-Bart Gewald, Sabine Luning and Klaas van Walraven (eds.). *The Speed of Change. Motor Vehicles and People in Africa, 1890-2000*. Leiden: Brill: 1-18.
Gough, Katherine V., Graham A. Tipple and Mark Napier. 2003. 'Making a Living in African Cities: The Role of Home-based Enterprises in Accra and Pretoria', *International Planning Studies*, 8(4): 253-277.
Grasseni, Cristina (ed.). 2007. *Skilled Visions: Between Apprenticeship and Standards*. Oxford: Berghahn.
Hansen, Karen Tranberg and Mariken Vaa (eds.). 2004. *Reconsidering Informality: Perspectives from Urban Africa*. Uppsala: Nordiska Afrikainstitutet.
Hart, Keith. 1970. 'Small-scale Entrepreneurs in Ghana and Development planning', *Journal of Development Studies*, 6(4): 104-120.
---. 1973. 'Informal Income Opportunities and Urban Employment in Ghana', *Journal of Modern African Studies*, 11(1): 61-89.
Ingold, Tim. 2000. *The Perception of the Environment: Essays on Livelihood, Dwelling and Skill*. London: Routledge.
Ingold, Tim and Jo Lee Vergunst (eds.). 2008. *Ways of Walking: Ethnography and Practice on Foot*. Aldershot: Ashgate.
Katz, Jack. 1999. *How Emotions Work*. Chicago: University of Chicago.
King, Rudith. 2006. 'Fulcrum of the Urban Economy: Governance and Street Livelihoods in Kumasi, Ghana'. In: Alison Brown (ed.). *Contested Space: Street Trading, Public Space and Livelihoods in Developing Cities*. Rugby: Practical Action Publishing: 99-118.
Klaeger, Gabriel. 2009. 'Religion on the Road: The Spiritual Experience of Road Travel in Ghana'. In: Jan-Bart Gewald, Sabine Luning and Klaas van Walraven (eds.). *The Speed of Change. Motor Vehicles and People in Africa, 1890-2000*. Leiden: Brill: 212-231.

Lee, Jo and Tim Ingold. 2006. 'Fieldwork on Foot: Perceiving, Routing, Socialising'. In: Simon Coleman and Peter Collins (eds.). *Locating the Field: Space, Place and Context in Anthropology*. Oxford: Berg.
Lefebvre, Henri. 2004. *Rhythmanalysis: Space, Time, and Everyday life*. Translated by Stuart Elden and Gerald Moor. London: Continuum.
Lyng, Stephen. 2008. 'Edgework, Risk and Uncertainty'. In: Jens Zinn (ed.). *Social Theories of Risk and Uncertainty: an Introduction*. Oxford: Blackwell: 106-137.
---. (ed.) 2005. *Edgework: the Sociology of Risk-Taking*. New York: Routledge.
Lyon, Fergus. 2003. 'Trader Associations and Urban Food Systems in Ghana: Institutionalist Approaches to Understanding Urban Collective Action', *International Journal of Urban and Regional Research*, 27(1): 11-23.
---. 2007. 'Institutional Perspectives on Understanding Street Retailer Behavior and Networks: Cases from Ghana'. In: John C. Cross and Alfonso Morales (eds.). *Street Entrepreneurs: People, Place and Politics in Local and Global Perspective*. London: Routledge: 164-179.
Merleau-Ponty, Maurice. 1962. *Phenomenology of Perception*. Translated by Colin Smith. London: Routledge.
Merriman, Peter. 2007. *Driving Spaces: a Cultural-Historical Geography of England's M1 Motorway*. Malden: Blackwell.
Overå, Ragnhild. 2007. 'When Men do Women's Work: Structural Adjustment, Unemployment and Changing Gender Relations in the Informal Economy of Accra, Ghana', *Journal of Modern African Studies*, 45(4): 539-563.
Quayson, Ato. 2010. 'Signs of the Times: Discourse Ecologies and Street Life', *City & Society*, 22(1): 77-96.
Robertson, Claire. 1983. 'The Death of Makola and other Tragedies: Male Strategies against a Female-Dominated System', *Canadian Journal of African Studies*, 17(3): 469-495.
---. 1984. *Sharing the Same Bowl: a Socio-Economic History of Women and Class in Accra, Ghana*. Bloomington: Indiana University.
Roitman, Janet and Achille Mbembe. 1995. 'Figures of the Subject in Times of Crisis', *Public Culture*, 7(2): 323-352.
Rosa, Hartmut. 2009. 'Social Acceleration: Ethical and Political Consequences of a Desynchronized High-Speed Society'. In: Hartmut Rosa

and William E. Scheuerman (eds.). *High-Speed Society: Social Acceleration, Power, and Modernity.* University Park: Pennsylvania State University: 77-112.

Rosa, Hartmut and William E. Scheuerman, (eds.) 2009. *High-Speed Society: Social Acceleration, Power, and Modernity.* University Park: Pennsylvania State University.

Sheets-Johnstone, Maxine. 1999. 'Emotion and Movement. A Beginning Empirical-Phenomenological Analysis of their Relationship', *Journal of Consciousness Studies*, 6(11/12): 259-277.

Tomlinson, John. 2007. *The Culture of Speed: the Coming of Immediacy.* London: Sage.

Urry, John. 2009. 'Speeding Up and Slowing Down'. In: Hartmut Rosa and William E. Scheuerman (eds.). *High-Speed Society: Social Acceleration, Power, and Modernity*, University Park: Pennsylvania State University: 179-200.

Weiss, Brad. 1996. *The Making and Unmaking of the Haya lived World: Consumption, Commoditization and Everyday Practice.* Durham, N.C.: Duke University.

Yankson, Paul W.K. 2000. 'Accommodating Informal Economic Units in the Urban built Environment: Petty Commodity Enterprises in the Accra Metropolitan Area, Ghana', *Third World Planning Review* 22(3): 313-334.

---. 2007. 'Street Trading and Environmental Management in Central Accra: Decentralisation and Metropolitan Governance in Ghana', *Research Review NS*, 22(1): 37-55.

The Transnational Choice

Young Tuareg Traders between Niger and Nigeria

TILMAN MUSCH

In speaking about Tuareg migrations to Nigeria, one often thinks about 'classic' examples of caravan-trading or of seasonal labour migrations to urban centres. This chapter deals with a different case: young Tuareg who travel between Niger and Nigeria in order to experience a 'new' and 'urban' way of life. Their main activity is trading (*faire du commerce*) in products from Nigeria. However, trading seems to be more a means to finance the foreign experience than to be an objective per se. The motivation for migrating is not just to earn money but an interest in the foreign, a wanderlust, a search for adventure and, not least, an interest in Nigeria as an example of a 'modern' and 'urban' way of life, as well as for prosperity and consumption.[1]

Searching for the new, trading in contemporary goods in daily use and participating in an urban culture contribute to a concept of life which seems

---

1   Ethnographic data in this chapter is based on work with young traders who are not simply 'interviewed persons' but rather friends or coevals. I was especially able to gather the most interesting information at the *Fada*, the meeting of (young) people. The method 'convenient' to the *Fada* may be called the '*Faakaray* method': the Zarma word *faakaray* means 'chatting' and 'joking' with coevals, independently of age or gender.

to have nothing to do with the 'traditional' lifestyle of rural Tuareg.[2] However, the migrants do not simply live in their new urban worlds, they are also closely linked to their original social environment. Thus, it is reasonable to call them 'transnational' migrants maintaining 'multi-stranded social relations linking the societies of origin and settlement'. They 'develop and maintain multiple relations – familial, economic, social, organizational, religious, and political – that span borders' (Glick-Schiller *et al.* 1992: IX; see also Wimmer and Glick-Schiller 2003).

The present chapter investigates the mobile way of life of these young urban migrants. The aim is to explain their migrations not as a constraint, as a conventional view might see it, but rather as a choice. In pursuing this point, I will first try to explain the appeal of Nigeria as a symbol of a global urban modernity. Then I will describe the migrants and their migrations in order to account for their mobile way of life and trading activities. This presentation leads to a discussion of the transnational character of their migratory life and to the following question: How do the migrants manage to link the rural and the urban? In the last part, I will try to deepen the idea of a 'transnational choice' as a means to realize an independent and 'modern' way of life.

NIGERIA: THE 'INVISIBLE CITY'

The term 'invisible city' (De Boeck and Plissart 2004) designates a city linked to a multitude of representations and meanings. Thus it can also mean an urban way of life which is – contrary to the 'rural' way of life –

---

2   Concerning the 'traditional' way of life in the Imanan canton based on agriculture, horticulture and breeding, see Guillaume (1974). The Imanan canton is located to the north of Niamey, before the town of Filingué. The Hausa canton of Kurfey is located to its north. Other neighbouring cantons belong to the Zarma, who are also present in Bonkoukou. The Tuareg of the Imanan speak Tamashek and Zarma; the latter is widespread among the younger generation and seems to be displacing Tamashek. This is important, as a kind of 'Hausaisation' will be mentioned below in the case of the migrants. However, 'Hausaisation' is determined not by proximity to the canton of Kurfey, but by contact with the Hausa of Maradi, Zinder and northern Nigeria.

linked to experiences of modernity and the consumption of 'modern' goods. The urban way of life may serve as a recipient of all kinds of dreams and imaginations. Is it therefore possible to say that Nigerian urban agglomerations are 'invisible cities' for young Tuareg migrants?

The question is worth asking, all the more as it is usually Europe, especially France, that is seen as attracting West Africans and inducing them to migrate. In this context, it is interesting that Europe does not seem to signify anything anymore for these young migrants: what served as an example for the generation of their parents has now lost its interest.[3] It is also significant that, during our conversations, the migrants showed little interest in the fact that I was living in Paris at that time. It was much more interesting to them that, like them, I too had travelled to Nigeria. *Avoir fait le Nigeria* ('having done Nigeria') was a common phrase of much greater importance than origin or skin colour.

The reasons for turning away from Europe are banal: Europe has practically become unreachable, its merchandise is too expensive, and objects of European origin coming to Africa are second-hand, renovated, or reconverted and adapted several times to the African environment. Products from Europe are therefore no longer 'European', but alienated from Europe. Europe is beyond reach and therefore no longer of interest.

Nigeria, on the contrary, is reachable. It is possible for migrants to experience Nigeria, which is, for them, characterized by a 'modern' and 'urban' life, as well as by prosperity and consumption. The reasons for Nigeria having become an example of 'modernity' are in part due to the economic development of the country:

"Nigeria's deposit of high quality crude – combined with a fourfold leap in world market price – was received as a blessing from providence. Nigeria's newly found 'God-given' wealth reunited the nation with unprecedented prosperity, portending a state-directed industrial revolution that would be lubricated by oil. As petroleum revenues poured in, an ambitious national development plan invested in parastatal industries, education, hospitals, and mass media, matched by a boom of imported commodities ranging from staple foods and raw materials to expensive technology and luxury goods." (Apter 2005: 22)

---

3 Political reasons, such as France's highly dubious attitude towards Africa, also seem to play a role in this loss of attractiveness.

Nigeria's oil-fed boom after the Biafra war (1967-70), followed by mass imports and the mass production of goods and by changes in the national education and health sectors, seems to represent an example of success and prosperity and promises a different, 'urban' and 'modern' way of life. However, none of the young traders could even define precisely what was attractive about Nigeria's 'modernity', except by answering: *C'est bien, le Nigéria* ('Nigeria is good'), *C'est plus bon qu'ici* ('It's better than here') or *Le Nigéria, c'est cool* ('Nigeria is cool').[4]

Not least, the self-made boom may explain the strong national pride of Nigerians, as well as their orientation towards personal wealth and success. According to several informants who had spent some time in Nigeria, the example of this country must be followed. On the individual level, following this example means migrating to Nigeria, trading in goods of Nigerian origin and using them. In other words, it means appropriating Nigeria by travelling there, receiving lived experiences and consuming 'as Nigerians'. However, by consuming 'as Nigerians' and by becoming owners of foreign merchandise, the young Tuareg trader also acquires the social status of somebody who is not only the owner of appreciated things but also of a lived experience unknown to those 'who stayed at home'. Migrating to Nigeria and 'appropriating' it may thus also mean alienation from the 'original' rural environment.[5]

---

4 Another important 'destination' of migration for Tuareg was Libya (Gregoire 1999: 215 ff.). However, the young traders did not want to migrate to Libya, which would have meant doing physical work for them.

5 The property of a 'foreign' object (or experience) also alienates its owner from his original local environment. According to Hahn, 'alienation leaves the space for an irrevocable entanglement with the object of alienation. Even though the value may be contested and the usage decreasing, the objects will remain in a relationship with the person on the level of meaning and handling' (Hahn 2008: 86). Concerning the attractiveness of foreign goods and the alienation of their owner, Krüggeler writes: 'During the early post-Independence period, elites of the southern sierra, on the other hand, were not so much worried that lagging behind Lima consumer trends could cause them economic disadvantages. They feared that Lima's attempts to emphasize imported ideas of progress and civilization by adopting European consumption behavior could lead to even further social and political marginalization of interior elites. For them, copying the con-

Furthermore, due to their frequent journeys to Nigeria, there has been a kind of 'Hausaisation' of these young Tuareg, whose fathers usually wear the Tuareg veil (*tegelmust*) and the tunic (*tekatkat*), and who speak in Tamashek among themselves. 'Hausaisation' is anyhow not expressed by clothing[6] – men as well as women prefer 'Western' clothes – but rather by the use of the Hausa language and by musical preferences (e.g. Hausa music and Hausa clips downloaded on mobile phones). 'Hausaisation' thus does not lead to assimilation to traditional Hausa culture but means rather the appropriation of a regional way of life and of consumption. 'Hausa' means many things for the young migrants: Nigeria, a world of foreign objects, trading and travelling, Nigerian musicals, films with Indian choreographies, music with Hausa texts and, not least, personal freedom which, however, does not exist in the 'traditional' milieu in the way the migrants claim it for themselves.

Migrating to Nigeria and appropriating foreign goods of mostly non-African origin constitutes not only a consumption-based lifestyle but also a way to get in touch with the world. As emphasized already by Malaquais (2004), Salazar (2010) and Weiss (2002), 'African' urbanity and its way of life is closely connected to European, Asian or American referents. Thus, for young migrants who would have financial and administrative difficulties in going to Europe or the United States, their 'inner-African' mobility offers them the ability to travel virtually to other continents by making use of 'foreign' cultural representations.[7] In the introduction to the present vol-

---

sumption patterns of the capital's upper class served the purpose of trying to close a growing social gap between Lima and the provincial elites' (Krüggler 1997: 38f.).

6   As is the case among the Tuareg of Zinder when they wear Hausa clothes (Waibel 1998: 192).

7   However, this 'foreignness' can also be relativized. Besides the 'global' character of goods and experiences, one should not forget that they also become 'Africanized'. Referring to the use of bicycles in Burkina Faso, Hahn (2008) emphasizes that a 'global' good, during the process of appropriation, is alienated from its original existence. This means that, during the decades of its existence, a bicycle incurs several modifications – and also repairs – with the objective of making or remaking it functional for African conditions. Many goods of Chinese origin, as well as the fact that urban 'Nigerian' culture orientates itself

ume Hahn speaks of the 'hybrid character' of African cities, which makes them attractive for migrants: 'This hybrid character and the often enthusiastic appreciation of cultural phenomena from all parts of the world (...) generate the power for the cities' momentum of expansion' (Hahn, this volume, p. 15). In a similar way, travelling to Nigerian cities and acquiring 'modern' and 'urban' products is a means for young transnational migrants to appropriate 'the world'. The meanings 'the world' can have for them are numerous. Urban life-worlds may be perceived not only as they are 'in reality', but also as they are imagined by every individual. Nigeria is not only a country as it may 'really' be, but also an 'invisible city' which allows all kinds of references to a worldwide urban modernity. Finally, by connecting the invisible city to the rural village of origin, migrants contribute to spreading the idea of modern urban life among their coevals, who, in their turn, link their own dreams to it.

TYING THE URBAN TO THE RURAL

Earlier studies have already shown that African rural-urban migrants are able to tie together the 'original' life-world of the village with that in the city (Cohen 1969; Epstein 1961; Gutkind 1965; Gugler 1971). Frequent journeys between the one and the other allow them to maintain or to strengthen these ties. Using data from eastern Nigeria, Gugler (1971) describes urban dwellers as integrated not only in their new urban environment but also in their original rural one. The 'multi-stranded social relations' (Glick-Schiller *et al.* 1992: IX) establish transnational relations between the environment of origin and the new destination.

Who are the transnational migrants described in the present chapter? In the following, I will outline the way of life, travel and trade of the young Tuareg I was able to speak with. How are they tying the urban to the rural? To answer this question, I will emphasize their special type of migration, which does not fit into classical schemata circumscribing the move by

---

towards contemporary Indian music or Indian film clips, can also be subjected to 'Africanization': the clips are based on Indian models, but the actors are Africans; the mobile phone is produced in China, but its melodies are 'African' ones (often of popular Nigerian music), etc.

means of a 'point of departure' linked to a 'destination'. Thus, one can represent the 'rural' and the 'urban' not as opposites but as components of a social and geographical network.

The young migrants[8] see themselves as 'traders' and explain the necessity of their migration through this. 'Trading' by migrating allows one to experience the 'example' of Nigeria, but also to participate in its prosperity and thus find a means of subsistence. Trading journeys to Nigeria, where young Tuareg buy products of mostly Chinese origin in order to resell them in Niger, can take several weeks.

Celibate young men often import objects of some value or prestige such as mobile phones or other electronic devices. They also import motorcycles or sometimes used cars. In this case, there is a progression concerning the merchandise: most migrants begin with small objects like mobile phones and then, after acquiring some wealth, import motorcycles, or in the ideal case even cars. This progression towards the 'more valuable' also designates an increase in the personal prestige of the trader. The migrants travel frequently, although they obey neither a seasonal calendar nor any other form of regularity. Often they depend on opportunities, for example, saving a certain amount of money or shipping a car by a relative living in Europe or the United States that has to be collected in the port of a coastal town.

The migrants travel to places which seem to be 'the most interesting' to them. However, those interviewed could not explain whether they were using the word 'interesting' in an economic or in some other sense. As they are free from family obligations and have no obligations to pursue agriculture, the time spent on the route is of minor importance. A trading trip can include longer stays in Nigeria or the towns of Zinder and Maradi (Niger), as well as ample visits to friends. An exact balancing of the travel costs in

---

8   All the persons I spoke with – celibate men and women between 16 and 26 years who attended school for some years and thus acquired some knowledge of French – originate from the former Tuareg aristocracy of the Imanan canton and its principal village, Bonkoukou. Their precise origins and biographical backgrounds are relevant in so far as they are not former Tuareg slaves. The migrants interviewed never do or did agricultural work, although today even aristocrats sometimes do this kind of labour. In contrast to this, the former Tuareg slaves split their time between migration, working as hired labourers and seasonal agricultural activities.

relation to distance and time does not seem to play a role, and trading trips are at the same time seen as an adventure: *Il faut voyager. Tu vois du nouveau. Tu ne peux pas rester toujours au même endroit* ('One has to travel. You see new things. You cannot always stay in the same place').

A trading trip can also lead the migrants to other countries: several of those interviewed went to Cotonou in order to trade in cars, as customs there were lower and friends had recently acquired a house there. Another station for them was or may be China: a visa can easily be acquired, and the objective is to load and ship a container with cheap merchandise.

My informants do not export anything to Nigeria, as trading in agricultural products (in demand there) does not correspond to the 'modern' image of a trader of mobile phones or motor cycles: *J'amène les portables, les motos. Ça, c'est bien. La pomme de terre, nous, on ne s'occupe pas de ces choses-là* ('I take mobile phones and motor cycles. That's fine. Potatoes, we don't handle them').[9]

The celibate young women among the migrants, some of whom already have illegitimate children left with their extended family in Niamey or the Imanan canton, seem to be completely independent, and their stays in Nigeria – sometimes also in other countries – can last for several months. They

---

9 The objects imported to Niger – from mobile phones to used cars – are often first used by the trader himself, who shows them to everybody during the period of use before offering them for sale. This phase of self-use can last for several days or even longer. As foils, intended to protect the object before its regular use, are often not removed even by the regular owner for several years, one can hardly know whether the trader is the regular user of an 'unpacked' object or whether he is using it only sporadically. This may also be a selling-strategy: if the trader is seen using 'his' object by anyone interested in buying it, the value of the latter and its 'promise of prestige' increase. In consequence, the resultant sales revenues may also increase. This is all the more the case as the trader can pretend that he does not really want to sell the object. Hahn describes the strategies of mobile phone users in Burkina Faso that tend to reduce, or abolish, costs. Such strategies include, for example, not calling or selling a phone credit before it expires, or 'flashing', that is, ringing someone to induce his callback. The strategies of young Tuareg traders who buy only on credit and use the merchandise (especially mobile phones) themselves in order to sell them later at a profit can also be seen as such a 'zero budget strategy' (Hahn and Kibora 2008: 104).

mostly trade in objects of lesser value like shoes and clothes, but in rare cases also in mobile phones.

Such trading trips are not orientated, as far as the merchandise is concerned, towards the calculation of profit and loss. Travel expenses and subsistence, as well as a certain income, are financed by male colleagues. Persons in this group can thus be compared to women working in the gold-digger environment in Burkina Faso (Werthmann 2007), who enter into relatively durable partnerships with men and are 'co-financed' by the latter.[10] An important motivation for this group is the search for personal freedom, which is described by Ouedrago, in another context, as 'working, taking risks, being free' (Ouedrago 1995). The component 'working', however, seems of minor importance for the migrants concerned, which also distinguishes them from Werthmann's informants. When I asked female migrants what they had done in recent months, their answer, accompanied by a wide smile of satisfaction, was, for example: *Rien! Je fais rien. Je suis là seulement!* ('Nothing. I don't do anything! I am just here!').[11]

When looking at the traders described above, it is clear that their migration serves two things. First, it allows them to go to a neighbouring country, experience the Nigerian example and live a 'modern' way of life characterized by consumption and personal liberty. Secondly, it provides them with the means of subsistence necessary for travelling. As a motivation for migration, however, the desire to experience the foreign is more prominent than the need to finance personal subsistence.

---

10 A future, more detailed study of the female group of migrants I describe above may be interesting in order to study gender in the context of migration, as it has been done by, for example, Olurode and Trager (1995) and in a more recent work by Lambert (2007) on Jola women (Senegal).

11 I will not discuss whether this attitude is a particularity of the women of the Tuareg aristocracy, who formerly indeed did not do physical labour, as all the work was done by slaves. However, the villagers of Bonkoukou – among them several members of the former aristocracy – emphasized that an upper-class woman was not able to work. This judgment may, of course, be exaggerated, as the generally precarious situation also concerns the aristocracy, and as slavery is now illegal and too expensive. Nevertheless, during several stays in Bonkoukou I always saw the female migrants in the homesteads of their families, relaxing on mats.

It is not the fact of migrating itself which is new to Tuareg society. On the contrary, there is a long tradition of migration to the south in order to trade or to earn money through other activities. However, the conception of life of the young urban migrants described here and their self-identification with a world of consumption seem to differ from the 'classical' examples of migration described briefly below.

Such 'classical' examples of Tuareg migrations to Nigeria are caravan-trading, seasonal labour or small-scale trade in mostly horticultural products.[12] In these cases, migration is closely connected with the economy of the 'homeland' and is subjected to a seasonal calendar. One can even speak of the strong economic integration of 'expatriate' activities into the 'homeland' economies. The prevailing motivation is the necessity to contribute to the latter, not a personal desire to be free and to experience the new.

As the cases of young Tuareg migrants presented above are not comparable to 'classic' examples of migration, their movements do not conform to 'aetiological' viewpoints of migration either. Klute and Hahn (2007) criticize the aetiological tendency in migration studies, which is characterized by the so-called 'push and pull factors'. The former leads persons to migration, the latter determines the choice of destination. Criticism of this aetiological tendency refers to the biased sedentary perspective of the logic of 'push and pull factors'. This perspective assumes that migration is an exception and a rupture with the place of origin requiring specific 'factors' for its explanation.[13]

---

12 Tuareg of the Kel Ewey and Kel Gress came and still come with their caravans to Kano, Katsina and Jigawa in order to sell or barter the horticultural products of the Aïr Mountains, salt and dried meat with Hausa in exchange for millet, cloth and objects of daily use (Spittler 1998: 170; Bernus 1981: 228f.). Male and mostly celibate Tuareg searched and still search for labour opportunities in the towns of Nigeria in order to earn enough to get married or to acquire livestock. For example, many former slaves (*buzu*) work as night-watchmen in Kano (Armstrong 1967: 269ff.). Small-scale traders export horticultural products and import products of daily use and of mostly minor financial value (clothes, shoes, dinnerware, etc.) to Niger.

13 From this perspective, the migrant is 'a person who uproots himself from his original home and moves to a new place where he settles and establishes new links' (Labo 2000: 1).

The migration of these young Tuareg has no spatially determined 'destination'. Is it a city in Nigeria where foreign life can be experienced? Is it a place along the route where the young migrants stay with friends? Is it even the homeland, where the migrants become, due to their trading activities, persons of higher social status? Or is the 'destination' connected to the route itself and to the fact of being a migrant?[14] The impossibility of identifying 'destinations' and 'origins', or even of speaking about a 'temporary settlement', is a specific feature of the present case. The young migrants live on the route, in several places and virtually also on other continents. They live somewhere *in between*, and their way of life is consequently *transnational* (Hahn, this volume: 14).

The difficulty or even impossibility of determining a clear destination thus excludes adopting an aetiological approach. People are not mobile 'because' of better conditions at the destination. 'Destination', in this context, can mean, among other things, two in particular: experiencing the new abroad, and showing the foreign to those left at home. The 'destination' provides an opportunity to appropriate, live and display the foreign. This may be manifested in the concrete objects of trade or, more abstractly, in the experience of 'urban' Nigeria and the 'invisible city'.

Avoiding an aetiological approach also means avoiding speaking about a 'rupture' between the rural environment of origin and the new urban life of the young migrants. As already mentioned, journeys between the 'two worlds' are frequent and contribute to conserving and strengthening social ties. It is of particular importance to establish networks between the society of origin and the new environments of the migrants. Furthermore, the migrant returning to his 'home' brings with him the example of the experienced new, concretely in the form of the object of consumption shown, given or sold in his village, and abstractly in the urban way of life being demonstrated of which the migrant is the representative. Linking in this way the urban experience to the rural environment and thus making the whole world virtually accessible to the village population contributes to creating transnational experiences in a rural context too.

---

14 The persons concerned, of course, do not call themselves 'migrants' but, as already mentioned, 'traders', and an imminent migration is described in terms of travelling: *je vais voyager* ('I am going to travel').

THE TRANSNATIONAL CHOICE

Above, transnationalism was defined as a way of life linking the rural society of origin and the new urban environments. Transnationalism is experienced by the young Tuareg migrants through their frequent journeys and their trading activities. However, although mobility has the potential to link the 'old' and the 'new', the transnational experience also represents the risk of alienation: new worlds are discovered by the migrants and new experiences are lived. How do they fit in with the traditional way of life of the society of origin?

The transnational migrants appropriate completely new ways of life and experience new life-worlds, which alienate them from their traditional environment. Furthermore, the fact that the migrants see themselves as traders has a symbolic value: trading implies appropriating, and appropriating foreign products means, for the migrants, not only becoming their owner but becoming, as their owner, foreign themselves.

However, as also mentioned, the migrants are not so much traders as travellers. Eventually, alienation occurs even before migrating, and it can be seen as the motivation for the move rather than its product. The young urban Tuareg migrants, due to their wishes of a modern life and emancipation as well as motives, which were prior to their first departure, risk being alienated from the 'traditional' society of their 'homeland', and in particular from their parental generation.[15] Leaving is then simply a justification for their alienation from those who have stayed 'at home'.

First, this is due to the fact that Nigeria is considered by everybody, including non-migrants, as an example of a better life. When a migrant returns, changes in his way of life are explained by the experience of Nigeria. As Nigeria serves as an example, the 'modern' way of life cannot be wrong, even if those who stayed 'at home' do not want to live and experience it.

Secondly, migrants justify their travels by their trading activities. As they earn a certain income, as they finance themselves and perhaps also some relatives 'at home', and, as their existence as traders contributes to a higher social status, their 'different' way of life is, if not understood, at

---

15 A fortiori when female migrants are concerned who have illegitimate children they conceived already in Bonkoukou and not only en route.

least accepted by others. It is considered as something necessary and as contributing to a better future for everyone. In this sense, the widespread supposition that migration is necessarily related to alienation serves not only as an explanation for differences but also as their justification. The 'alienated', despite his otherness, remains a fully accepted member of his 'traditional' society, thereby maintaining social coherence. Thus migration not only makes it possible to live a particular, sometimes different way of life; it also provides an explanation of this way of life to 'the others'. In this sense, migration is not a constraint, while transnationality is a choice.

In a similar way, foreign goods and experiences are also shared in order to manage alienation.[16] By linking the urban and the rural, the transnational migrant brings the 'invisible city' into the village and may thus create a desire among his coevals to discover new and foreign experiences. Sharing the foreign means also inciting others to migrate, to experience the new and to make their own 'transnational choices'.

REFERENCES

Apter, Andrew. 2005. *The Pan-African Nation: Oil and the Spectacle of Culture in Nigeria*. Chicago: University of Chicago.
Armstrong, R. 1967. 'The Nightwatchmen of Kano', *Middle Eastern Studies*, 3(3): 269-282.
Bernus, Edmond. 1981. *Touaregs nigériens: unité culturelle et diversité régionale d'un peuple pasteur*. Paris: Éditions de l'Office de la recherche scientifique et technique d'Outre-Mer.
Cohen, Abner. 1969. *Custom and Politics in Urban Africa: A Study of Hausa Migrants in Yoruba Towns*. Berkeley: University of California.

---

16 According to Hahn (2008), and as already mentioned above, ownership may lead to the alienation of the owner from his social environment. However, Hahn also confines the idea of alienation through ownership: social coherence must not be put into question by alienation, as the mechanism of giving away and donating contributes to the integration of the bought object and the 'reintegration' of its original owner into the local context. Thus, sharing virtually transnational experiences may also lead to the reintegration of their owners into the social context.

De Boeck, Filip and Marie-Françoise Plissart. 2004. *Kinshasa: Tales of the Invisible City*. Tervuren: Luidon.

Epstein, Arnold L. 1961. 'The Network and Urban Social Organization', *Rhodes-Livingstone Journal*, 29: 29-62.

Glick-Schiller, Nina, Linda Basch and Cristina Blanc-Szanton. 1992. 'Towards a Definition of Transnationalism: Introductory Remarks and Research Questions'. In: Nina Glick-Schiller (ed.): *Towards a Transnational Perspective on Migration: Race, Class, Ethnicity, and Nationalism Reconsidered*. New York: New York Academy of Sciences: IX-XIV.

Gregoire, Emmanuel. 1999. *Touaregs du Niger: le destin d'un mythe*. Paris: Karthala.

Gugler, Josef. 1971. 'Life in a Dual System: Eastern Nigerians in Town, 1961', *Cahiers d'Etudes Africaines*, 11(3): 400-421.

Guillaume, Henri. 1974. *'Les nomades interrompus': introduction à l'étude du canton Twareg de l'Imanan*. Niamey: Centre Nigérien de Recherches en Sciences Humaines.

Gutkind, Peter C. W. 1965. 'African Urbanism, Mobility and the Social Network', *International Journal of Comparative Sociology*, 6: 48-60.

Hahn, Hans Peter. 2008. 'Appropriation, Alienation and Syncretization: Lessons from the Field'. In: Afe Adogame, Magnus Echtler and Ulf Vierke (eds.). *Unpacking the New: Critical Perspectives on Syncretization in Africa and Beyond*. Berlin: Lit: 71-92.

Hahn, Hans Peter and Ludovic Kibora. 2008. 'The Domestication of the Mobile Phone: Oral Society and New ICT in Burkina Faso', *Journal of Modern African Studies* 46: 87-109.

Klute, Georg and Hans Peter Hahn. 2007. Cultures of Migration: Introduction. In: Hans Peter Hahn and Georg Klute (eds.). *Cultures of Migration: African Perspectives*. Berlin: Lit: 9-27.

Krüggeler, Thomas. 1997. 'Changing Consumption Patterns and Everyday Life in Two Peruvian Regions: Food, Dress, and Housing in the Central and Southern Highlands (1820-1920)'. In: Benjamin Orlove (ed.). *The Allure of the Foreign: Imported Goods in Postcolonial Latin America*. Ann Arbor: University of Michigan: 31-66.

Labo, Abdullah. 2000. 'The Motivation and Integration in the Nigerian-Niger Border Area: A Study of Magama Jibia'. In: IFRA-Ibadan (ed.). *Trans-Border Studies*. Ibadan: IFRA: 1-32.

Lambert, Michael. 2007. 'Politics, Patriarchy, and New Tradition: Understanding Female Migration among the Jola (Senegal, West Africa)'. In: Hans Peter Hahn and Georg Klute (eds.). *Cultures of Migration: African Perspectives*. Berlin: Lit: 129-148.

Malaquais, Dominique. 2004. *Douala / Johannesburg / New York: Cityscapes Imagined*. Cape Town: Isandla Institute.

Olurode, Lai. 1995. 'Women in the Rural-Urban Migration in the town of Iwo in Nigeria'. In: Jonathan Baker and Tade Akin Aina (eds.). *The Migration Experience in Africa*. Uppsala: Nordiska Afrikanstitutet: 298-302.

Ouedrago, Jean-Bernard. 1995. 'The Girls of Nyovuuru: Dagara Female Labour Migrations to Bobo-Dioulasso'. In: Jonathan Baker and Tade Akin Aina (eds.). *The Migration Experience in Africa*. Uppsala: Nordiska Afrikanstitutet: 303-320.

Salazar, Noel B. 2010. 'Towards an Anthropology of Cultural Mobilities', *Journal of Migration and Culture*, 1(1): 53-68.

Spittler, Gerd. 1998. *Hirtenarbeit: Die Welt der Kamelhirten und Ziegenhirtinnen von Timia*. Köln: Köppe.

Trager, Lilian. 1995. 'Women Migrants and Rural-Urban Linkages in South-Western Nigeria'. In: Jonathan Baker and Tade Akin Aina (eds.). *The Migration Experience in Africa*. Uppsala: Nordiska Afrikanstitutet. 268-288.

Waibel, Gabi. 1998. *Sesshaftwerdung und Sozialer Wandel bei den Tuareg Zinders (Niger)*. Hamburg: Institut für Afrikastudien.

Weiss, Brad. 2002. 'Thug Realism: Inhabiting Fantasy in Urban Tanzania', *Cultural Anthropology*, 17: 93-124.

Werthmann, Katja. 2007. 'Dans un monde masculin: le travail des femmes dans un camp de chercheurs d'or au Burkina Faso'. In: Elisabeth Boesen and Laurence Marfaing (eds.). *Les nouveaux urbains dans l'espace Sahara-Sahel. Un cosmopolitisme par le bas*. Paris: Karthala: 295-322.

Wimmer, Andreas and Nina Glick-Schiller. 2003. 'Methodological Nationalism, the Social Sciences and the Study of Migration: An Essay in Historical Epistemology', *International Migration Review*, 37(3): 576-610.

The Issue of the Diaspo in Ouagadougou

LUDOVIC KIBORA

INTRODUCTION

Ouagadougou, the capital of Burkina Faso, has been a centre of commercial transactions since pre-colonial times (Skinner 1974), with a tradition of hosting people of different origins. West African traders from both the coast and the Sahel used this place for stop-overs and during bridging periods of low market activity, indicating that exchanges between the different populations of the region have a long history (Hien 2003). Whereas traders constituted an important stream of in-migration, there was also a considerable level of out-migration. Young Mossi men and women went to the colony of Côte d'Ivoire, where there was a crucial need for labour on the coffee and cacao plantations (Mandé 1992; Bi 2003).

This intermingling of populations has some positive aspects, but today it often leads to problems of incomprehension. This shifting valuation of intercultural contacts due to the rise of the notion of identities has been addressed by the historian Issiaka Mandé as follows:

"There has always been an important flow of populations in inner Africa. Colonial administration created frontiers and new ethnographic interpretations that crystallize this point. One builds identities that are opposed to others; this will provoke a certain number of nationalist movements." (Mandé 1999: 2)

After independence, many Burkinabe who lived in Côte d'Ivoire returned to their country of origin. Some of them returned for good, while others just wanted to see their homeland and then leave again. They are now called *Paweto* ('those who stayed in the bush') or *Kosweogo* ('those who lingered in the bush').

Since the beginning of the violent conflicts in Côte d'Ivoire, return migration of Burkinabe who were born in Côte d'Ivoire or spent most time of their childhood there increased considerably. Many of them are young people who want to study at the University of Ouagadougou. This group of returning migrants gathering in urban centres is referred to as *Diaspo*, a diminutive of the word 'Diaspora', used here specifically for educated young people living in Ouagadougou with a Burkinabe nationality and a migratory background related to their stay in Côte d'Ivoire.

The *Diaspo* are sensitive regarding questions of identity and are often confronted with problems of integration. As the present analysis of their situation will make clear, their situation can also serve as a starting point for an anthropological analysis of social change. The *Diaspo* have already attracted some scholarly awareness, especially by historians (Mandé 1999; Batenga 2003) and sociologists (Zongo 2003). This contribution will focus on the concept of *Diaspo* as such and on its social implications by examining these young people's life-worlds in Ouagadougou and by thinking about their perspectives of integration in their home country. The documentation presented here is the result of literature research, interviews conducted in Ouagadougou in the '*Diaspo* setting' and participant observation in Ouagadougou from 2000 to 2009.

In the first section, the term *Diaspo* and its usage in Burkina Faso will be discussed. In the second section, social questions related to the marginal situation of this youth group will be addressed in detail.

FROM DIASPORA TO DIASPO

According to the *Petit Larousse illustré* (Larousse 2003), the term 'Diaspora' means 'the totality of members of a dispersed people throughout the world staying in contact with each other'. This dispersal may have a number of causes, varying from war to trade or the simple desire for a change of scene. Following Stéphane Dufoix (2004), the word 'Diaspora', which was first used in the Septuagint, was originally used for the Jewish people. It expressed 'the divine will' to disperse the chosen people.

Wars and other social upheavals in the twentieth century have certainly contributed to the enrichment of the concept and its expansion. Still according Dufoix, it was especially in the 1990s that new fields of research in the social sciences put this word on the agenda. During the last ten years 'diaspora policies', that is policies of states aimed at identifying parts of its population living beyond the borders of the state's territory (Ragazzi 2009: 379). At that time, the social sciences were tackling the issues of globalisation and 'transcendentalism', the post-modern movement in philosophy and the culturalist movement in anthropology. All these issues in particular were connected to the situation of migrant populations. Thus, the term 'Diaspora' makes it possible to address groups that are regarded as a homogeneous entity in a socio-cultural sense, even though they do not share the same national identity compared to the majority of the country of residence. In a research overview of this topic, Dufoix wrote:

"For about the last ten years, the scientific use of the term 'Diaspora' has undergone an amazing inflation in the field of the social sciences. Formerly reduced to certain 'peoples'(Jews, Armenians, afterwards Indians and Chinese), it progressively expanded until it encompasses at the present time more than fifty populations. The notion of Diaspora is at the heart of a number of recent and renewed questionings recently found in the field of the social sciences: postmodernism, globalisation and nationalism." (ibid.)

Following Dufoix, the first genuine attempt to construct a conceptual model founded on precise criteria was made by William Safran in 1991:

"I suggest [...] that the concept of Diaspora be applied to expatriate minority communities whose members share several of the following characteristics: 1) they, or their ancestors, have been dispersed from a specific original 'center' to two or more 'peripheral', or foreign regions; 2) they retain a collective memory, vision, or myth about their original homeland – its physical location, history, and achievements; 3) they believe that they are not – and perhaps cannot be – fully accepted by their host society and therefore feel partly alienated and insulated from it; 4) they regard their ancestral homeland as their true, ideal home and as the place to which they or their descendents would (or should) eventually return – when conditions are appropriate; 5) they believe that they should, collectively be committed to the maintenance or restoration of their original homeland and to its safety and prosperity; and 6) they continue to relate, personally or vicariously, to that homeland in one way or another, and their ethnocommunal consciousness and solidarity are importantly defined by the existence of such a relationship." (Safran 1991: 83-84)

This conceptual approach makes it possible to highlight the differences between the general concept of Diaspora and the term *Diaspo*. For example, Diaspora generally indicates a population not living in its place of origin, while the term *Diaspo* in Burkina Faso characterizes returning young migrants in their parent's home country. The term *Diaspo* itself originates from the student milieu. It is impossible to tell whether its first use was initiated by nationalists to refer to students born abroad or whether those coming from abroad used it for themselves. Following its widespread use, it has been commonly adopted, even though it has pejorative connotations for some persons.

The advantage of this term seems to be that, according to its users, it shares some characteristics following the conceptual definitions mentioned above. In particular it points to the suffering of those who have grown up in Côte d'Ivoire and were forced to leave the place of their childhood due to political conditions. *Diaspo* evolved particularly in the course of the mass arrival of many young Burkinabe from neighbouring Côte d'Ivoire because of the crises threatening the country since the beginning of the millennium. But the diminutive term *Diaspo* has undergone a problematic evolution from sympathy in the beginning to a more critical evaluation because of the discomfort felt among those living together with the local population.

OVERVIEW OF A RETURN TO THE COUNTRY OF ORIGIN

Many Burkinabe have lived in Côte d'Ivoire since the colonial period, when they mostly worked on the coffee and cacao plantations. The constitution of this immigrant group has a long history. Already during French colonisation, the Upper Volta was considered unproductive and in 1932 was therefore divided between Niger, Côte d'Ivoire and what is today Mali. At that time, the only valuable resource appeared to be the region's manpower. Therefore, men and women were brought in great numbers to Côte d'Ivoire to work on the plantations. The economic haemorrhaging continued with the construction of the railroad from Abidjan to Niger that connected Abidjan with Ouagadougou in 1954. Numerous workers were brought from Upper Volta to work on this railway construction site. Thus Upper Volta became a pool of cheap labour for the French colonisation in West Africa.

However, at independence in 1960 many people decided to stay in Côte d'Ivoire. There was an agreement between Félix Houphouët Boigny, president of Côte d'Ivoire, and Maurice Yaméogo, president of Burkina Faso, then Upper Volta, which even encouraged many Burkinabe to join their brothers in Côte d'Ivoire. Manifold advantages attracted tireless workers to Côte d'Ivoire. Among them was the ease with which foreigners could acquire land. Many managed to acquire their own plantations (Schwartz 2000). Considering the difficult conditions for agriculture in the areas of origin like the central plateau, where the soil is not always fertile, the opportunity to make one's living in Côte d'Ivoire offered a substantial improvement in income-generating opportunities.

After some years in Côte d'Ivoire, many came back to their country of origin riding new bicycles, carrying radios on their shoulders and wearing modern clothes. These scenes caused jealousy in the home villages, influencing many young men to make their own experience of emigration to Côte d'Ivoire. Farm work, kitchen help, all occupations that were not filled by Ivorian citizens were almost entirely occupied by Burkinabe. Some became rich, while others lost everything for different reasons. But the population that stayed behind in Burkina Faso very generally perceived them as successful migrants, and so the influx continued. The 1998 census in Côte d'Ivoire listed 3,954,550 foreigners living in the country, roughly two thirds of them were Burkinabe.

With the growth of the Ivorian population and the structural crisis of the capitalist world system with the fall in prices for raw materials such as coffee and cacao, which did not spare Côte d'Ivoire, foreigners were used as scapegoats for the economic problems that arose everywhere. Therefore, the number of emigrants who sent their children to school in Burkina Faso increased noticeably from the beginning of the 1980s.

While education in many parts of the region was shaken by repeated crises (strikes followed by closures of universities in Mali, Togo and Senegal in the 1980s, etc.), Burkina Faso was seen as stable and the school system as of good quality. That encouraged Burkinabe migrants living in Côte d'Ivoire to send their sons back to Burkina Faso to settle them there. In addition every Burkinabe under 23 years systematically received registration and a scholarship at the University of Ouagadougou after his school-leaving exam. These circumstances encouraged many Burkinabe students to return to their country, especially when conditions for higher education and access to the field of administration in Côte d'Ivoire began to become complicated. Indeed, a policy of preferring nationals, called the 'ivorisation' of the administrative field, reduced the chances of many young Burkinabe who had completed their education in Côte d'Ivoire to find jobs in the civil service there.

This wave of return migration was sharply accelerated by the economic crisis that hit Côte d'Ivoire from the beginning of the 1980s. To get the national budget back on its feet again, residence permits for foreign citizens were introduced, as well as a policy of discrimination against non-nationals. In addition there was an inhuman treatment of foreigners by a corrupt police force with frequent extortions in public. This difficult evolution pushed many Burkinabe back to their country of origin.

The death of President Houphouët Boigny in 1993 was followed by a growth of xenophobia in the country. This tendency led to a violent outburst with the events in Tabou in 1999, where several Burkinabe were massacred in an Ivorian village because they were cultivating land that the locals had given to them. As a consequence, the government of President Bédié promoted and established the term *ivoirité*, which referred to a concept of nationalist policy. This conflict led to the expulsion of 15,000 Burkinabe (Schwartz 2000: 56). The crisis culminated on 19 September 2002, when part of the Ivorian army rebelled against the regime of Laurent Gbagbo. As a consequence, immigrants of all social categories followed the students and young intellectuals. An operation called *Bayiri* (return to one's native country) was organized by the Burkinabe state to repatriate those who wanted to return. Officially more than 365,997 people came back to Burkina Faso between 2002 and 2004 (PNUD 2005). For many younger people and students, this mass return constitutes a permanent return to their parent's home country. This group is now confronted with the challenge of integrating into their own country.

THE LIFE OF THE DIASPO IN OUAGADOUGOU: BETWEEN INTEGRATION AND RETREAT INTO ONESELF

"It's a pleasure for me to send this open letter to you because it is strictly forbidden to apply for different selection procedures as a civil servant, especially when you are born in Côte d'Ivoire, received your school-leaving exam before 2000 (in 1999 as in my case) and are, as the only evidence, provided only with a provisional attestation of this exam due to the Ivorian crisis. What discrimination! Are we all sons and daughters of this beloved country Burkina Faso or not?"

This outcry by Jean-Marie Kaboré was published in the daily newspaper *Le Pays*, number 3628, on 24 May 2006 under the title 'Selection procedure: discriminatory manoeuvres'. Even though it might seem exaggerated, this text expresses one of the major difficulties with which the *Diaspo* are confronted in Burkina Faso. The administrative problems create feelings of frustration on the part of many returning young migrants, who feel they are treated like strangers in their own country. Stuck in a situation where returning to the country of immigration (often the country of birth) is too dangerous, these young people display a wish to establish themselves in the Burkinabe society and are, depending on their different problems, often forced to gather in groups to make them remember the country from which they emigrated.

Initially, the *Diaspo* were predominantly pupils and they had great fun in behaving as the 'social elite'. They felt, in an evolutionary sense, as if they were superior, compared to those of their own generation who had not experienced the same adventure. Due to the fact that they came from a more developed country, they believed they were 'better connected'. This specific capacity was expressed in the more fashionable life they led than their brothers, who had stayed in the country. Their way of imitating a western style made it easy to distinguish them from the local population. Most of them spent their holidays with their parents, who had stayed in Côte d'Ivoire, and so they were able to return to Burkina Faso with the latest fashions (of clothes and music), thus representing their own sort of people. At school, in college and at university, Burkinabe from Côte d'Ivoire were just regarded as Ivorian. They gathered at public places (night clubs, discos, bars, etc.) and played the latest music hits, as known from Abidjan.

For example, the term *maquis* to denote bars and other popular small restaurants in Ouagadougou has been imported from Abidjan by the *Diaspo*.

But many pupils and students had problems in integrating because their parents tried to associate them with family life in Ouagadougou without making any effort to introduce them to their father's village of origin as the basis of the family. Moreover, once the young people had left their villages to live in Ivorian cities, they never intended to return for longer periods to their villages of origin, therefore they never intended to maintain a close relationship with those who stayed behind. Dockers, laundresses or workers, those who had never taken up a school career, had undergone such a metamorphosis in a socio-professional sense that they despised working in the fields. In this context, the young people organized their lives among their friends, with whom they shared the same experience of emigration and the same problems. The forced repatriation that directed many migrants to their villages of origin was a psychological shock for many of them because they had often left home more than twenty years earlier, and therefore nobody expected them to return any more.

The question of identity, which is connected to the integration of the *Diaspo*, has been especially relevant because of the impossibility of returning to Côte d'Ivoire for political reasons. Being stuck in this fashion, young people in urban contexts adopted various strategies of integration. Many of them established relations with their extended family, cautiously but deliberately. At the same time, most of them also declared their solidarity with each other in an opportunistic way. In reality many had no orientation in their country of origin, yet in spite of suffering from the harsh conditions of re-migration, many *Diaspo* developed remarkable socio-economic initiatives. Students with a background of immigration even established associations of solidarity referring to their 'Ivorian origin'.

On the campus of Ouagadougou, one can notice a number of clubs, each representing a particular group of *Diaspo*. These are, among others: the CAS (club amitié solidarité = friendship solidarity club), a group of students from Moyen Comoé in Côte d'Ivoire; NAB (Nouvelle Alliance pour les Burkinabè de l'Agneby = New alliance of Burkinabe from Agneby), a group of those from the region of Agboville; 2A-ED (Association des étudiants anciens élèves de Dabou = Student Association of former pupils from Dabou) and, more discreet in appearance, ASEBE (Association des Scolaires et Etudiants Burkinabè de l'Extérieur = Association of Burkinabe pupils and students from abroad). Those responsible for 2A-ED, which was officially recognized by the authorities in March 2005, show a particular dynamism by promoting the usefulness of such groups in relation to the difficulties the *Diaspo* are confronted with concerning integration in their own country. These associations are most often the continuation, i.e. the transfer of similar clubs, which attracted young Burkinabe in Côte d'Ivoire. They support the integration of the newcomers at school, at university and in society. For the young *Diaspo* they function as a basis of understanding and solidarity. At the moment there are about ten associations of this kind in Ouagadougou, most often constituted by former pupils from Dabou, Daloa, Agneby, Soubré, Yamoussoukro, etc. Since 2004 attempts to create an umbrella organisation have been undermined by disputes over the leadership. But in the sense mentioned above, these associations supply a need that is not met by the official authorities. The historian Issiaka Mandé describes this as follows:

"These 'cultural hybrids' form collective characteristics, encircle the cultural field and prescribe even a language; we are thus confronted with the creation of an ethnicity." (Mandé 1999: 1)

In the quest for a place in society, the groups of *Diaspo* gave reasons for the emergence of small informal groups among the local students. Those who established themselves on the campus of Ouagadougou are called *Tenga* or *Tenguiste* (meaning 'soil' or 'home' in the national language, Mooré). In contrast to the *Diaspo*, they never migrated. They sometimes solve their disputes with the *Diaspo* violently. These incidents of the '5/5', as they are called in the jargon of the *Diaspo*, mark a real battle between the *Diaspo* and the *Tenga*, beginning in the students' hostel of *Patte d'Oie* in Ouagadougou and carrying along with it all the student hostels of the city. This conflict, which emerged from differences during the election of hostel representatives, made the gap between the two groups visible to everyone in the city. Based on interviews with members of these groups, it is possible to determine their respective perspectives. The *Diaspo* are considered to speak French with an Ivorian accent (leaving out many articles and preferably using Ivorian jargon). They are said always to dress fashionably, at the edge of extravagance. The *Diaspo* are also criticized for their inclination to excitement in all circumstances and for being far too pleasure-seeking. They are also characterized as very daring, having no fear in putting into action what they think to be good.

In contrast to this, the *Tenga* are said to have a local accent in French, and most of them speak several local languages. They prefer to dress in a simple and discreet manner and are characterized as rather quiet and reserved. The typical meeting place for *Tenga* is the road side with a bench and some green tea. They are also seen as much more hesitant.

These criteria, used to distinguish students called *Diaspo* from those called *Tenga*, are rather arbitrary and used occasionally to describe one or the other camp. Using the results of a questionnaire distributed during a study in 1999 to 197 students (111 native-born and 86 *Diaspo*), Moussa Batenga (1999), a teacher of history at the University of Ouagadougou, was able to generate similar statements through interviews. The *Tenga* think that the *Diaspo* have a sense of superiority, that they lack politeness and that they are rebellious, though they acknowledge that *Diaspo* are open-minded, dynamic and act in solidarity. In contrast to this, the *Diaspo* think that *Tenga* are not very cooperative, are passive and too reserved. In the perception of the *Diaspo*, the *Tenga* have the merits of being studious, polite and modest. This attempt to categorise the two student groups based on their geographical origin is evidence of a genuine problem of integration.

The *Tocsin* association was founded in March 1997 to deal among other things with this difficult contrast in mutual perceptions. Its members are individuals from the Burkinabe administration; most of them spent their childhood in Côte d'Ivoire and are very familiar with the phenomenon of the difficult or even failed integration of the returning migrants. In a television debate entitled 'Burkina Faso and the world: migration and Diaspora', broadcast in April 2006, the president of *Tocsin*, Albert Ouédraogo, warned of the risks that could be caused in the long run by the name *Diaspo* and the fact that it is opposed to the term *Tenga*. *Tocsin* tries to intervene to promote the integration of *Diaspo* and reminds the government of the need to take the situation seriously, otherwise it could lead to a rise in intolerance and opposition between these two categories of Burkinabe.

However, this polarity is relativized by the fact that one can find *Diaspo* and *Tenga* within the same family. Similarly, the *Diaspo* do not all belong to the same ethnic group. Each socio-cultural group in Burkina Faso has its section of both *Diaspo* and *Tenga*. Public recognition of this fact could help to avoid a tendency towards rancour and unjustified emphasizing of ethnic aspects. Nevertheless the problems of integration can be solved for those who have decided to consider Côte d'Ivoire only as a country of immigration. Mamadou Zongo of Ouagadougou expresses this very well:

"The difficulties they (*Diaspo*) are confronted with depend on a learning process of integration because in reality the return to the country is an opportunity to find out the difference and thus needs a lot of effort to adapt oneself in many respects (climatic, culinary, cultural, etc.)." (Zongo 2003: 8)

This is why the creation of associations seems to be more intense at the level of schools and the university, where young people often have no orientation. As for socio-economic integration (work, marriage, etc.), the restructuring of social ties creates new relations and social cohesion. It is thus hard to believe that the *Diaspo* represent a permanent social phenomenon. The newcomers will take as an example their predecessors who managed to find a place in society much earlier. It is the administration's task to find a solution for the most frequent difficulties (concerning personal documents, diplomas, etc.) and to initiate opportunities to catalyse the social game to provide for the rest.

Conclusion

In Burkina Faso there is, strictly speaking, no immigration service, but rather an integration service, and even a department for regional cooperation and integration. From an empirical point of view and according to the research carried out for this article it can be estimated that there is at least one *Diaspo* in every Burkinabe family. The feeling of stigmatization of this important and dynamic minority is a phenomenon that should not be underestimated. Many young people returning from Côte d'Ivoire say that the name *Diaspo*, which they accepted earlier with pride, sounds more and more like an insult to them. Therefore, they react by using the term *Tenga* as a synonym of the popular Ivorian term *Gaou* (meaning 'savage', 'uncivilized').

This affects thousands of Burkinabe, most of them young, who are heading for or are destined to play an important role in the country's socio-economic life. The concretization of frustrations that have been restrained for a long time can lead in many cases to an attitude that is critical of social cohesion. The *Tocsin* association has taken many students under its wing and organizes actions in this field to make especially the integration of returning migrants easier. In particular *Tocsin* does not miss any opportunity to emphasize the future role of the young educated elite for Burkina Faso, provided integration is successful.

It is of great importance that the authorities take measures to solve what at the moment can be considered the 'problems of papers' that Burkinabe are confronted with when they were born in Côte d'Ivoire or acquired their documents there. It is important that – on the national level – experiences from the other side of the border will be acknowledged as a richness that can be adapted to local knowledge and that may become an advantage for the future development of Burkina Faso.

REFERENCES

Bassolet, Angèle. 'Sans pays! Langue, exil et self-identitè diasporique'. http://motspluriels.arts.uwa.edu.au/MP2303abo.html (accessed 20 January 2012)

Batenga, Moussa W. 2003. 'Le milieu universitaire de Ouagadougou: L'insertion des étudiants burkinabè venant de la Côte d'Ivoire'. In: Catherine Coquery-Vidrovitch and Issiaka Mandé (eds.). *Etre étranger et migrant en Afrique au XXième siècle. Volume 1*. Paris: Harmattan. 325-338.

Clifford, James. 1994. 'Diaspora', *Cultural Anthropology,* 9(3): 302-338.

Cohen, Robin. 1997. *Global Diasporas. An Introduction.* London: UCL.

Compaoré, Maxime and Pierre Claver Hien (eds.). 2003. *Histoire de Ouagadougou des origines à nos jours.* Ouagadougou: DIST/CNRST.

Coquery-Vidrovitch, Catherine and Mandé Issiaka. 2003. *Etre étranger et migrant en Afrique au xxème siècle.* Paris: Harmattan.

Dufoix, Stéphane. 1999. 'L'objet diaspora en questions', *Cultures & Conflits,* 33/34: 147-163.

---. 2004. *De 'Diaspora' à 'diasporas'. La dynamique d'un nom propre.* Intervention à l'université de Paris I, 6 March 2004. Paper presented at: http://histoire-sociale.univ-paris1.fr/Sem/Dufoix-paris1.pdf (accessed 20 January 2012)

Dufoix, Stéphane. 2004. *Généalogie d'un lieu commun 'Diaspora' et sciences sociales*. http://barthes.ens.fr/clio/revues/AHI/articles/preprints/duf.html (accessed 20 January 2012)

Gnangoran, Yao Bi. 2003. 'La mise sous tutelle de la Haute Volta, actuel Burkina Faso (1932-1944)'. In: Yenouyaba G. Madiéga and Oumarou Nao (eds.). *Burkina Faso. Cent ans d'histoire 1885-1985*. Paris: Karthala: 736-767.

Gueye, Abdoulaye. 2001. *Les intellectuels africains en France. Préface de Babacar Sall*. Paris: Harmattan.

Hall, Stuart. 1990. 'Cultural Identity and Diaspora'. In: Jonathan Rutherford (ed.). *Identity, Community, Culture, Difference*. London: Lawrence & Wishart: 222-237.

Hien, Pierre Claver. 2003. 'Les frontières du Burkina Faso: genèse, typologie et conflits (1885-1985)'. In: Yenouyaba G. Madiéga and Oumarou Nao (eds.). *Burkina Faso. Cent ans d'histoires 1885-1985*. Paris: Karthala: 695-720.

Kaboré, Jean-Marie. 2006. *Concours direct: des manœuvres discriminatoires*. Ouagadougou: Le Pays.

Larousse. 2003. *Petit Larousse illustré (éd.2004)*. Paris: Larousse.

Mandé, Issaka. 1992. *Migrations et développement économique: la main-d'œuvre voltaïque en Côte d'Ivoire de 1947 à 1960*. Paper presented at Conférence de l'Association canadienne des Études africaines.

Mandé, Issaka. 1988. *Les émigrés burkinabè en Côte d'Ivoire dans la tourmente des recompositions identitaires en Afrique*. Québec: Département de sociologie, Université Laval.

Mandé, Issaka, Stéfanson Blandine and Konaté Doulaye (eds.). 2005. *Historiens africains et la mondialisation: actes du 3e congrès international des historiens africains, Bamako, 2001*. Paris: Karthala.

PNUD/BIT. 2005. *Rapport général des travaux du séminaire sur l'intégration*, Ouagadougou: PNUD.

Prévélakis, Georges. 1996. *Les réseaux des diasporas*. Paris: Harmattan.

Ragazzi, Francesco. 2009. 'Governing Diasporas', *International Political Sociology*, 3: 378-397.

Safran, William. 1991. 'Diasporas in Modern Societies: Myths of Homeland and Return', *Diasporas*, 1(1): 83-99.

Schwartz, Alfred. 2000. 'Le conflit foncier entre Krou et Burkinabè à la lumière de "l'institution kroumen"', *Afrique contemporaine*, 193: 56-66.

Skinner, Elliot P. 1974. *The Transformation of Ouagadougou*. Princeton: Princeton University.

Tokpa, Jacques. 2003. 'La contribution de la Haute-Volta à la mise en valeur de la Cote d'Ivoire: La question de la main d'œuvre mossi 1919-1947'. In: Yenouyaba G. Madiéga and Oumarou Nao (eds.). *Burkina Faso. Cent ans d'histoire 1885-1985*. Paris: Karthala: 1385-1404.

Van Hear, Nicholas. 1998. *New Diasporas: The Mass Exodus, Dispersal and Regrouping of Migrant Communities*. London: Routledge.

Zongo, Mamadou. 2003. 'La diaspora burkinabè en Côte d'Ivoire: trajectoire historique, recomposition des dynamiques migratoires, rapport avec le pays d'origine', *Revue Africaine de Sociologie* 2(7): 113-126.

Haalpulaar Migrants' Home Connections
Travel and Communication Circuits

ABDOULAYE KANE

The transnational linkages of Senegal River Valley villages with the outside world are becoming more and more global due to the existence of vital village diasporas in Europe and North America. The great majority of the villages in the Senegal River Valley are connected with village diasporas in different places in Africa (Dakar, Libreville, Ponte Noire), Europe (France, Belgium and Italy) and the United States. This chapter examines the various ways in which these Haalpulaar[1] diasporas around the world continue to maintain strong relations of solidarity with their rural communities through constant transnational practices.

The Haalpulaar are generally involved in a circular type of migration, and even those who brought their families to their host countries continue to keep home in mind. The majority of Haalpulaar are therefore engaged in transnational practices that bring together their host countries and communities of origin. Although practices of money transfers have been well studied, there are a number of social remittances and interventions of migrant networks that are less well known.

---

1 The Haalpulaar are a sedentary Fulani group living in the Senegal River Valley, i.e. the border areas between Senegal and Mauritania. They are Muslims with a very rigid social hierarchy reminiscent of the Indian caste system. For their important role in the dissemination of Islam and the Tijaniyya Sufis, cf. Robinson (1985).

The goal of this chapter is to examine the evolution of the ways in which Haalpulaar migrants in Dakar and abroad have maintained connections with the people they left behind. I will discuss the revolution in communication technologies and how they have dramatically changed the relations of Haalpulaar with their families in the Senegal River Valley villages and small towns. I will argue that Haalpulaar villages have all become 'remotely global' in the sense Piot (1999) uses it in discussing Kabre communities. Haalpulaar villages are all connected to the outside world through small diasporas established in African, European and North American cities. The flows of people, money, information, images and material goods in both directions have a lasting impact on the social life of these villages.

The chapter is divided into three sections. The first section examines the connections between the Senegal River Valley, Dakar and Haapulaar migrants in North America and Europe. The creation of business ventures connecting the three places and the constant travelling between the capital city and the Senegal River Valley villages for a host of reasons are analysed. The second section focuses on the transnational practices of communication between migrants in North America and Europe and their country of origin. The changing nature and content of the communication flows, we shall see, is related to the progressive revolution of communication technologies and their rapid penetration to remotely located areas in Africa. The third section examines the paradoxes of the flow of communications between villages in the Senegal River Valley on the one hand and the Senegal River Valley and its diasporas in Dakar, France and the United States on the other hand. Such communications are instantaneous between the villages and their migrants abroad, while remaining still very slow between the different villages of the Senegal River Valley.

URBAN-RURAL CONNECTIONS AND TRANSNATIONAL BUSINESS VENTURES

Every day hundreds of people take buses, minivans and small cars from Haalpulaar villages to Dakar for various reasons (to pay a visit to relatives, to attend a marriage, to pursue studies, to be treated as a patient, to look for a job, or to take a train or an airplane to foreign countries). In the bus station in Dakar or Pikine, hundreds of Haalpulaar travellers come every morning to board a mini bus or *sept (7) places* (car with seven seats) to go back to their rural homes. The Haalpulaar in Dakar are connected to their rural homes through frequent travel.

There is a continuous flow of people between Dakar and the Senegal River Valley villages. The majority of first-generation migrants in Dakar go back regularly to visit their parents. There are also annual caravans organized by migrants to celebrate *the Maouloud*,[2] the prophet Mohamed's birthday, to attend *Ziarras*[3] for local religious saints, or to spend *Tabaski*[4] or *Korite*[5] with their families. People also travel to their villages during life-cycle events such as funerals, marriages or naming ceremonies.

With the increasing number of means of transportation, the Senegalese capital has become relatively close to the Senegal River Valley villages. Dakar is about 700 km from Thilogne in the middle valley, and it takes the minivans about eight to nine hours to go between the two places. The theoretical separation of cities and villages in Africa does not reflect the fluidity of exchanges and the complex ways in which the two spaces enmesh with each other through travel and connections. There are people like Magueye who restlessly travel between Dakar and their rural home. There are hundreds of Magueyes who are neither villagers nor urbanites, their vital space being in between the two spaces.

---

2 *Maoloud* is a religious feast that celebrates the birthday of the Prophet Mohamed. Two to three days prior to the night of celebration, thousands of minivans and buses leave Dakar to go to Tivaoune, Kaolack, Medina Gounass, Touba and a record number of villages in the Senegal River Valley, where it has become a tradition to celebrate Maoloud with villagers living in Dakar. The villagers in Dakar rent a minivan or bus and spend three to four days in their rural homes.

3 *Ziarra* is a visit to pay respect to religious leaders and saints. In Senegal the followers of the Islamic Sufi orders visit regularly their sheikh or religious guide. They can also make a visit to the tombs of the venerated founders or highly regarded sheikhs of their Sufi order known as Tariqa.

4 *Tabaski* is the religious celebration of Abraham's sacrifice. It is called in Arabic Eid Al Kabir.

5 *Korite* is the religious feast celebrating the end of Ramadan.

Magueye, fifty years old, with three wives and fourteen children, travels more than twenty times a year between Dakar, where he lives with his family, and Thilogne, his village where part of his extended family is still living. I know Magueye personally as he is my neighbor in Golera, a neighborhood of Thilogne. I have travelled several times with him in both directions between Dakar and Thilogne. The last time I travelled with him was in the summer of 2008. He was always looking for an opportunity to travel without paying his ticket. Whenever I come to Dakar, he would come to see me and ask me not to leave him in Dakar. I avoided travelling with him a number of times by telling him I was not going straight to Thilogne. I usually stopped in St. Louis for few days before continuing to Thilogne. But I did travel with him more frequently from Thilogne to Dakar. I asked Magueye why he travelled so restlessly between the two places. He replied that he is 'a people's person. People need me in most of the social events that take place in Thilogne or among Thilognese in Dakar', he continued. It is true that he is often invited by *Torobbe* and *Sebbe* families to perform as a *Ñeeño* during marriage celebrations.[6]

Magueye is from the social corporation of pottery-makers, which belongs to the larger *ÑeeñƁe* social category that includes all social-professional groups and the praise singers. The *ÑeeñƁe* play an important social function during family ceremonies. They usually speak on behalf of the noble families. They act as intermediaries between the grooms' and brides' families by negotiating engagements and marriages. Magueye goes back to his village whenever there is a family ceremony. He goes to present his condolences whenever there is a death in his family or neighborhood. He accompanies returnees from Europe, North America or Central Africa

---

6 The Haalpulaar social structure has three major hierarchical social groups, themselves divided into subgroups. At the top of the social hierarchy are the Rimbe or nobles composed of several endogamous subgroups, namely the Torobbe, the Sebbe, the Subalbe, and the Jawambe. In the middle of the social hierarchy are the Neenbe, comprising mainly manual workers such the Waylube or Blacksmiths, the Lawbe or Woodworkers, the Sakeebe or leather workers, the Mabube or weavers, and praise singers who are known as Awlube or griots. The Neenbe, on top of their usual manual work, also have the social function of serving as social intermediaries between Rimbe families. At the bottom of the social hierarchy are the Maccube, said to be the descendents of slaves.

when they go from Dakar to Thilogne. He also serves as a guide for the returnees in Dakar, helping them make their purchases of gifts in Dakars markets by bargaining on their behalf. The travelling back and forth between Thilogne in Dakar is a business for Magueye, who earns most of his income by participating as a *Ñeeño* in family ceremonies and guiding returning migrants in both Dakar and Thilogne.

Between 1998 and 2003, Magueye ran a money transfer business in collaboration with Bathie, his noble friend in New York City. Magueye developed a close relationship with Bathie after the latter came back from the US to celebrate his marriage in 1990. Magueye guided Bathie in Dakar and helped him buy clothes for his fiancée and close relatives, and he went with him to visit them in Dakar. He advised him about the appropriate gift for each relative they visited. He travelled with him back to Thilogne and helped to organize his marriage ceremony. To thank him for his time and service, Bathie gave Magueye 200,000 CFA Francs ($ 350) and two locally fashionable boubous. Bathie's wife gave him 40,000 CFA Francs ($ 60) and one boubou. Moreover, Magueye received a smaller gift from Bathie's extended family, in total about 350,000 CFA Francs ($ 500).

After he went back to New York, Bathie, who was a trader at that time, started to explore the money transfer business. He contacted Magueye and asked him to serve as his local operator in Dakar. He opened a bank account in a local bank and made a 'procuration' arrangement with Magueye so that the latter could withdraw money from his bank account. Bathie operated wire transfers of large sums of money in New York. As his partner in Dakar where the remittances are sent, Magueye paid out remittances he received from Bathie to recipients on a daily basis.

Magueye and Bathie opened a small office in Grand Yoff, a popular neighborhood in Dakar where Magueye received the faxes that Bathie sent every day containing the list of money transfer recipients. The office had a large desk and three chairs, a fax machine and two telephone booths. The office was used to pay out the money transfers and also acted as a 'telecentre' (callshop) which operates as public telephone booth. The office attracted a lot of Haalpulaar migrants in Dakar and became a *grand place* where people came to share information and talk to other people from their villages.

The transfer money business in Dakar also served Thilogne and its environs, especially the Agnam villages. Magueye hired Amadou to act as a middleman between Dakar and Thilogne. Amadou would carry large sums of money to Thilogne and spend two days paying out money transfers to recipients before coming back to Dakar, where he would spend some three days before returning in another mission. During the four years that the transfer business existed, Amadou was literally in between Thilogne and Dakar. He was known to mini-van, 7 places and bus drivers, shopkeepers and restaurant owners along the road. He was also used by both villagers and migrants in Dakar as a carrier of letters, oral messages, information and goods between the two places.

The money transfer business collapsed in 2003 because there was no formal accounting system following the operations in Dakar and New York. Bathie blamed Magueye for the failure of the business, claiming that Magueye adopted a lifestyle that was beyond his means. He married a third wife, finished constructing his house in Dakar and indulged in outrageous levels of consumption. Magueye's account of the reasons for the bankruptcy of the transfer business was that Bathie stopped paying him and Amadou the usual monthly commissions. He started to withdraw money to pay himself and Amadou. For Magueye the reason of the collapse was that Bathie was arrested in New York and fined $50,000 for selling counterfeit shoes. In order to pay his fine and avoid prison, he sacrificed the transfer business.

What one learns from this story is the interconnectedness between international destinations, the Senegalese capital and the Senegal River Valley villages. There are hundreds of business ventures involving Haalpulaar immigrants in different destinations and the people they left back home. Although trust is a major problem, as the money transfer business described above seems to indicate, this does not prevent Haalpulaar immigrants in global cities from being involved in a variety of business ventures that exploit the opportunities related to the home connections. Diagne, 48 years old, runs an informal freight-forwarding business allowing Haalpulaar immigrants who want to send home machinery, electronic equipment, cars and extra luggage to do so by paying less than freight businesses in French airports or harbors. Ba, forty years old, runs a money transfer business between Paris, Dakar and Thilogne. Contrary to Bathie's money transfer, Ba relies exclusively on family members. His business partner in Dakar is his father, a retired accountant who worked for a local bank in Dakar. In Thilogne, Ba collaborates with his brother, who runs a modern bakery belonging to Ba. Both Diagne's and Ba's business ventures are working perfectly well.

Coming back to the connections between Dakar and the Senegal River Valley villages, one can come to the conclusion that Magueye's case is an extreme one. Few people travel frequently between their village of origin and the Senegalese capital. It is difficult to beat Magueye's record of twenty trips per year between Thilogne and Dakar. However, there are thousands of people involved in this back and forth travel between Dakar and the Senegal River villages. Penda, 54 years old, lives in Dakar with her family. She owns a clothes shop in a local market in Parcelles Assainies and goes to Thilogne about five times a year. She is very influential in her extended family because she attends all family ceremonies, whether they take place in Dakar or in Thilogne. In 2007, she travelled three times to Thilogne in one month. She came first for the marriage of her sister's daughter and two weeks after going back to Dakar was informed that her uncle had fallen seriously ill, so she came back to see him. She left again after three days for Dakar; five days later her uncle passed away. She returned to Thilogne with a group of relatives to present her condolences. They rented a minivan with eighteen seats and travelled by night. After five days Penda went back to Dakar.

When I talked to Penda about these frequent trips to the village, she acknowledged that they are tiring but added that she had no choice but to go back to her rural home for funerals and marriages. For her it is unthinkable to stay in Dakar when there is a happy or unhappy social event in her extended family. She explains:

"When my son and my two daughters were getting married, my relatives from both my mother's and father's side came from Fouta to attend. When I lost my son in Italy in 2003, my relatives from Thilogne rented two minivans to come to present their condolences. What I am doing is just paying back the support and kindness of my relatives to me and my family. I just ask God to continue to give me the strength and the means to accomplish these family obligations. When you have your relatives or neighbors in grief because they have lost their loved ones, it is important to be seen and to share their pain." (Interview with Penda in Parcelles Assainies Unité, 24 July 2008)

Most Haalpulaar men and women in Dakar share Penda's view of how important it is to come back home during the funerals of their extended family members. As she explains, villagers also come to Dakar to give their condolences to their family members living in the city.

Another category of movements back and forth between villages and the city are those made by students. In many villages in the Senegal River Valley there are only elementary and middle schools. Therefore, after finishing school, students have to go to Matam, St. Louis or Dakar to continue their studies. During the academic year, the villages are empty because of the absence of most of the young people. They return at the end of the academic year for the summer holidays, stimulating village life by organizing soccer competitions between neighborhoods of the same village or between villages. They also organize sketches and cultural performances and participate in educating the local population in health and environmental issues.

TRANSNATIONAL PRACTICES OF COMMUNICATION

In the relatively short history of their migration to France, maintaining connections with home has always been very important to the Haalpulaar. In particular, the worldwide technological revolution of the past two decades in the realm of telecommunications has enabled Haapulaar migrants to benefit from the rapid global circulation of information, goods, images and ideas. Having had to rely on letters during the 1960s and 1970s as the only way to communicate with family and friends back in the Senegal River Valley, in the 1990s and 2000s Haalpulaar migrants stated that the increasing availability of cell phones in the West and at home was dramatically changing the frequency and nature of communication between the nodes of their migrant networks. The cheaper rates for cell and satellite phones and cards meant that a migrant in Paris could call home on a regular basis.

One of the obvious ways in which transnational migrants maintain connections with home is through the establishment of communication channels between themselves and the people they left in their home communities (Rouse 1991: 13; Clifford 1997: 246-247). The accessibility of cell phones in even the most remote areas of the globe makes contacting one's relatives and friends at home an integral part of the migration experience. Such means of communication have linked individuals and groups in post-industrial metropolises with their counterparts in remote localities that once quenched the thirsty imaginations of anthropologists in the self-deluded search of the pristinely exotic. One personal story will bring home the way in which the cell phones have revolutionized the way we communicate across long distances.

During the summer of 2003, I was travelling with my family between Dakar, the capital of Senegal, and Thilogne, my home town situated in the Senegal River Valley. My wife, who had arrived from France a week earlier, was equipped with a cell phone she purchased in Dakar that she used to inform her mother, who lives in Compiegne, a small city north of Paris, of our plans to travel overland to my village. We left Dakar in the early hours of the morning hoping to arrive in Thilogne before sunset. We did not know, however, that the road on which we were travelling had been cut by heavy rains, about 25 km away from my home town. Our arrival at the point where the road was cut left us at a loss over what to do, especially as my wife realized that she had no credit on her cell phone with which to call and alert my family of our situation. After about half an hour, my wife's cell phone started ringing. It was my mother-in-law calling from the comfort of her living room in Compiegne informing us of an announcement she heard on a Senegalese radio station, to which migrants in France can listen to via satellite, about the condition of the road from Dakar to Thilogne. Having told her we were standing right at the point at which the road was cut, we asked her to call my parents in Thilogne and have them call my wife's phone. Soon afterwards the phone rang, and in half an hour a neighbor of my parents had come in his car to pick us up.[7]

What do we learn from this story? It is clear that the new technologies, in this case satellite radios and cell phones, have created very complex (in some cases absurd) circuits of communication in which distance is not always the most relevant factor determining the ability to contact someone living in another village or town. Our proximity to Thilogne did not obviate the need for the intermediary role played by my mother-in-law in France between us and my parents. In demonstrating on the one hand the closeness with which members of the diaspora can participate in events back home, and on the other the relative scarcity of access to means of communication that still exist in rural Senegal, this experience struck me as a reminder both

---

7   Based on the author's experience in August 2003.

of how far we have come and how far we still have to go in connecting the Senegal River Valley with the rest of the world.

During my fieldwork in New York, Cincinnati, Memphis and in France, I witnessed first-hand the daily phone calls of my informants. Besides husbands and fathers calling their wives and children, I was interested in phone calls to local actors in Haalpulaar films, which are widely watched by Haalpulaar migrants as one of the preferred forms of entertainment after work. The conversation of Issa with a local actor whom he has never met but who has become a close friend visiting his family back home at his request is a case in point of how long-distance phone calls are central not only to maintaining connections with family members, but also to establishing new relationships and friendships across vast distances.

In their living room on the third floor in an old building in Fulton Street, Brooklyn New York, Issa, 48 years, greeted me with a nod and continued his telephone conversation with one of the rising stars of Haalpulaar movies: Yacine.
'Are you with my sister? Did they treat you well?'
'Give the telephone to my sister. I want to talk to her.'
'Aminata, go and get from Pape, the shopkeeper, everything you need for the kottungu, I will send the money at the end of the week. Did you buy the sheep for the dinner? Make sure everything is well done. You know Yacine is really a great friend.'
After half an hour of discussion, Issa started passing the telephone around, asking his friends to talk to the local actress who had come to visit his home in Thilogne. Sidy, one of Issa's friend, burst out from time to time: ' Thiom! walay ka daanaan' - 'You have what none of your age group members have.'
After the telephone had been passed around, Issa asked me to talk to Yacine. Although I did not know her, I politely took the telephone and did like everybody else:
'Allo, this is Abdoulaye, a friend of Issa! Is it right that you are in Thilogne?'
'Yes, I am in your very welcoming village. Everybody is nice to me', she replied.
Not knowing what else to say, I continued:
'I like your movies. Every time I watch them I want to go back home.'
'Thank you, I appreciate your support. I really cannot pay my fans in America. People are calling me, sending money, and many of you when you come back would do everything to come and see me', she said.
'Thank you, I am passing the telephone to Issa', I replied.

Issa continued the conversation for another ten minutes before hanging up the telephone and starting to greet me properly. He has never met Yacine in person but has watched all her movies and started to call her in 2002. Since then they have become good friends, and he calls her very frequently to see how she is doing. Issa admitted to me that he and many other Haalpulaar migrants send her money because they want to support her, knowing that she does not get much from her movies. The irony is that Yacine is better known in the diaspora, where her movies are circulating and valued by nostalgic and homesick Haalpulaar migrants, than in Senegal, where until recently locally made movies circulated in limited circles. It is Haalpulaar migrants who are returning home who are bringing these movies back to their rural homes and introducing them to the local audience.

The telephone encounter between Issa and Yacine is a metaphor of the increasing frequency and volume of the communication between Haalpulaar in the diaspora and their home communities. The telephone has become a central object in Haalpulaar migrants' lives. It has become the most important tool in achieving the goal of keeping home in mind. It is through telephone conversations that transnational social spaces are realized (Linda Bash 1994; Appadurai 1996; Vertovec 2009). Through telephone conversations, Haalpulaar migrants remind villagers of their presence during both happy and unhappy events, congratulating new couples, comforting people facing illnesses, presenting condolences to those who have lost their loved ones, consulting marabouts and traditional healers for illness and misfortune, and carrying out their social obligations towards their families and communities while living and working in global cities.

In 2006, while undertaking research in Thilogne, I attended a funeral in the Ndongo compound. Siley, the oldest son of the deceased, could not talk to people who were coming to present their condolences because he was busy on the phone. He asked his uncle to meet people and accept their condolences on his behalf. Siley's cell phone was ringing constantly. People were calling him from around the world to present their condolences. He counted more than a hundred calls the first day and another sixty to seventy calls the second day. He said he felt really humbled that people in the diaspora remembered him and his family during this difficult time. He said he talked to people he had not seen or heard from for thirty years. Most of the callers sent money to the family to take care of the funeral expenses. This practice has become the norm because parents left in the Senegal River

Valley make sure that their sons and daughters living abroad are informed about the deaths of close relatives, neighbors and friends so that they can call to present their condolences and send money to support the grieving family. Also in the diaspora news of deaths circulates rapidly between Haalpulaar around the world, and migrants who have lost a loved one receive numerous phone calls from their diaspora community, as Siley did in his home village.

Other moments of intense communication between migrants and their families in the Senegalese River Valley are celebrations of religious holidays. It is often the people left behind who initiate the communication and ask for help to face the important expenses of religious celebrations. They ask for money to pay for fabrics and tailors to make sure that everyone in the household has new clothes for the occasion. Women ask for money to bring their jewelry to blacksmiths to make them shiny. Families also need cash to pay the contributions to age-group clubs, which use the money to entertain their members, as well as at the end of Ramadan (Julde Korka) and the festival of Abraham's sacrifice (Eid Adha). During these occasions migrants call their parents, uncles and aunts to ask forgiveness and receive blessings.

The celebration of the Prophet Mohammad's birthday, known as Maoloud, stands out as a moment of intense communication between Haalpulaar migrants and their home communities. Haalpulaar migrants from Thilogne are organized around neighborhood associations which sponsor the religious activities related to the Maoloud. They send money to buy a cow to be killed to feed the neighborhood and its guests, most of whom came to sing the prophet praise songs, recite the Koran, or give sermons during the whole night of celebrations.

The communications between Haalpulaar in France and in the United States and the people left in their villages is most often realized via satellite. One of the 'hot' commodities used by Haalpulaar migrants in the United States is the satellite calling card. The companies that offer satellite communication services have been targeting African immigrants in both Europe and the United States by designing cards with a map of Africa and pictures related to the continent. 2 Africa, 247 Africa, African Party, African Dream, African Line, Bongo Africa, African Cousin, Afri World, Africa Select, etc. are some of the names given to satellite phone cards offered by INMARSAT, SATWEST, ITECH TELECOM, GLOBAL PAPA, etc.

Calling cards that work via satellite connections are the most frequently used systems of communication. Along Fulton Street in Brooklyn there are several small shops owned by Haalpulaar and Fulani Guineans that sell calling cards. Also among the Haalpulaar there are migrants who buy calling cards wholesale and resell them by going from door to door along Fulton Street. These sellers are also involved in retailing Haalpulaar movies, as well as a variety of ethnic products, from clothes and shoes to hats and prayers beads. The situation in the United States is very similar to France, where Haalpulaar usually buy calling cards from small retailers in the foyers. The foyer, apart from being a vertical village, is also a place of community business where blacksmiths, tailors, hairdressers and small vendors of ethnic products sell by following the rules of African social life, with bargaining, credit and the usual social hierarchies based on age, gender and belonging to social corporations.

The widespread use of the telephone in communications between the migrants and their home villages is a very recent phenomenon. Until the end of the 1980s, there were only a few landlines in the villages of the Senegal River Valley. Electricity came to the villages of the Valley situated along National Road No. 2 between 1988 and 2000. At the end of the 1990s thousands of households were linked up to the electricity and telephone networks. The number of landlines was four in the whole village of Thilogne in 1988. The number of landlines in the same village jumped to 178 in 2003. For someone like myself, who had an uncle who served as manager of the local post office in Thilogne during the 1970s and early 1980s, this development is a big revolution.

I remember the time when the public was at the post office and how people who wanted to place calls to Dakar had to wait for four to six hours without any guarantee that their calls would get through. In my uncle's living room, we could hear his loud voice: 'Allo! Allo Dakar! Allo! Allo Dakar!' After several tries, he would often tell the customers that they needed to come back in the late afternoon or very early in the morning and try again. The village could spend days and sometimes weeks without any telephone signal.

Now times have changed. The great majority of households have electricity and a landline telephone in their compound. However, there is a correlation between the households that have telephone lines and the migrations of their members. It is migrants who often made sure their rural houses have a telephone to make communication with home more frequent. They are the ones who pay the connection fees and who also take care of the telephone bills.

Since the beginning of 2000, another revolution has been sweeping the Senegal River Valley villages with the invasion of cell phones. Everybody, young boys and girls, adult men and women, and even a few old people walk around with their little gadget in their hands, hanging from their necks or put in their pockets or handbags. When I debarked in Thilogne in 2008 with an old Nokia, everybody thought I was joking. They could not believe that the university professor I am had such low self-esteem to carry such an old-fashioned cell phone. The young people were carrying very sophisticated cell phones like Blackberries, Sidekicks and cell phones with two lines. They obtain their cell phones from people in the diaspora or from Mauritanian black markets in Kaedi, Rosso and Nouakchott.

One of the common uses of the cell phone is 'bipping', which consists in calling a number and letting it ring only once in the hope that at the other end a husband, a father, a daughter, a wife or a friend will call back and therefore take over the costs of the call. Before proceeding to an analysis of the significance of this rapid increase in the means and volume of communications between the Haalpulaar and their rural communities, I would like to return briefly to the long history and evolution of communications between those who went away and those who remained behind in the Senegal River Valley.

The methods Haalpulaar migrants have used to communicate with home have gone through various stages, and have depended on the means available to particular migrants in their host communities. Until the end of the 1970s, the letter was the only means of communication that Haalpulaar migrants and their families at home could use to keep in touch. Very often even postal services could not be relied upon, and letters were carried by people traveling between home villages and cities.

Moussa, 57 years old, arrived in France in 1971. He remembers when the letter was the only way to communicate with his family in the Senegal River Valley. He would enclose the letters with the money he was sending to his parents, siblings and other relatives every month. The content of his letters consisted of greetings, inquiries about people's health and instructions on how the money ought to be distributed. Moussa showed me a pile of the letters he had received in return from family members and friends, which were often filled with various demands for help with household expenses, home construction, school fees, medical bills and family ceremonies.

Some migrants have preferred to send home tapes they have recorded, as a means of both communication and entertainment. In addition, migrants going back and forth between Senegal and France would make the rounds to compounds where the families of fellow migrants resided to record the voices of the latter's wives and kids, which they would play for the absent husband or father upon returning to their host community. Tape recorders served as valuable gifts to fiancés and wives, who used them to entertain friends and guests. By the end of the 1980s, however, video cameras added a whole new dimension to the ties linking the diaspora with home. Nowadays, images of life in the Senegal River Valley are present in the foyers of Paris.

A few Haalpulaar migrants even use Youtube accounts to post videos recorded while they were visiting their villages. This creates the exciting possibility to give migrants from the same village but living in different countries simultaneous access to footage from home, which is made all the sweeter if the footage includes a naming ceremony or a marriage. The internet in general plays a role in making easier the longstanding practice of Haalpulaar migrants sending home edited video footage of their lives in France.

The new information technologies have compressed time and space and made communication with home more instantaneous and frequent for Haalpulaar migrants. The practices of transnationalism have been facilitated by the revolution in telecommunications, with the rapid expansion of landlines and cellular phones in the Senegal River Valley. In the 1970s, the landlines were limited to the post offices in major villages. In the 1980s, privileged families of politicians and wealthy business owners were able to have landline telephone connections in their houses. The rapid expansion of landline connections started in the 1990s with the electrification of the villages along the National Road No. 2 and the determination of migrants abroad to have landline telephones installed in their newly built concrete houses. A decade later, in the middle of the 2000s, cell phones have become ubiquitous and accessible to almost all, men and women, young and old, rich and poor alike. Here again, migrants are at the forefront of the cellular revolution because they are the ones who often came back with cell phones as gifts for their family members and friends.

The use of telephones, both landlines and cell phones, was until recently oriented to the satisfaction of maintaining connections between migrants abroad and their home communities in the Senegal River Valley. At the local level, few people used the cell phone as tool of communication between families scattered in several villages. This created paradoxes in the circulation of information between different villages and their diasporas around the world. The information circulated with greater fluidity between a local village and its diaspora in France or the United States than between two nearby rural communities. The following section explores these paradoxes by describing a case study of the way in which information about a death went from the village where the death had occurred to Cincinnati before coming back to Dakar and only then to the village from which the deceased women originated.

THE STRANGE CIRCUITS OF COMMUNICATION: WHEN MIGRANTS LIVING ABROAD ARE BETTER INFORMED ABOUT HOME THAN THE VILLAGERS

The telephone has become the most used medium of communication between migrants in the United States and the people they left behind. The telephone has in many ways redefined the relationships that Haalpulaar migrants have with their families and communities in the Senegal River Valley. The men who left their families behind are now able to monitor on a daily basis what is going on in their family lives, giving them the ability to discipline their children, dictate decisions to their wives and negotiate credit with shopkeepers.

At the same time, the telephone has facilitated the fluidity of information between the migrants and their home villages. The village's news does not take long to reach the migrants' communities abroad. News of a death, for example, can reach family members in France and the United States before it reaches family members in Dakar or in some remote areas of the Senegal River Valley, which could be just fifty miles away from the place where the news originated. In the summer of 2002, we followed a fascinating case of how the news of a death circulated from a village to the outside world.

Diey and her cousin were travelling from Thilogne to Ndiafane, a small village next to the Senegal River, where her sister was married to a migrant who was in New York City at that time. They travelled from Thilogne to Galoya by car, then they rented a traditional boat to go to Ndiafane. Unfortunately the boat sunk in the middle of the river and none of them knew how to swim. The boat owner was not able to save them. The news of what had happened reached Ndiafane, and an expedition of young men was able to fetch the bodies in the early evening, and Diey's sister identified her and her cousin. She immediately called her husband in New York City. Her husband called Diey's brother in Cincinnati, who in turn made several phone calls to Dakar to his immediate family members.

People in Thilogne, which was just fifty miles away from Ndiafane, did not know what had happened until the next morning, when they started to receive phone calls from the United States, France and Dakar, places in which the news was circulating from one migrant community to the next through family, neighborhood and friendship networks. Everybody in Thilogne was surprised that they got the news the last. (Interview with Thiam in Thilogne, August 2002)

This story shows the complexity of how information circulates in an era of globalization. What is remarkable is the fluidity of information originating from home to different diasporic communities. The lack of fluid communication between rural places in Senegal separated by only short distances is also striking. However, the use of cell phones is rapidly changing the way Haalpulaar villages communicate with each other. There has been an exponential rise in the number of people owning cell phones in the Senegal River Valley, making communication between villages more fluid than in even the very recent past. Another development worth mentioning here is the appearance of community radios in Pete, Thilogne, Ourosogui and Matam, which reach Haalpulaar villages on the other side of the border in Mauritania or Mali and have contributed fundamentally to increasing the channels of communication between remote areas and the more accessible areas along National Road No. 2 to the Senegalese Capital. Now news of births, marriages and deaths is publicized by the community radios, making it accessible to all listeners across the Senegal River Valley.

Conclusion

The anthropology of transnational migration, with its associated global flows of money, images and ideas, provides a necessary framework for understanding the relations that Haalpulaar migrants maintain with their rural homes. The strength and spontaneity of the connection between migrants and the people they have left behind questions the relevance of the role that physical proximity plays in migrant networks. Nowadays, migrants and villagers create and share social spaces and social fields every day, and their relationships are not constrained by physical distance or the existence of political boundaries (Bash and Blanc 1996).

This chapter has demonstrated how travel and the use of new communication technologies have made the connections between Haalpulaar migrants in Dakar and abroad and their rural communities more instantaneous and fluid. The connection between migrants in Dakar and their rural homes was often made possible through restless travel between two places by a variety of people for a variety of reasons. Various business ventures initiated in the Haalpulaar diaspora abroad contribute to the increased mobility between Dakar and the Senegal River Valley villages. The connections between rural and urban areas challenge any notion of the two places as separate entities. The continuous flow of people between the two areas makes it more and more difficult to draw boundaries between them.

The connections between Haalpulaar migrants living abroad and their rural homes are often kept up through daily communications, which paradoxically operate along local-global axes rather than local-local or local-national axes. The result is that migrants living abroad are often better informed of what is going on in their home villages than their family members in Dakar or in other neighbouring villages of the Senegal River Valley, as shown by the example of how information about the deaths of Diey and her cousin was circulated.

REFERENCES

Appadurai, Arjun (ed.) 2001. *Globalization*. Durham: Duke University.
Appadurai, Arjun. 1996. *Modernity at Large: Cultural Dimensions of Globalization*. Minneapolis: University of Minnesota.
Basch, Linda G., Nina Glick-Schiller and Cristina Szanton Blanc. 1994. *Nations Unbound: Transnational Projects, Postcolonial Predicaments, and Deterritorialized Nation-States*. Langhorne: Gordon and Breach.
Daffé, Gaye. 2008. 'Les transferts d'argent des migrants sénégalais.' In: Momar Coumba Diop (ed.). *Le Senegal des migrations: Mobilité, identité et societés*. Paris: Karthala: 105-131.
D'Alisera, JoAnn. 2004. *An Imagined Geography: Sierra Leonean Muslims in America*. Philadelphia: University of Pennsylvania.
Daum, Christophe. 1992. *L'immigration ouest-africaines en France: une dynamique nouvelle dans la vallée du fleuve Sénégal?* Paris: Panos.
---. 1993. 'Quand les immigrés construisent leurs pays', *Homme et Migrations*, 1165: 13-17.
---. 1998. *Les associations de Maliens en France: Migration, développement et citoyenneté*. Paris: Karthala.
Faist, Thomas. 2008. 'Transnationality in North and South: Concept, Methodology and Venues for Resarch'. In: Remus Gabriel Anghel, Eva Gerharz, Gilberto Rescher and Monika Salzbrunn (eds.). *The Making of World Society. Perspectives from Transnational Research*. Bielefeld: transcript: 25-50.
Kane, Abdoulaye. 2005. 'Les diasporas africaines et la mondialisation', *Horizons Maghrébins*, 53: 54-61.
---. 2000. 'Diasporas villageoises et développement local en Afrique: le cas de Thilogne Association Développement', *Hommes et Migrations*, 1229: 96-107.
Lambert, Michael. 2002. *Longing for Exile: Migration and the Making of a Translocal Community in Senegal (West Africa)*. Portsmouth: Heinemann.
Levitt, Peggy. 2000. *The Transnational Villagers*. Berkeley: University of California.
Manuh, Takyiwaa (ed.). 2005. *At Home in the World: International Migration and Development in Contemporary Ghana and West Africa*. Accra: Sub Saharan Publishers.

McGaffey, Janet and Rémy Bazenguissa-Ganga. 2000. *Congo-Paris: Transnational Traders on the Margins of the Law*. Bloomington: Indiana University.

Mazzucato, Valentina. 2008. 'Transnational Reciprocity: Ghanaian Migrants and the Care of their Parents back Home'. In: Erdmute Alber, Sjaak van der Geest and Susan Reynolds Whyte (eds.). *Generations in Africa*. Berlin: Lit: 91-108.

Piot, Charles. 1999. *Remotely Global: Village Modernity in West Africa*. Chicago: University of Chicago.

Quiminal, Cathérine. 1991. *Gens d'ici, gens d'ailleurs: migration Soninké et transformation villageoise*. Paris: Christian.

Robinson, David. 1985. *The Holy War of Umar Tal: the Western Sudan in the Mid-Nineteenth Century*. Oxford: Clarendon.

Rouse, Roger. 1991. 'Mexican Migration and the Social Space of Postmodernism', *Diaspora*, 1(1): 8-23.

Schmitz, Jean. 2007. 'Des migrants aux "notables" urbains: les communautés transnationales des gens du fleuve Sénégal (Sénégal/Mali/Mauritanie)'. In: Elisabeth Boesen and Laurence Marfaing (eds.). *Les nouveaux urbains dans l'espace Sahara-Sahel: Un cosmopolitisme par le bas*. Paris: Karthala-ZMO.

Stoller, Paul. 2002. *Money Has No Smell: The Africanization of New York City*. Chicago: University of Chicago.

Tall, Serigne Mansour. 2005. 'The Remittances of Senegalese Migrants: a Tool for development?' In: Takwiah Manuh (ed.). *At Home in the World: International Migration and Development in Contemporary Ghana and West Africa*. Accra: Sub Saharan Publishers: 153-170.

Timera, Mahamet. 1996. *Les Soninké en France: D'une histoire à une autre*. Paris: Karthala.

---. 2002. 'Social Trajectory of Sahalian Youth in France'. In: Deborah Bryceson, and Ulla Vuorela (eds.). *Transnational Family: New European Frontiers and Global Networks*. London: Berg: 147-154.

Epilogue

Images and Spaces

KRISTIN KASTNER

As elaborated in the previous chapters, different rhythms of movement and forms of mobility are intrinsic to urban life-worlds. Movement and mobility encompass migration, displacement and accelerated social mobility and have been appropriated as multifaceted strategies of urban survival and accumulation, but also of control (Simone 2003). African cities show remarkable growth rates and are highly attractive for nearly half the continent's population, despite their harsh living conditions. However, the social realities of the residents and their aspirations, interactions and trajectories are vastly unknown to scholars and policy-makers (Landau 2010: 170). This book aims to make a contribution to reducing this asymmetry by analysing urban life-worlds in motion as described from the perspectives of their protagonists.

When dealing with different types of mobility, contradictory forms like immobility and forced mobility should be considered as well. Thus, the eviction of squatters in Nigerian cities which forces the inhabitants to look for new homes (Nwaka) or the forced return of the *Diaspo* from Côte d'Ivoire back to Burkina Faso due to Ivorian nationalist politics (Kibora) shape urban life-worlds as much as more voluntary forms of mobility. These forms include the frequent journeys of Haalpulaar between the Senegal River Valley villages and the capital of Dakar (Kane) and the *wanderlust* that entices young Tuareg traders – both women and men – to travel from Niger to Nigerian cities (Musch).

Physical mobility and migration go along with the hope for social mobility as a driving force, which is most obvious in the case of Cameroonian scammers (Frei) and youth (Tazanu), Senegalese migrant women (Gemmeke) and Ghanaian street hawkers (Klaeger).

These different forms of movement and mobility have been considerably facilitated and accelerated by the introduction and continuing appropriation of new media in Africa. They have created complex transnational circuits of communication and flows of images, ideas, goods and money between rural and urban areas, as well as to and from cities in other African countries, Europe and the United States. Thus, the ever-growing urban centres in Africa have become important nodes of ties ranging from rural regions to so-called global destinations. In this way, migrants and mobile people themselves become conduits of information, money and values and, as go-betweens, tie home villages and local communities to their city of residence and urban centres around the world, as Landau points out (2010: 181).

The present contributions on urban life-worlds in motion remind me of my own research with undocumented Nigerian migrants in Morocco and Spain and their ways of moving in and between cities, their ways of perceiving them and of dealing with their mostly involuntary stay before taking the next step on their long journey to Europe.

The migrants' transitional lives between hidden movements, times of immobility and forced mobility due to deportation reveal some crucial aspects of what being mobile in and between urban spaces means. Taking the restriction on mobility and the negation of free movement as a starting point for approaching issues of mobility may be a rewarding step to gaining better insight into the phenomena of movement and mobility.

Since Nigerian migrants lack official documents, they are forced to move as inconspicuously as possible. On their strenuous way from Nigeria overland to Europe they take pick-ups and must even walk long distances in order to cross the Algerian Sahara and reach Morocco. When travelling to the cities of Rabat or Tangier in the very north of Morocco, they often do so by hiding in or under trains. From these cities they plan the crossing of one of the borders between Morocco and Spain, between Africa and Europe.

Their clandestine movements also leave traces in the migrants' vocabulary, which has partly been created on the road. The notions of *beating* and *staying trankil* describe their particular ways of moving and staying still whilst trying to avoid contacts with authorities that would most probably lead to deportation to the neighbouring border zones. Nigerians call cities where life is stressful because of the constant fear of deportation *hot* places. The port city of Tangier, just seventeen kilometres from the Spanish coast, is commonly known by Nigerian migrants to be very *hot* because of the high police presence. Conversely, *cool* places in Morocco and later on in Europe allow a 'rest of mind' thanks to relatively free movement. This may be the case in bigger cities like Rabat and Casablanca. On the other hand, in Tangier migrants try to be as invisible as possible and live in secret *coded houses*, which they only leave at dusk. When moving in the city, they choose routes and detours that differ from those taken by the locals. Moreover, Nigerian migrants adopt various roles as tourists, students or pregnant women in order to pass as 'normal' citizens and to avoid police harassment. In sum, the life-worlds of Nigerian migrants are shaped by various forms and rhythms of (im)mobility and by the migrants' (re)actions when confronted with them.

Nigerian migrants in Morocco have created alternative social spaces in the urban realm as a reaction to the difficulties related to their presence in the public sphere. By appropriating the rooftops as meeting points – normally used by the local population exclusively for drying clothes and putting up a satellite dish – they adopt new spaces for gathering together, doing business and preparing for the next step on their journey to Europe.

In many cases, the migrants are forced to remain in Morocco much longer than expected, and their involuntary stay may last for several years before they finally succeed in crossing one of the European borders. While living in this state of immobility without a clear endpoint in sight, images and dreams about European cities evolve: the harsher their life-world, the more intense and colourful becomes the European dream.

Imagination is intimately tied to people's expectations, regardless of whether they are real travellers or whether they travel in their imagination (Malaquais 2006: 17). Although physically present in their cities, they live elsewhere in their minds. It is the very immobility – when 'things are not moving', as one of Frei's interlocutors put it (this volume) – and the impossibility of leaving their place that nourish ideas and ideals about mobility (Malaquais 2004: 4). Thus, the *imaginaire* as a social practice (Appadurai 1996: 31) is constitutive of daily life, and the 'imagined foreign worlds' (Gardner 1993: 1) become symbols and metaphors far beyond mere geographical references. Following Vigh, it is 'through the social imaginary that we locate ourselves in the word, position ourselves in relation to others and seek to grasp that sphere of our existence which we have not yet experienced but which we act towards in anticipation' (Vigh 2008: 20). Imagination has indeed strong real(istic) features, as we can observe in most of the contributions in this volume. Given the volatility of the population, which, as a consequence, leads to relatively thin social networks and low levels of trust between ethnic and national groups, as well as within one and the same group (Landau 2010: 175), I argue that imaginations are crucial for human life-worlds and that their force to move mountains helps city dwellers not only to endure the daily struggle for survival but to go far beyond it.

Cities or places within the city mean different things to different people – a statement that holds true for different groups of city dwellers, as well as for researchers. Whilst Nwaka stresses the urban poor and their daily hardship in Nigeria's informal cities, the same Nigerian cities may be the favourite 'modern' destinations of the young Tuareg traders described by Musch. Thus, on the one hand, images of Nigerian cities are related to poverty, informal arrangements, slums and forced mobility due to the evictions from informal settlements by state officials; on the other hand, Nigerian cities are symbols of urban modernity for those traders and migrants of choice whose journeys and trading with 'modern' and 'urban' goods make them feel connected to the wider globalized world. It is not only in the Cameroonian city of Molyko described by Tazanu that the same urban space generates different meanings and experiences depending on whether or not one is a migrant. Although the two groups share the same space, they do so in different ways and according to their means. And in Dakar's popular neighbourhoods like Pikine, Grand Yoff or Parcelles Assainies, some of those *diskettes* and *marabouts* described by Gemmeke may come across the frequent travellers in Kane's contribution.

In the case of Nigerian transmigrants who consider Tangier a mere stepping stone on their way to Europe, the difference between being a clandestine Nigerian migrant or a Moroccan local is even more striking. Either they use completely different urban spaces, or they share similar realms but during different times of the day.

Mobile people are, in many cases, trespassers of various kinds: they cross boundaries within the city and, by frequently going back and forth between it and their villages, they blur the boundaries between the rural and urban life-worlds. Thus, as Kane stresses in this volume, 'the theoretical separation of cities and villages in Africa does not reflect the fluidity of exchanges and the complex ways the two spaces enmesh into each other through travel and connection'. Musch follows the same line of reasoning when he argues that the rural and urban should not be perceived as opposites, 'but as components of a social and geographical network'. These flows of people and information of various kinds, of goods and money, are multi-directional: they result in the interconnectedness of formerly remote villages with the global world, as well as in the introduction of rural practices in the urban space. *Rurbanization* denotes a phenomenon where city dwellers adopt agricultural activities in urban and peri-urban areas, which grants them more autonomy in their daily struggle for well-being or mere survival.

Apart from transgressing physical boundaries, mobile people also overstep social and moral ones. Changes in role and social status are often displayed on one's body, which becomes a marker of distinction and conspicuous consumption. Thus, Cameroonian *bushfallers* (migrants who come back home for visits) and scammers adopt a distinctive habitus that renders them most visible in the urban space. Their bodies look 'fresh', as described by Tazanu, and this expression not only refers to the relatively clear skin of recently arrived migrants, but to a whole set of attitudes: By showing off, wearing trendy clothes and accessories or riding flashy cars, they distinguish themselves from those who – at least physically – have not left the city. The *Diaspo* in Ouagadougou also distinguish themselves from those compatriots who have no biographical connections to Côte d'Ivoire and consciously maintain this gap by wearing distinctive clothes or by listening to music from Abidjan.

However, *bushfallers* and *scammers* are not exclusively admired for displaying their success, and the *Diaspo* often feel like strangers in their country of origin. Movement and mobility thus create not only deterritorialized realms and transnational social spaces, but also locally embedded conflicts about contested values. Tazanu puts it in a nutshell by characterizing the urban life-world as 'a playground where success and disenchantment clash and are fuelled by the realities of migration and the visible material success that comes with migrating' (this volume).

Conversely, migrant *marabouts* in Dakar choose to maintain a rural habitus (Gemmeke). By doing so, they provide a connection to the countryside through language, dress and various artifacts that form a source of power and identity. In this context, the countryside is associated with the 'pure' and 'real' as opposed to life in Dakar, which is linked to the emergence of new and 'urban' problems, especially for female clients. These examples suggest that life-worlds also move because of the '*emotive* engagement' of the people involved, as emphasized by Klaeger (this volume). Thus, *hot* and *cool* cities always depend on the perspectives and situations of those who are in motion.

By looking at the different life-worlds in motion presented in this volume, different modes and levels in the authors' uses of the notion 'life-world' are noticeable. Following Edmund Husserl (1986 [1907]) and, more recently, Schütz and Luckmann (1975), who defined *Lebenswelt* as the world of immediate lived experiences, our intention was to collect a range of life-worlds in and beyond cities in Africa and to approach the impressive spectrum of urban life-worlds between creativity and despair. As a framing approach for the contributions in this book, we therefore chose a phenomenological perspective that seeks detailed descriptions of how people immediately experience space, time and the world in which they live (Jackson 1996: 12). With this volume we want to trace those phenomena that are constitutive of *cityness*, a word coined by Simone (2010), a term that captures 'those elements of city life that cannot be captured, least of all by the organizing categories of modern social science' (Lemert 2009: x). As a result, we understand *cityness* and *urban life-worlds* as complementary terms. Both try to capture surprises and contradictions and emphasize local ways of living and people's life-worlds instead of the abstract planned city per se. This approach acknowledges that cities in Africa are 'constantly changing, evolving, and mutating entities that resist efforts seeking to capture their essence, to categorize them in accordance with pre-established classification schemes, or freeze them into rigid molds' (Murray – Myers 2006: xiii).

Consequently, we consider it more appropriate to stress relationships, connections and linkages than to identify and measure attributes (ibid.).

Most of the present authors do not deal with the notion of 'life-world' in theoretical terms. This tendency reflects the current state of the art, where the use of 'life-world' points to a rather vague and general term to describe common features of human life. Nevertheless, the encompassing concept of 'life-world' holds the potential for contributing to an emerging field of research, which may concede a new liberty in investigating urban phenomena. To grasp the life-worlds of urban dwellers in a phenomenological sense allows the integration of new forms and levels of research. Urban life, its different rhythms and directions can be captured by additionally making use of methods developed by the field of sensorial anthropology. Participant observation could be complemented by perception-orientated methods and studies into soundscapes (Pink 2008; Shine 2010). Noises and smells, as well as alternative portraits of the city created by rumours, images and imaginations, are constitutive of city dwellers' life-worlds and reveal crucial aspects of the dynamic, shifting and at the same time locally embedded realities of urban dwellers.

Phenomenological approaches can grasp what is beyond surface appearances. Thus, following Simone (2004a), it is people, not pipes, that matter most. The reality of urban life-worlds replaces *the* city as the object of study. I suggest that this perspective challenges the problematic practices of applying analytical and policy tools drawn mostly from European and North American experiences to manage cities and their residents, as criticised by Simone (2004b). Focussing on life-worlds contributes to a better understanding of urban realities in Africa, which are still only partly known.

References

Appadurai, Arjun. 1996. *Modernity at Large: Cultural Dimensions of Globalization*. Minneapolis: University of Minnesota.

Gardner, Katy. 1993. 'Desh-Bidesh: Sylheti Images of Home and Away', *Man*, 28(1): 1-15.

Husserl, Edmund. 1986 (1907). *Die Idee der Phänomenologie: Fünf Vorlesungen*. Edited and introduced by Paul Jannsen. Hamburg: Meiner.

Jackson, Michael. 1996. 'Introduction'. In: Michael Jackson (ed.). *Things as They Are: New Directions in Phenomenological Anthropology*. Bloomington: Indiana University: 1-50.

Landau, Loren B. 2010. 'Inclusion on Shifting Sands: Rethinking Mobility and Belonging in African Cities'. In: Caroline Wanjiku Kihato *et al.* (eds.). *Urban Diversity. Space, Culture, and Inclusive Pluralism in Cities Worldwide*. Washington D.C.: Woodrow Wilson Center: 169-186.

Lemert, Charles. 2009. 'Foreword'. In: AbdouMaliq Simone. 2010. *City Life from Jakarta to Dakar*. New York: Routledge: ix-xii.

Malaquais, Dominique. 2006. 'Villes flux: imaginaires de l'urbain en Afrique aujourd'hui', *Cosmopolis: de la ville, de l'Afrique et du monde*, 100: 17-37.

---. 2004. 'Douala / Johannesburg / New York: Cityscapes Imagined', *Dark Roast Occasional Paper Series*, 20: 1-21.

Murray, Martin J. and Garth A. Myers (eds.). 2006. *Cities in Contemporary Africa*. New York: Palgrave.

Pink, Sarah. 2008. 'An Urban Tour: the Sensory Sociality of Ethnographic Place-Making', *Ethnography*, 9(2): 175-196.

Schütz, Alfred and Thomas Luckmann. 1975. *Strukturen der Lebenwelt*. Neuwied: Luchterhand.

Shine, Jennifer. 2010. *Movement, Memory and the Senses in Soundscape Studies*. Simon Frazer University (Vancouver). www.sensorystudies.org /?page_id=389 (accessed 20 December 2011)

Simone, AbdouMaliq. 2004a. 'People as Infrastructure: Intersecting Fragments in Johannesburg', *Public Culture*, 16(3): 407-429.

---. 2004b. *For the City Yet to Come: Changing African Life in Four Cities*. Durham: Duke University.

---. 2003. *Moving Towards Uncertainty: Migration and the Turbulence of African Urban Life.* Paper prepared for Conference on African Migration in Comparative Perspective. Johannesburg, South Africa, 4-7 June, 2003.

Vigh, Henrik. 2008. 'Crisis and Chronicity: Anthropological Perspectives on Continuous Conflict and Decline', *Ethnos*, 73(1): 5-24.

Abstracts and Information on Authors (in alphabetical order)

'I GO CHOP YOUR DOLLARS'
Scamming Practices and Notions of Moralities among Youth in Bamenda, Cameroon (pp. 41-72)

Urban youth in Bamenda, the Anglophone Northwest Province of Cameroon are dealing with difficult situations regarding scarcity of jobs, high levels of corruption, political tensions, and lacking prospects for their future. In such an environment, various options of making a living are considered. A new 'type of business' has emerged since mid of the first decade of the new millennium, which is compelling in public cyber cafés in town: The notion 'scamming' derives from 'scam' (fraud, cheat, deceit), and is referring to internet related illegal business practices. Scamming practices have become possible by the accessibility of space transcending communication and information media, as internet and mobile phone, which offer opportunities to get in contact with potential business partners (or scam victims) worldwide, access online advertising, buying and selling, easy transnational money transfer, and, furthermore, the anonymity of a 'virtual space'. Scamming practices have, above all, an impact on the local setting and society, where they stimulate critical narratives about new media use, youth's position in society, and moral legitimacies of social mobility. Scammers are seen to trespass conventional societal hierarchies and norms by displaying wealth acquired by illegitimate means, and status in peer groups. Since migrating abroad has become a more and more difficult venture, scamming is an alternative pathway to success for some youth. However, scamming seems not to be a substitution for 'making it' in a morally accepted way, but a temporary strategy to 'survive'.

Bettina Frei has studied Social Anthropology at the University of Basel, Switzerland. She has conducted her PhD research in the North West Province in the Anglophone part of Cameroon, and in Switzerland. Her forthcoming PhD thesis is focussed on the use of new media, mobility, and social transformation, entitled: 'Sociality revisited? Liveness, and the use of internet and mobile phone in urban Cameroon'. Research and writing have been carried out in the framework of an interdisciplinary African-European research programme at the University of Basel.

WOMEN AND MAGIC IN DAKAR
Rural Immigrants Coping with Urban Uncertainties
(pp. 73-100)

In Parcelles Assainies, a sandy outskirt of Dakar permanently resembling a gigantic excavation site, the waiting rooms of esoteric experts (marabouts) are daily abounding with a mostly female clientele. Especially the female experts are extremely popular. They deal daily with essential gender issues at the heart of Senegalese society: polygamy, female celibacy, infertility and the migration of men (leaving their wives and children behind) to the diaspora. In Dakar, these problematic issues are magnified. Here women fight in a fiercely competitive environment for housing, jobs and suitable marriage partners. Marabouts play an important role in this urban environment where opportunities and insecurities interrelate. They offer divination sessions for more insight into the thoughts and intentions of family members, spouses, and neighbours. Their spells should make landlords forget to collect the rent, superiors and colleagues secure jobs, and co-wives insane, leave the house, or even die. Marabouts thus offer tools for containing, expressing, and producing feelings of fear, anxiety, frustration, and jealousy. What is more, women typically tend to continue to consult marabouts in Dakar when they migrate abroad themselves. Their marabouts thus connect Dakar and the diaspora trough telephone, Western Union, and the travels of their incantations, amulets, and jinns (spirits). Taking examples from fieldwork in Parcelles Assainies, this chapter discusses the ambiguous position of female marabouts in gendered challenges of life-worlds in Dakar.

Amber Gemmeke is a researcher at the Anthropology Department of Bayreuth University, Germany. Her research interests include religious authority, media, African migration to Europe, transnational religious networks, and religious change in Europe. Amber Gemmeke published on Senegalese female marabouts in, among other journals and edited volumes, *Africa* and *Codesria Bulletin*. She is currently carrying out research on West African religious experts in the Netherlands, with a specific focus on their use of media.

INTRODUCTION
Urban Life-Worlds in Motion (pp. 9-28)

Although cities in Africa play an important role as drivers for the political and societal change on this continent, urban life-worlds have for long been a neglected field in anthropological studies. The present article aims at pointing to two more recent approaches that might complement the earlier studies – mainly from cities in the so-called copper belt – that focused on cultural change and modernization through the experience of the urban. The key to a broader understanding of current urban life-worlds is mobility and migration, as it is expressed through the new paradigm of transnationality. Furthermore, globalization has contributed to the circulation of images about urban worlds, which have been appropriated in urban contexts in Africa and thus have become part of the local representation of other worlds. Urban life-worlds in Africa blur the boundaries of territoriality and locality. They are part of multiple networks that span around the world, through images, but also through experiences and expectations of those who engage in personal migration projects. By directing the awareness to the different rhythms of the urban, Henri Lefebvre provides a very well fitting metaphor in order to describe the rapid changing of the form of cities in Africa, but also of the way of life of those living there.

Hans Peter Hahn is Professor for Anthropology with special focus on African studies at the University of Frankfurt. His regional specialization is West Africa (Togo, Ghana and Burkina Faso). His research interests are oriented towards material culture, consumption and the impact of globalization on African societies. He recently edited a book on 'Consumption in Africa' (Lit, 2008), focusing on understandings of household economies in Africa. He was engaged in several projects of museum cooperation in Togo (1996-2000), and participated in a research program on globalization in Africa (2000-2007). His publications include articles on consumption in Africa (2011), the perception of the material world and an introductory book on material culture (2005).

HAALPULAAR MIGRANTS' HOME CONNECTIONS
Travel and Communication Circuits (pp.187-206)

This chapter examines the various ways Haalpulaar diasporas around the world continue to maintain strong relations of solidarity with their rural communities through constant transnational practices. The goal of this article is to examine the evolution of the ways in which Haalpulaar migrants in Dakar and abroad maintained connection with the people they left behind. I point out the revolution in communication technologies and the way it dramatically changes the relation that Haalpulaar have with their families in the Senegal River Valley villages and small towns. I argue that the Haalpulaar villages have all become 'remotely global' in the sense Piot (1999) applied this notion in the case of Kabre communities. The Haalpulaar villages are all connected to the outside world through their small diasporas established in African, European and North American cities. The flows of people, money, information, images and material goods in both directions have a lasting impact on the social life of these villages.

Abdoulaye Kane is an Associate Professor of Anthropology with a joint appointment between the Department of Anthropology and the Center for African Studies at the University of Florida. He is a specialist of migration in the Senegal River Valley and he has published a book, several articles and book chapters on various aspects of Haalpulaar transnational experiences. He co-edited two books that are forthcoming. The first edited volume with Hansjörg Dilger and Stacey Langwick is on 'Medicine, Mobility, and Power in Global Africa' and the second edited volume with Todd Leedy is on 'African Migrations: Patterns and Perspective'. Both volumes will be published with Indiana University Press. His most recent article appeared in *Anthropology Today* on 'Migrants' Associations and Charity in home communities'.

EPILOGUE
Images and Spaces (pp. 207-216)

When dealing with different types and rhythms of mobility, contradictory forms like immobility and forced mobility should also be considered since they shape urban life-worlds in Africa as much as more voluntary forms of mobility. Moreover, imaginations are crucial for human life-worlds and their force to move mountains helps city dwellers not only to endure the daily struggle for survival but to go far beyond it. Despite its rather vague use, the concept of 'life-world' holds the potential for contributing to an emerging field of research. To grasp the life-worlds of urban dwellers in a phenomenological sense allows the integration of new forms and levels of research: Noises and smells as well as alternative portraits of the city created by rumours, images and imaginations, are constitutive of the city dwellers' life-worlds and reveal crucial aspects of the dynamic, shifting and at the same time locally embedded realities of urban dwellers. This perspective challenges the problematic practices of applying analytical and policy tools drawn mostly from European and North American experiences.

Kristin Kastner studied anthropology at the LMU University in Munich. She conducted extensive fieldwork with Nigerian migrants in Morocco and Spain. In 2011 she completed her Ph.D. thesis entitled 'Between Suffering and Styling. Nigerian migrant women on both sides of the Strait of Gibraltar' at BIGSAS (Bayreuth International Graduate School of African Studies). She currently works at the Institut für Ethnologie, Goethe-University in Frankfurt.

THE ISSUE OF THE DIASPO IN OUAGADOUGOU
(pp.173-186)

People in Burkina Faso have a centuries-old tradition of migrating to neighbouring countries on the West African coast. As a consequence, important minorities have settled in countries like Côte d'Ivoire and Ghana, where they own plantations and real estate. This chapter is less concerned with Burkinabe residents in Côte d'Ivoire than with those who have left this country due to the violent riots since the turn of the millennium. In Ouagadougou, these people are called *Diaspo*. Many of them are young, and they have actively adopted the term *Diaspo* in order to distinguish themselves from the *Tenga*, a term for the native-born population. This opposition signals the emergence of serious problems of integration. How have these problems come about? What are the perspectives for integration for these young people, who often feel like foreigners in their own country? This chapter aims to clarify some of the conflicting issues between these groups of young urban men and women.

Ludovic Ouhonyioué Kibora obtained his Ph.D. in Social Anthropology from the University Denis Diderot, Paris 7. He is Associate Professor at the University of Koudougou and the University of Ouagadougou and senior researcher at the Institut des Sciences des sociétiés in Ouagadougou. Currently he is Head of Department of socio-economic and development anthropology at INSS.

MOVEMENTS INTO EMOTIONS
Kinetic Tactics, Commotion and Conviviality among Traffic Vendors in Accra (pp. 131-156)

This article provides an ethnographic insight into the life-world of hawkers and traffic vendors on the Ofankor Road in northern Accra (Ghana). On this busy urban through-road, female and male hawkers in their teens and early twenties provide a range of products to travellers passing in the usually slow-moving city traffic. The article first explores the ways in which hawkers encounter and occupy the road as a space of movements and differential speeds. Hawkers' activities depend on and respond to the varying volume and velocity of passing vehicles with their very own movements. These involve moving with and alongside traffic and 'chasing' cars and customers, all part of hawkers' aim to keep up with the vehicles' speeds, get closer to customers, hastily exchange goods against cash and compete with fellow hawkers. Building on this, the article examines how the bodily and kinetic practices create a life-world by the roadside that is largely characterised by joviality and mixed emotions, resulting from the hawkers' idiosyncratic ways of engaging with and reacting to their own bodily manoeuvres and efforts. The traffic vendors' daily work thus makes for a life-world that is 'moving' – both in a corporeal and emotional sense, and expressed in sociabilities that are formed ambiguously through solidarity, humour, self-irony, mockery and spitefulness.

Gabriel Klaeger is currently completing his PhD in Anthropology at SOAS (University of London) and works at the Institut für Ethnologie (Goethe University Frankfurt). His PhD thesis deals with roads, automobility, speeds and risks and is based on ethnographic fieldwork conducted on and alongside the Accra-Kumasi road in Ghana. His current research with traffic vendors in urban Ghana forms part of the research programme 'Travel and Roadside Communities' set up by Kurt Beck (University of Bayreuth) and the author and funded by the German Research Foundation (DFG).

THE TRANSNATIONAL CHOICE
Young Tuareg Traders between Niger and Nigeria
(pp. 157-172)

This article deals with the case of young Tuareg migrants who travel between Niger and Nigeria in order to experience a 'new' and 'urban' way of life. Although the main activity of the migrants is trading with products of Nigeria, the motivation for migrating is located elsewhere and not in the simple gain of money: in the interest for the foreign, wanderlust, the search for adventure and, not least, in the interest in Nigeria as an example for an 'urban' way of life as well as for prosperity and consumption. Notwithstanding their highly mobile way of life, the young migrants are not only integrated in their new urban world, but also closely linked to their original social environment, and thus legitimately can be called 'transnational' migrants. The aim of the chapter is to explain the migrations of these young urban migrants not as constrained but as a 'transnational choice' which seems to be a means to realize an independent and 'modern' way of life.

Tilman Musch holds a doctoral degree in Social Anthropology. He is specialised on pastoral communities in West Africa and Central Asia. Currently he is carrying out research in the Republic of Niger and in Nigeria. His main interests are related to the subfield of spatial anthropology: land-tenure, extraction of mineral resources in nomadic transhumance areas, migration and new urban mobile lifestyles.

THE URBAN POOR, THE INFORMAL SECTOR AND ENVIRONMENTAL HEALTH POLICY IN NIGERIA
(pp. 29-40)

Poverty and rapid urbanization are two of the mayor challenges facing Africa today. One of the primary concerns of the Millennium Development Goals of the UN-Habitat is to improve the lives of millions of slum-dwellers around the world and to reduce the number of people without sustainable access to good drinking water and sanitation. This chapter examines how urban poverty and urban life-worlds have developed in Nigeria and other African countries over the last fifty years, the extent to which government policies have helped or constrained cities and the urban poor, and how poverty leading to slum conditions can be alleviated and reversed in order to reduce social tensions and worsening disparities in access to basic urban services. Some African governments have adopted a misguided policy of blaming the victims, trying in vain to repress and outlaw the informal sector by forcibly evicting hundreds of thousands of so-called squatters from urban slums. Current research suggests that the path to urban sustainability in Africa lies in building more inclusive and socially equitable cities. The central argument here is that human development and welfare ought to be at the centre of the concern for sustainable urbanization in Africa, and that greater priority should be given to the health and development concerns of the poor. The chapter concludes with some general reflections on the future of African cities, what form they will take, and how the changes needed to make these cities healthier, more productive, inclusive and equitable, as well as better able to meet people's needs, can be brought about.

Geoffrey I. Nwaka, MA (Birmingham), PhD (Dalhousie), Professor of History and former Dean of Postgraduate Studies at Abia State University, Uturu, Nigeria. He was guest researcher/visiting scholar at a number of research institutes and universities in Europe, Australia and North America. His research interests are in historical and contemporary urban issues, environmental protection, and African development. He is author of several scholarly publications and served in government during 1991-99 as Special Advisor to the Governor of Imo State.

'THEY BEHAVE AS THOUGH THEY WANT TO BRING HEAVEN DOWN'
Some Narratives on the Visibility of Cameroonian Migrant Youths in Cameroon Urban Space (pp.101-130)

This article centres on urban commentaries directed at visiting Cameroonian migrant youths, often known as *bushfallers*. On their visit to Cameroon, besides being conspicuously visible in urban areas, the migrants' presence provokes remarks on success, morality, consumerism, life abroad, etc. In a way that seems rebellious to conventional local urban youths' way of life, *bushfallers* often indulge in materialistic/consumerist activities and lifestyles that are usually only associated with Westerners and the local elite. These lifestyles testify the migrants' success and achievements abroad. In no other sphere is the visibility as apparent as in urban settings where the media increasingly portray lifestyles and consumerist activities of both the Western world and the local elite. Even though the visible consumerist way of life is secretly admired by non-migrants, the ideal public opinion is that the *bushfallers* are spoilt. Such perception subjects them to suspicion, scorn and jealousy as deduced from remarks about their moral uprightness and success when they periodically and temporarily share the same urban life-world with non-migrant youths.

Primus M. Tazanu just finished his PhD in Media Anthropology at the University of Freiburg, Germany. His thesis is entitled 'Being Available and Reachable: New Media and Cameroonian Transnational Sociality'. The study uncovers what has become of Cameroonian transnational friendships and family ties in the age of the mobile phone and internet. He holds a BSc in Sociology and Anthropology from the University of Buea (Cameroon), a MSc in Development and International Relations from the University of Aalborg (Denmark) and a postgraduate diploma in International Migration and Ethnic Relations from the University of Malmö (Sweden).